HIGHBROW / LOWBROW

The William E. Massey Sr.
Lectures in the History of
American Civilization
1986

Teuer *Febuero* *89*

HIGHBROW / LOWBROW

The Emergence
of Cultural Hierarchy
in America

LAWRENCE W. LEVINE

Harvard University Press

Cambridge, Massachusetts

London, England • *1988*

This book is printed on acid-free paper, and its binding materials
have been chosen for strength and durability.

Library of Congress Cataloging-in-Publication Data

Levine, Lawrence W.
Highbrow/lowbrow.

(The William E. Massey, Sr. lectures in the history
of American civilization ;   )
Includes index.
1. United States—Popular culture. 2. Arts—United
States. I. Title. II. Series.
E169.1.L536 1988   973   88-11021
ISBN 0-674-39076-8 (alk. paper)

For my friends

Herbert Gutman
Warren Susman
John William Ward

Whose deaths in 1985 took from us
their vision, their generosity,
and their laughter

Contents

Illustrations

Acknowledgments

S EVERAL INSTITUTIONS played a significant role in the creation of this book: the John D. and Catherine T. MacArthur Foundation provided a generous long-term fellowship, which allowed me to pursue questions that had been agitating me.

The University of California at Berkeley, in addition to all the other considerations it has shown me since I joined its faculty in 1962, was understanding in granting me time for the pursuit.

The Smithsonian Institution, particularly the National Museum of American History and the Woodrow Wilson International Center for Scholars, brought me to Washington, D.C., for the academic years 1981–82 and 1982–83, respectively, and allowed me to begin to work on the problems of this book in the midst of Washington's scholarly treasures and intellectual stimulation. I am particularly grateful to Roger Kennedy, James Billington, Prosser Gifford, and Michael Lacey for all they did to facilitate my research and make me feel welcome.

The Library of Congress, which once again has been my intellectual center away from home, gave me access to sources and people—especially the staff of the Motion Picture, Broadcasting, and Recorded Sound Division—which have been crucial to this and future research projects.

Harvard University's invitation to deliver the William E. Massey Sr. Lectures in the History of American Civilization in 1986 led directly to this volume. I am especially grateful to David Herbert Donald and Stephan Thernstrom of the History of American Civilization Program, which was my host during my stay in Cambridge.

I tried out various sections of this book in lectures and seminars at the following institutions whose faculty, staff, and students gave me the encouragement and criticism necessary to scholarship: the Hungarian Academy of Sciences, Budapest; the

National Museum of American History; Johns Hopkins University; Yale University; the University of Minnesota; the State University of New York at Stony Brook; the Woodrow Wilson International Center for Scholars; the Resident Associates Program of the Smithsonian Institution; the University of Maryland, College Park; the Shelby Cullom Davis Center, Princeton University; Claremont Mckenna College; Stanford University; the University of California, Berkeley.

Many friends and colleagues freely shared their ideas with me in the spirit of community that scholars like to speak of but don't always achieve: Daniel Aaron, Susanna Barrows, Sacvan Bercovitch, Ivan Berend, Ira Berlin, Marcus Cunliffe, Jonathan Elkus, Samuel Haber, Peter Hanak, O. B. Hardison, John Higham, William R. Hutchison, Robert Kelley, Joseph Kerman, Jackson Lears, Leon Litwack, Leo Marx, Peter Marzio, Elaine Tyler May, Lary May, Robert Middlekauff, Sidney Mintz, Susan Moeller, David Montgomery, Phyllis Palmer, Ed Quinn, Michèle Root-Bernstein, Charles Rosenberg, Roy Rosenzweig, Mary Ryan, Irwin Scheiner, Carl Schorske, the late Henry Nash Smith, Werner Sollors, Alan Trachtenberg, Wilcomb Washburn, Fred Weinstein, Gabrielle Weber-Jarich, and Larzer Ziff.

Several excellent graduate students—Madelon Powers, Mary Odem, Michael O'Malley, Nina Silber, Burton Peretti, Mary Regan, and Larry Glickman—helped me to locate and often make sense of some of the materials on which this book is based. In addition, I have had many unofficial research assistants among my students and friends who have aided me significantly by sending me news clippings, playbills, programs, and an assortment of helpful source materials and references to books and articles.

Diane Hamilton shared her expertise with me in helping to locate and select the illustrations.

Three scholars allowed me to read unpublished material of particular relevance to this work: Peter Buckley sent me several unpublished papers as well as parts of his dissertation, "To the Opera House: Culture and Society in New York City, 1820–1860," while he was still writing it. Charles Shattuck let me see the manuscript of the second volume of his *Shakespeare on the American Stage*, which is subtitled *Booth and Barrett to Sothern and Marlowe.* Katherine Preston sent several chapters of her dissertation-in-progress, "Travelling Opera Troupes in the United States, 1825–1860," as well as an unpublished paper. These were acts of generosity and trust that I deeply appreciate.

Samuel Brylawski frequently shared his home with me during my stays in Washington and always shared his impressive knowledge of American culture and the treasures of his Recorded Sound Reference Center at the Library of Congress. Brian Horrigan and Amy Levine invited me to share the warmth of their home, the astuteness of their perceptions, and their vast knowledge of opera during my trips to Washington. Cynthia Wolloch also opened her home to me in Washington and at a crucial juncture in my research pointed me firmly in the direction of the Folger Shakespeare Library. My Washington family—Bill, Harriet, Burton, and Susan Taylor, and Randi Glickberg—augmented the pleasures of that city for me. Annette Melville and Scott Simmon discussed my work, led me to sources, and gave me the gift of their company both in Washington and San Francisco.

I owe particular thanks to those who read and helped me improve the final draft. William R. Taylor, Ronald Walters, John Kasson, David Grimsted, and Katherine Preston, who are working on closely related projects, gave me the considerable benefit of their knowledge and insights. My fellow Berkeley historians Martin Jay and Henry May scrutinized the final draft with their characteristic care and perception, offered a number of important suggestions, and saved me from errors of fact and judgment. Leo Lowenthal, who began to think about these problems before I was born, read drafts, engaged in long conversations, and allowed me the privilege of his wisdom and his friendship. Dorothy Shannon, who worked with me as a secretary, also functioned as an intellectual confidant who proofread and criticized the final manuscript to its great benefit. Elizabeth Hurwit of Harvard University Press edited the manuscript and helped me to guide it into print. Aida Donald of Harvard University Press gave me good advice, pushed me when I needed pushing, and always made it clear to me that she believed in this project. Above all, my wife, Cornelia Levine, took time from her own work in German history to read drafts of everything several times over and endure an endless stream of verbal thoughts, worries, and queries, both significant and trivial. Although I may not always have acceded to her invariably independent, thoughtful criticisms, I have always benefited from them, and this work is better in myriad ways because of her.

The writers of a time hint the mottoes of its gods. The word of the modern, say these voices, is the word Culture.

Walt Whitman,
Democratic Vistas (1871)

Prologue

I WAS STANDING in the halls of the Woodrow Wilson Center in Washington, D.C., a few years ago chatting with a scholar who had just seen several Buster Keaton films. He was so enthusiastic and admiring of Keaton's skills that I relaxed my usual reserve when discussing such matters with my fellow academics. "Yes," I agreed, "Keaton was a great artist." I had rung the bell inadvertently and my colleague was about to prove Pavlov correct once again. He appeared puzzled for a moment and then came the familiar adjectival correction: "A great *popular* artist." Some time later I spoke at a symposium that accompanied a superb exhibit of Grant Wood's art. When the museum director was thanked publicly by the show's curator for his cooperation and his willingness to present the work of a painter whose artistic credentials have been under attack since he was first exhibited, the director called out from his seat in the very last row of the auditorium: "Just don't bring me Norman Rockwell next time!" It got a laugh, and like all jokes it had a message: There were, he was taking pains to make clear, depths beyond which even someone brave or foolish enough to exhibit Grant Wood could not be induced to sink.

Recently, the *San Francisco Chronicle* columnist Gerald Nachman attended a performance of Rossini's *Barber of Seville* and wondered why operagoers would put up with its "silly and sentimental" libretto when Broadway producers continually refused to revive musicals by Jerome Kern, Irving Berlin, George Gershwin, or Richard Rodgers on the grounds that "although the score is terrific, the book is laughable." If operas originally had been written by Americans, Nachman suggested, "they'd be dismissed as moronic," and concluded: "I realized it must be the American reverence for all things European and our tendency to take for granted all things quintessentially American. I thought we were over that but it's too ingrained; we're patriotic about everything but our art." The idea that Americans, long after they declared their political independence, retained a colonial mentality in matters of culture and intellect is a shrewd perception that deserves serious consideration. So does what Nachman himself termed the "outrageous" argument that *Showboat*, *Guys and Dolls*, or *Babes in Arms*, might be compared favorably with *The Barber of Seville*, *Norma*, or *La Traviata*. In fact, is the idea of a serious comparison of American musicals and opera really so outrageous? Are we certain we would learn so little about opera, musicals, and our own culture from making it? Irreverence, however, has its limits and even as he was fashioning these bold suggestions and assertions, Nachman felt it necessary to place his iconoclasm in proper perspective by making a bow to the prevailing icons and traditional definitions: "Nobody's talking culture here. I'm talking enjoyment."[1]

These episodes are repeated in book after book; even in Raymond Carney's sensitive study of the film director Frank Capra, which maintains that Capra can be understood fully if he is placed within a larger tradition of post-romantic expressive culture in America. It is a refreshing and important approach to Capra, but here too we get the characteristic hedging. "Capra's work must be considered alongside the work of Hawthorne, Emerson, Homer, Whitman, Eakins, James, Sargent, and Hopper, to name only the most obvious examples," Carney insists on the second page of his preface, and then, *in the very next sentence*, the familiar barricades begin to appear: "I want to emphasize that in making comparisons between the work of Capra and these other artists I am not trying to equate their respective achievements or to dignify Capra with a fancy intellectual pedigree."[2] The problem of course is that to place a film director *alongside* noted authors and artists, rather than *under* them, is to risk eroding hierarchy, though in fact we might learn a great deal from the process.

Stuart Levine of the University of Kansas faced a similar dilemma. In the early 1970s he began to lecture about how scholars might approach the values and institutions of high culture, and argued that art forms were not necessarily the product of "cosmic truths, but are rather the result of certain peculiarities in the way in which our culture operates." He was surprised by the response his lectures generated: "On both occasions in which I presented these ideas, some people in the room misunderstood them, taking them to be an attack on the elite arts, a kind of cynical and even snide put-down of humanists on the part of a social scientist dabbling in the arts." When Levine put his ideas into print, he found it prudent to add some "confessional material"—a sort of cultural loyalty oath—which made his allegiances unmistakable:

> Let me say that I have no training in the social sciences beyond what my students have taught me, that for many years I made my living teaching American literature and the history of American painting, that I also have training in American architecture and American music, and that for a number of years before entering the academic world I supported myself as a professional concert musician. I still love all these arts, still perform from time to time, still spend happy hours in museums and concert halls . . . I carry many of the values described in this essay. But I refuse to believe that it is bad to attain sufficient detachment from them to recognize them for what they are—attitudes I hold, values by which I make judgments, but not necessarily universal truths.[3]

This world of adjectival boxes, of such crude labels as "highbrow," "middlebrow," "lowbrow," of continual defensiveness and endless emendations; this world in which things could not be truly compared because they were so rarely laid out horizontally, next to one another, but were always positioned above or below each other on an infinite vertical scale, had much to do with the genesis of this book and, I suspect, it will have more than a little to do with its reception. The latter will have to take care of itself, but let me here say a few words about the former. Let me, that is, heed the implicit counsel of the French historian Marc Bloch who in his posthumously published book, *The Historian's Craft*, spoke to his fellow historians of "the curious modesty which, as soon as we are outside the study, seems to forbid us to expose the honest groping of our methods before a profane public."[4]

The "honest groping" that helped lead to this volume began with a redundant discovery. More than a decade ago, while working on a study of Afro-American culture, I read through a series of minstrel shows to derive some more exact sense of how antebellum whites depicted black culture. What arrested my attention was the ubiquity of Shakespearean drama in the humor of the minstrels who would ask each other such riddles as, "When was England offered for sale at at very low price?" and answer, "When King Richard offered his kingdom for a horse," or lampoon the "Seven Ages of Man" soliloquy from *As You Like It:*

> All the world's a bar,
> And all the men and women merely drinkers;
> They have their hiccups and their staggerings . . .

That these and the other parodies related in the next chapter were popular with the extremely heterogeneous audiences which attended minstrel shows brought me to the realization that Shakespeare must have been well known throughout the society since people cannot parody what is not familiar. Although Shakespeare's widespread popularity was already known among theater historians and the relative handful of cultural historians who had bothered to study the nineteenth century stage, my "discovery" had a dynamic effect upon me. Being the product of my own society in which Shakespeare is firmly entrenched in the pantheon of high culture, I was surprised, and fascinated, by the notion that his plays might have been popular culture in the nineteenth century, but initially I resisted the idea. How could a playwright whom I had been taught to consider so formidable a talent as to be almost sacred, and whose plays were demanding even for educated readers in the twentieth century, have been accessible to the broad and far less well educated public a century earlier? It took a great deal of evidence to allow me to transcend my own cultural assumptions and accept the fact that Shakespeare actually *was* popular entertainment in nineteenth-century America.

The evidence was there, overwhelmingly, but that was only the beginning; I still had to struggle with the temptation—to which many scholars have succumbed—to be guided by my prior expectations and to dismiss the popularity of Shakespeare as aberrant or irrelevant since plain people could not possibly have appreciated him for the "right" reasons: not for his poetry or philosophy or wisdom but for his buffoonery, lewdness, sensationalism. This urge has assumed many forms. Take the following sentence from a 1974 history of mid-nineteenth-century American society and culture written by a scholar who has pioneered in the study of, and taught us an enormous amount about, American popular culture:

> Shakespeare was tremendously popular (in Philadelphia sixty-five performances in 1835 alone) but his plays were either produced as vehicles for a popular star—like Edwin Booth's Lear or Forrest's Macbeth—or treated as blood-and-thunder spectacles, which accounted for frequent appearances of *Richard III, Othello, Julius Caesar*, and *The Merchant of Venice*.[5]

What was the purpose of this curious "*but*"? Did it really negate, or qualify, or explain the fact of Shakespeare's popularity in any meaningful way? The more I stumbled into these inescapable qualifiers, the more I concluded that their effective—though not necessarily deliberate—function was to protect the historian and the historian's culture. By inserting a strategic "but" here and there, scholars were shielded from having to confront the perplexing implications of Shakespeare's popularity, a popularity that challenged the very cultural expectations which had taught us to believe such a thing was improbable if not impossible. To avoid this cultural trap it was necessary to do what historians should always strive to do, however imperfectly they succeed: to shed one's own cultural skin sufficiently to be able to perceive Shakespeare, as nineteenth-century Americans perceived him, through the prism of nineteenth-century culture.

Before this could be accomplished there was still another problem: the difficulty I had believing that I was worthy to work on Shakespeare—another legacy of my own culture. Could I, a non-specialist, possibly possess the credentials necessary to do research involving a figure my culture had taught me to revere as one of the barely accessible Classic Writers who could be approached only with great humility and even greater erudition? It was only when a friend in Washington, D.C., tired of my dilatory tactics, made an appointment for me to speak with a librarian at the Folger Shakespeare Library and I found myself one morning actually sitting in that fine research center reading through playbills of nineteenth-century American productions of Shakespeare, that I began to feel myself treading familiar ground and realized that the dimensions of this historical problem were no greater than others I had investigated with some degree of success; that in fact a historian of American history with no special training in drama, and no special knowledge of Shakespeare, might just be able to bring a refreshing perspective to a neglected subject.

Nevertheless, cultural dispositions die hard and I continued to shove my slowly evolving article on Shakespeare's relationship to nineteenth-century Americans into my desk drawer at the slightest excuse. The drawer opened permanently only when I was invited to participate in a conference in Budapest in 1982 on the relationship between high and low culture. Perhaps the prospect of making my first public scholarly comment on Shakespeare in a foreign country appealed to me as less formidable than doing so in my own country. Whatever the reasons, I decided to roll the dice: if they accepted my proposal to contribute a paper demonstrating that Shakespeare was part and parcel of nineteenth-century American culture and speculating about the process by which he was transformed into high culture at the turn of the century, I would finally complete it. They did and I did. The fact that the paper was greeted with enthusiasm and that my American colleagues encouraged me to publish it, eroded whatever resistance remained in me. Indeed, once the article was published the opposite reaction set in and I began to play with the notion of expanding it and exploring to what extent the case of Shakespeare was *sui generis*: did the other elements of what was to become high culture at the turn of the century—symphonic music, opera, the fine arts—undergo the same transformation? How and when did the cultural categories I had been brought up to believe were permanent and immutable emerge? They clearly did not exist in the case of Shakespeare until the turn of the century. Was this true of other forms of expressive culture as well?

This question had become increasingly important to me as I continued my work on a study of American culture during the Great Depression and found myself hampered by the imprecise hierarchical categories culture has been carved into. How did one distinguish between "low," "high," "popular," and "mass" culture? What were the definitions and demarcation points? The arresting films of Frank Capra, one of the 1930s' best known and most thoughtful directors, were labeled "popular culture" as was the art of Norman Rockwell, the decade's most popular and accessible American painter. But the same label was also applied to a grade "B" movie produced with neither much thought or talent, or a Broadway musical comedy that closed after opening night. Why were all of these quite distinct expressions lumped together? What did they have in common? (It certainly was not "popularity"!) What distinguished them from other forms of expressive culture that carried different hierarchical labels?

Reading the literature that dealt with these categories was of little help. Writers like Dwight Macdonald were clever and passionate, but the categories they discussed seemed to me to be the subjective results of their own contemporary aesthetic priorities and judgments, with very few, if any, serious attempts at historical accuracy or empathy.[6] There were far more polemics concerning cultural categories than serious historical investigations; far more half-thought-through arguments than careful and relatively consistent definitions. Even as astute a scholar as Richard Chase appears not to have perceived the contradictions in his proposition that the terms "highbrow," "middlebrow," and "lowbrow" "work very well, and are in fact indispensable, in making large cultural formulations. But in applying them to individual authors the terms must be constantly re-examined."[7] More troubling was the tendency to equate the notion of culture with that of hierarchy so that to examine closely the manner in which the hierarchy of culture was erected, or to challenge the reasoning behind the hierarchy's parameters, was translated almost inevitably into an attack on the idea of culture itself. Cultural categories, which no one seemed able to define with any real precision, became fixed givens that one could be skeptical of only at the price of being accused of uncritical democratic relativism.

My own interest is not in attacking the notion of cultural hierarchy per se. Obviously we need to make distinctions within culture as within every other realm of human endeavor, although I do spend a fair amount of time wondering if by making those distinctions as rigidly hierarchical as we tend to, we are not limiting the dimensions of our understanding of culture, which could be furthered by having a more open and fluid set of divisions more conducive to facilitating truly complex comparisons we presently lack. Our comparative understanding might be furthered as well by adding to the almost exclusively aesthetic criteria of the present hierarchy, thematic criteria (the message of various forms of expressive culture), functional criteria (how various forms of expressive culture "work"), and quantitative criteria (to what extent various forms of expressive culture are diffused throughout the society). But at this point, debating the question of hierarchy concerns me less than examining the *nature* of the hierarchy we are debating. If the cultural categories we utilize are the product of a specific historical moment—like the political categories "right" and "left," which currently do as much to obfuscate as to enlighten—then the immediate question is less whether we should employ hierarchical categories than whether we should employ *frozen* categories ripped out of the contexts in which they were created. The only way to decide this is to learn more about the categories and their development.

These were the questions troubling me when Harvard University invited me to deliver the 1986 William E. Massey Sr. Lectures in the History of American Civilization. I seized the opportunity to extend my Shakespeare inquiry into other areas of expressive culture. This volume is the direct result of Harvard's invitation. The first chapter is a greatly expanded version of my 1984 article, "William Shakespeare and the American People: A Study in Cultural Transformation."[8] Chapters 2 and 3 are an expanded and revised version of the three Massey Lectures, which were collectively entitled: "The Fragmentation of American Culture."

One of the central arguments of this book is that because the primary categories of culture have been the products of ideologies which were always subject to modifications and transformations, the perimeters of our cultural divisions have been permeable and shifting rather than fixed and immutable. To accept this thesis is to accept a picture of the American cultural past and present that departs considerably from the images most of us have learned to accept, which is never an easy thing to do. This may explain the charges of nostalgia that have been leveled against me when I have presented parts of this thesis in papers and lectures. It is not a charge I understand very well. I certainly am not nostalgic for the disorderly crowds of the nineteenth century; I do not want my audiences to shout me down when they disagree, or make me repeat sentences they find particularly stirring, or indulge in riots when they find the conditions in the auditorium not to their liking. These are not the conditions I yearn to work under, and I have not one shred of desire to see them return. Nevertheless, such conditions did offer greater degrees of choice and freedom of action to audiences than they were later to experience and did render them participants as well as spectators. It is my purpose to show the extent to which these conditions once prevailed, to speculate about why they disappeared or at least diminished, and to wonder about what was lost to our culture in their demise.

If a sense of loss does permeate this book—and I suspect it does—it has to do with the loss of what I perceive to have been a rich shared public culture that once characterized the United States. As I trust the following chapters make clear, I do not mean to imply that the Americans of the past were the creators and products of a stable, unvarying, undifferentiated culture. On the contrary, American culture, from the very outset, was a divided one, replete with ethnic, class, and regional distinctions. It was this very cultural variety that fascinated a visitor like Tocqueville and led him to speculate at such length about the forces capable of uniting this heterogeneous people. What I mean, in referring to a shared culture, is that in the nineteenth century, especially in the first half, Americans, in addition to whatever specific cultures they were part of, shared a public culture less hierarchically organized, less fragmented into relatively rigid adjectival boxes than their descendants were to experience a century later.

I have no illusions of having solved the conundrum I first confronted when I read those minstrel shows more than a decade ago. I have meant to open not close doors, to raise as well as answer questions, to stimulate as much as to convince, and to lure as many other scholars as possible into asking comparable questions and pursuing related lines of research concerning the development of American expressive culture and the vocabulary we use to describe and comprehend it.

One

William Shakespeare
in America

Mark twain's treatment of Shakespeare in his novel *Huckleberry Finn* helps us place the Elizabethan playwright in nineteenth-century American culture. Shortly after the two rogues, who pass themselves off as a duke and a king, invade the raft of Huck and Jim, they decide to raise funds by performing scenes from Shakespeare's *Romeo and Juliet* and *Richard III*. That the presentation of Shakespeare in small Mississippi River towns could be conceived of as potentially lucrative tells us much about the position of Shakespeare in the nineteenth century. The specific nature of Twain's humor tells us even more. Realizing that they would need material for encores, the "duke" starts to teach the "king" Hamlet's soliloquy, which he recites from memory:

> To be, or not to be; that is the bare bodkin
> That makes calamity of so long life;
> For who would fardels bear, till Birnam Wood
>   do come to Dunsinane,
> But that the fear of something after death
> Murders the innocent sleep,
> Great nature's second course,
> And makes us rather sling arrows of outrageous fortune
> Than fly to others that we know not of . . .[1]

Twain's humor relies on his audience's familiarity with *Hamlet* and its ability to recognize the duke's improbable coupling of lines from a variety of Shakespeare's plays. Twain was employing one of the most popular forms of humor in nineteenth-century America. Everywhere in the nation burlesques and parodies of Shakespeare constituted a prominent form of entertainment.

Hamlet was a favorite target in numerous travesties imported from England or crafted at home. Audiences roared at the sight of Hamlet dressed in fur cap and collar, snowshoes and mittens;

they listened with amused surprise to his profanity when ordered by his father's ghost to "swear" and to his commanding Ophelia, "Get thee to a brewery"; they heard him recite his lines in black dialect or Irish brogue and sing his most famous soliloquy, "To be, or not to be," to the tune of "Three Blind Mice." In the 1820s the British comedian Charles Mathews visited what he called the "Nigger's (or Negroe's) theatre" in New York, where he heard "a black tragedian in the character of Hamlet" recite "To be, or not to be? That is the question; whether it is nobler in *de* mind to suffer, or tak' up arms against a sea of trouble, and by *opossum* end 'em." "No sooner was the word *opossum* out of his mouth," Mathews reported, "than the audience burst forth, in one general cry, '*Opossum! opossum! opossum!*'—prompting the actor to come forward and sing the popular dialect song "Opossum up a Gum Tree". On the nineteenth-century American stage, audiences often heard Hamlet's lines intricately combined with those of a popular song:

> Oh! 'tis consummation
>   Devoutly to be wished
> To end your heart-ache by a sleep,
>   When likely to be dish'd.
> Shuffle off your mortal coil,
>   Do just so,
> Wheel about, and turn about,
>   And jump Jim Crow.[2]

No Shakespearean play was immune to this sort of mutilation. *The Comedy of Errors* was performed as *Ye Comedie of Errours, a Glorious, Uproarous Burlesque. Not Indecorous nor Censorous, with Many a Chorus, Warranted Not to Bore Us, now for the First Time Set before Us. Richard III*, the most popular Shakespearean play in the nineteenth century, was lampooned frequently in such versions as *Bad Dicky*. In one New York production starring first-rank Shakespearean actors, a stuttering, lisping Othello danced while Desdemona played the banjo and Iago, complete with Irish brogue, ended their revelries with a fire hose. The comedic form made it possible to touch upon extremely sensitive issues. In a southern parody of *Othello*, for example, Othello and Desdemona were allowed to sing together, "Dey say dat in the dark all cullers am de same." In Kenneth Bangs's version of *The Taming of the Shrew*, Kate ended up in control, observing that, although "Shakespeare or Bacon, or whoever wrote the play . . . studied deeply the shrews of his day . . . the modern shrew isn't built that way," while a chastened Petruchio concluded, "Sweet Katharine, of your remarks I recognize the force: / Don't strive to tame a woman as you would a horse." Serious or slapstick, the punning was endless. In one parody of the famous dagger scene, Macbeth continues to put off his insistent wife by asking, "Or is that dagger but a false Daguerreotype?" Luckily, Desdemona had no brother, or Othello "might look black and blue," a character in *Othello* remarked, while one in *The Merchant of Venice* observed of Shylock, "This crafty Jew is full of *Jeux d'esprit!*" Throughout the century, there was an impressive number of parodies with such titles as *Julius Sneezer*, *Roamy-E-Owe and Julie-Ate*, *Hamlet and Egglet*, *Desdemonum*, and *Much Ado about a Merchant of Venice*.[3]

These full-fledged travesties reveal only part of the story. Nineteenth-century Shakespearean parody most frequently took the form of short skits, brief references, and satirical songs inserted into other modes of entertainment. In one of their routines, for example, the Bryant's Minstrels playfully referred to the famous observation in Act II of *Romeo and Juliet*:

> Adolphus Pompey is my name,
>   But that don't make no difference,
> For as Massa Wm. Shakespeare says,
>   A name's of no significance.

The minstrels loved to invoke Shakespeare as an authority: "you know what de Bird of Avon says 'bout 'De black scandal an' de foul faced reproach!'" And they constantly quoted him in appropriately garbled form: "Fust to dine own self be true, an' it must follow night and day, dou den can be false to any man." The significance of this national penchant for parodying Shakespeare is clear: Shakespeare and his drama had become by the nineteenth century an integral part of American culture. It is difficult to take familiarities with that which is not already familiar; one cannot parody that which is not well known. The minstrels' characteristic conundrums would not have been funny to an audience lacking knowledge of Shakespeare's works:

> When was Desdemona like a ship?
> When she was Moored.[4]

IT IS NOT surprising that educated Americans in the eighteenth and nineteenth centuries knew their Shakespeare so well that John Quincy Adams, who was born in 1767, could write, "at ten years of age I was as familiarly acquainted with his lovers and his clowns, as with Robinson Crusoe, the Pilgrim's Progress, and the Bible. In later years I have left Robinson and the Pilgrim to the perusal of the children; but have continued to read the Bible and Shakespeare." What is more interesting is how widely Shakespeare was known to the public in general. In the last half of the eighteenth century, when the reading of Shakespeare's plays was still confined to a relatively small, educated elite, substantial numbers of Americans had the chance to see his plays performed. From the first documented American performance of a Shakespearean play in 1750 until the closing of the theaters during the American Revolution,* Shakespeare emerged as the most popular playwright in the colonies. Fourteen to fifteen of his plays were presented at least one hundred and eighty—and one scholar has estimated perhaps as many as five hundred—times. Following the Revolution, Shakespeare retained his position as the most widely performed dramatist, with five more of his plays regularly performed in an increasing number of cities and towns.[5]

Not until the nineteenth century, however, did Shakespeare come into his own—presented and recognized almost every-

---

*In 1774 the Continental Congress discountenanced and discouraged "every Species of Extravagance and Dissipation, especially all Horse Racing, and all Kinds of Gaming, Cock Fighting, Exhibitions of Shews, Plays, and other expensive Diversions and Entertainments."

where in the country. In the cities of the Northeast and Southeast, Shakespeare's plays dominated the theater. During the 1810-11 season in Philadelphia, for example, Shakespearean plays accounted for twenty-two of eighty-eight performances. The following season lasted one hundred and eight nights, of which again one-quarter—twenty-seven—were devoted to Shakespeare. From 1800 to 1835, Philadelphians had the opportunity to see twenty-one of Shakespeare's thirty-seven plays. The Philadelphia theater was not exceptional; one student of the American stage concluded that in cities on the Eastern Seaboard at least one-fifth of all plays offered in a season were likely to be by Shakespeare. George Makepeace Towle, an American consul in England, returned to his own country just after the Civil War and remarked with some surprise, "Shakespearian dramas are more frequently played and more popular in America than in England." Shakespeare's dominance can be attested to by what Charles Shattuck has called "the westward flow of Shakespearean actors" from England to America. In the nineteenth century, one prominent English Shakespearean actor after another—George Frederick Cooke, Edmund Kean, Junius Brutus Booth, Charles Kemble, Fanny Kemble, Ellen Tree, William Charles Macready—sought the fame and financial rewards that awaited them in their tours of the United States.[6]

It is important to understand that their journey did not end with big cities or the Eastern Seaboard. According to John Bernard, the English actor and comedian who worked in the United States from 1797 to 1819, "If an actor were unemployed, want and shame were not before him: he had merely to visit some town in the interior where no theatre existed, but 'readings' were permitted; and giving a few recitations from Shakespeare and Sterne, his pockets in a night or two were amply replenished." During his travels through the United States in the 1830s, Tocqueville found Shakespeare in "the recesses of the forests of the New World," and observed, "There is hardly a pioneer's hut that does not contain a few odd volumes of Shakespeare. I remember that I read the feudal drama of *Henry V* for the first time in a log cabin." Five decades later, the German visitor Karl Knortz made a similar observation:

There is, assuredly, no other country on earth in which Shakespeare and the Bible are held in such general high esteem as in America, the very country so much decried for its lust for money. If you were to enter an isolated log cabin in the Far West and even if its inhabitant were to exhibit many of the traces of backwoods living, he will most likely have one small room nicely furnished in which to spend his few leisure hours and in which you will certainly find the Bible and in most cases also some cheap edition of the works of the poet Shakespeare.

Even if we discount the hyperbole evident in such accounts, they were far from inventions. The ability of the illiterate Rocky Mountain scout Jim Bridger to recite long passages from Shakespeare, which he had learned by hiring someone to read the plays to him, and the formative influence that the plays had upon young Abe Lincoln growing up in Salem, Illinois, became part of the nation's folklore.[7]

But if books had become a more important vehicle for disseminating Shakespeare by the nineteenth century, the stage remained the primary instrument. The theater, like the church, was one of the earliest and most important cultural institutions established in frontier cities. And almost everywhere the theater blossomed Shakespeare was a paramount force. In his investigation of the theater in Louisville, Cincinnati, St. Louis, Detroit, and Lexington, Kentucky, from 1800 to 1840, Ralph Leslie Rusk concluded that Shakespeare's plays were performed more frequently than those of any other author. Chicago, with slightly more than four thousand inhabitants, was barely incorporated in 1837 when productions of *Richard III* were being given in a theater improvised in the dining room of the deserted Sauganash Hotel. In Mississippi between 1814 and the outbreak of the Civil War, the towns of Natchez and Vicksburg, with only a few thousand inhabitants each, put on at least one hundred and fifty performances of Shakespeare featuring such British and American stars as Ellen Tree, Edwin Forrest, Junius Brutus Booth, J. W. Walleck, Charles Kean, J. H. Hackett, Josephine Clifton, and T. A. Cooper. Stars of this and lesser caliber made their way into the interior by boat, along the Ohio and Mississippi rivers, stopping at towns and cities on their way to New Orleans. Beginning in the early 1830s, the rivers themselves became the site of Shakespearean productions, with floating theaters in the form first of flatboats and then of steamboats bringing drama to small river towns.[8]

By mid-century, Shakespeare was taken across the Great Plains and over the Rocky Mountains and soon became a staple of theaters in the Far West. During the decade following the arrival of the Forty-niners, at least twenty-two of Shakespeare's plays were performed on California stages, with *Richard III* retaining the predominance it had gained in the East and South. In 1850 the Jenny Lind Theatre, seating two thousand, opened over a saloon in San Francisco and was continuously crowded: "Miners . . . swarmed from the gambling saloons and cheap fandango houses to see *Hamlet* and *Lear*." In 1852 the British star Junius Brutus Booth and two of his sons played *Hamlet*, *Macbeth*, *Othello*, and *Richard III* from the stage of the Jenny Lind and packed the house for the two weeks of their stay. In 1856 Laura Keen brought San Franciscans not only old favorites but such relatively uncommon productions as *Coriolanus* and *A Midsummer Night's Dream*. Along with such eminent stars from abroad, American actors like McKean Buchanan and James Stark kept the hunger for Shakespeare satisfied.[9]

But Shakespeare could not be confined to the major population centers in the Far West any more than he had been in the East. If miners could not always come to San Francisco to see theater, the theater came to them. Stark, Buchanan, Edwin Booth, and their peers performed on makeshift stages in mining camps around Sacramento and crossed the border into Nevada, where they brought characterizations of Hamlet, Iago, Macbeth, Kate, Lear, and Othello to miners in Virginia City, Silver City, Dayton, and Carson City. Walter M. Leman recalled the dearth of theaters in such California towns as Tod's Valley, Chip's Flat, Cherokee Flat, Rattlesnake, Mud Springs, Red Dog, Hangtown, Drytown, and Fiddletown, which he toured in the 1850s. In the Sierra town of Downieville, Leman performed *Richard III* on the second story of a cloth and paper house in a hall without a stage: "We had to improvise one out of the two billiard tables it contained, covering them with boards for that purpose." Such conditions were by no means confined to the West Coast. In earlier years, Leman had toured the Maine towns of Bangor,

Belfast, Orono, and Oldtown, not one of which had a proper theater, necessitating the use of church vestries and other improvisations. In 1816 in Lexington, Kentucky, Noah Ludlow performed *The Taming of the Shrew*, *Othello*, and *The Merchant of Venice* in a room on the second floor of an old brewery, next door to a saloon, before an audience seated on backless, cushionless chairs. In the summer of 1833, Sol Smith's company performed in the dining room of a hotel in Tazewell, Alabama, "on a sort of landing-place or gallery about six feet long, and two and a half feet wide." His "heavy tragedian" Mr. Lyne attempted to recite the "Seven Ages of Man" from *As You Like It* while "persons were passing from one room to the other continually and the performer was obliged to *move* whenever any one passed."[10]

Thus Shakespeare was by no means automatically treated with reverence. Nor was he accorded universal acclaim. In Davenport and neighboring areas of eastern Iowa, where the theater flourished in both English and German, Shakespeare was seldom performed and then usually in the form of short scenes and soliloquies rather than entire plays. As more than one theater manager learned, producing Shakespeare did not necessarily result in profits. Theatrical lore often repeated the vow attributed to Robert L. Place that he would never again produce a play by Shakespeare "no matter how many more he wrote." But these and similar incidents were exceptions to the general rule: from the large and often opulent theaters of major cities to the makeshift stages in halls, saloons, and churches of small towns and mining camps, wherever there was an audience for the theater, there Shakespeare's plays were performed prominently and frequently.[11] Shakespeare's popularity in frontier communities in all sections of the country may not fit Frederick Jackson Turner's image of the frontier as a crucible, melting civilization down into a new amalgam, but it does fit our knowledge of human beings and their need for the comfort of familiar things under the pressure of new circumstances and surroundings. James Fenimore Cooper had this familiarity in mind when he called Shakespeare "the great author of America" and insisted that Americans had "just as good a right" as Englishmen to claim Shakespeare as their countryman. At the dedication of Shakespeare's statue in Central Park in 1872, his familiarity to Americans was taken for granted. "Old World, he is not only thine," the inscription on the temporary pedestal proclaimed, and Bayard Taylor, in his commemorative poem, declared:

> He came, a household ghost we could not ban:
> He sat, on Winter nights, by cabin-fires;
> . . . . .
> He preached within the shadow of our spires;
> . . . and became
> The Master of our Thought, the Land's first Citizen![12]

Shakespeare's popularity can be determined not only by the frequency of Shakespearean productions and the size of the audiences for them but also by the nature of the productions and the manner in which they were presented. Shakespeare was performed not merely alongside popular entertainment as an elite supplement to it; Shakespeare was performed as an integral part of it. Shakespeare *was* popular entertainment in nineteenth-century America. The theater in the first half of the nineteenth century played the role that movies played in the first half of the twentieth: it was a kaleidoscopic, democratic institution presenting a widely varying bill of fare to all classes and socioeconomic groups.

During the first two-thirds of the nineteenth century, the play may have been the thing, but it was not the only thing. It was the centerpiece, the main attraction, but an entire evening generally consisted of a long play, an afterpiece (usually a farce), and a variety of between-act specialties. In the spring of 1839, a playbill advertising the appearance of William Evans Burton in *As You Like It* at Philadelphia's American Theater announced, "Il Diavolo Antonio And His Sons, Antonio, Lorenzo, Augustus And Alphonzo will present a most magnificent display of position in the Science of Gymnastics, portraying some of the most grand and imposing groups from the ancient masters . . . to conclude with a grand Horizontal Pyramid." It was a characteristically full evening. In addition to gymnastics and Shakespeare, "Mr. Quayle (by Desire)" sang "The Swiss Drover Boy," La Petite Celeste danced "a New Grand Pas Seul," Miss Lee danced "La Cachuca," Mr. Quayle returned to sing "The Haunted

Spring," Mr. Bowman told a "Yankee Story," and "the Whole" concluded "with *Ella Rosenberg* starring Mrs. Hield."[13]

Thus Shakespeare was presented amid a full range of contemporary entertainment. During the Mexican War, a New Orleans performance of *Richard III* was accompanied by "A NEW and ORIGINAL Patriotic Drama in 3 Acts . . . (founded in part on events which have occurred during the Mexican War,) & called: Palo Alto! Or, Our Army on the Rio Grande! . . . TRIUMPH OF AMERICAN ARMS! Surrender of Gen. Vega to Capt. May! Grand Military Tableau!" It would be a mistake to conclude that Shakespeare was presented as the dry, staid ingredient in this exciting menu. On the contrary, Shakespearean plays were often announced as spectacles in their own right. In 1799 the citizens of Alexandria, Virginia, were promised the following in a production of *Macbeth*: "In Act 3d—A Regal Banquet in which the Ghost of Banquo appears. In Act 4th—A Solemn incantation & dance of Witches. In Act 5th—A grand Battle, with the defeat & death of Macbeth." At mid-century, a presentation of *Henry IV* in Philadelphia featured the "Army of Falstaff on the March! . . . Battlefield, Near Shrewsbury, Occupying the entire extent of the Stage, Alarms! Grand Battle! Single Combat! DEATH OF HOTSPUR! FINALE—Grand Tableau."[14]

Shakespeare's position as part and parcel of popular culture was reinforced by the willingness of Shakespearean actors to take part in the concluding farce. Thus Mr. Parsons followed such roles as Coriolanus, Othello, Macbeth, and Lear by playing Ralph Stackpole, "A Ring-Tailed Squealer & Rip-Staver from Salt River," in *Nick of the Woods*. Even Junius Brutus Booth followed his celebrated portrayal of Richard III with the role of Jerry Sneak in *The Mayor of Garrat*. In the postbellum years Edward L. Davenport referred to this very ability and willingness to mix genres when he lamented the decline of his profession: "Why, I've played an act from *Hamlet*, one from *Black-Eyed Susan*, and sung 'A Yankee Ship and a Yankee Crew' and danced a hornpipe, and wound up with a 'nigger' part, all in one night. Is there any one you know of today who can do that?" It is clear that, as much as Shakespearean roles were prized by actors, they were not exalted; they did not unfit one for other roles and other tasks; they were not elevated to a position above the culture in which they appeared. Although David Garrick's *Catharine and Petruchio*, a condensation of *The Taming of the Shrew*, or his *Shakespeare's Jubilee*, consisting of scenes from a number of Shakespeare's plays concluding with a grand procession, were popular afterpieces, more frequently the final word of the evening was not Shakespeare's. *Hamlet* might be followed by such farces as *Fortune's Frolic* and *The Sultan; or, A Peep Into the Seraglio*, *The Merchant of Venice* by *The Lottery Ticket*, *Richard III* by *The Green Mountain Boy*, *King Lear* by *Chaos Is Come Again* on one occasion and by *Love's Laughs at Locksmiths; or, The Guardian Outwitted* on another, and, in California, *Romeo and Juliet* by *Did You Ever Send Your Wife to San Jose?*[15]

These afterpieces and *divertissements* most often are seen as having diluted or denigrated Shakespeare. I suggest that they may be understood more meaningfully as having *integrated* him into American culture. Shakespeare was presented as part of the same milieu inhabited by magicians, dancers, singers, acrobats, minstrels, and comics. He appeared on the same playbills and was advertised in the same spirit. This does not mean that theatergoers were unable to make distinctions between Shakespearean productions and the accompanying entertainment. Of course they were. Shakespeare, after all, was what most of them came to see. But it was a Shakespeare presented as part of the culture they enjoyed, a Shakespeare rendered familiar and intimate by virtue of his context.

In 1843 the curtain of the rebuilt St. Charles Theatre in New Orleans featured an arresting bit of symbolism: it depicted Shakespeare in a halo of light being borne aloft on the wings of the American eagle. Shakespeare was not only domesticated; he was humanized. Henry Norman Hudson, the period's most popular Shakespearean lecturer, hailed Shakespeare as "the prodigy of our race" but also stressed his decency, his humility, his "true gentleness and lowliness of heart" and concluded that "he who looks the highest will always bow the lowest." In his melodrama *Shakespeare in Love*, Richard Penn Smith pictured the poet not as an awesome symbol of culture but as a poor, worried, stumbling young man in love with a woman of whose feelings he is not yet certain. In the end, of course, he triumphs and proclaims his joy in words that identify him as a well-rounded human being to whom one can relate: "I am indeed happy. A poet, a lover, the husband of the woman I adore. What is there more for me to desire?" Nineteenth-century America swallowed Shakespeare, digested him and his plays, and made them part of the cultural body. The nature of his reception by nineteenth-century audiences confirms this conclusion.[16]

While he was performing in Natchez, Mississippi, in 1835, the Irish actor Tyrone Power observed people on the road hurrying to the theater. Their fine horses, ornate and often antique saddles, and picturesque clothing transported him back to Elizabethan England and "the palmy days of the Globe and Beargarden." Power's insight was sound; there *were* significant similarities between the audiences of Shakespeare's own day and those he drew in America. One of Shakespeare's contemporaries commented that the theater was "frequented by all sorts of people old and younge, rich and poore, masters and servants, papists and puritans, wise men etc., churchmen and statesmen." The nineteenth-century American audience was equally heterogeneous. In both eras the various classes saw the same plays in the same theaters—though not necessarily from the same vantage point. Until mid-century, at least, American theaters generally had a tripartite seating arrangement: the pit (orchestra), the boxes, and the gallery (balcony). Although theater prices fell substantially from 1800 to 1850, seating arrangements continued to dovetail with class and economic divisions. In the boxes sat, as one spectator put it, "the dandies, and people of the first respectability and fashion." The gallery was inhabited largely by those (apprentices, servants, poor workingmen) who could not afford better seats or by those (Negroes and often prostitutes) who were not allowed to sit elsewhere.* The pit was dominated by what were rather vaguely called the "middling classes"—a "mixed multitude" that some contemporaries praised as the "honest folks" or "the sterling part of the audience."[17]

---

*The *Daily Picayune* in New Orleans commented on March 14, 1844, "The playgoing portion of our negro population feel more interest in, and go in greater numbers to see, the plays of Shakespeare represented on the stage, than any other class of dramatic performance."

All observers agree that the nineteenth-century theater housed under one roof a microcosm of American society. This, the actor Joseph Jefferson maintained, was what made drama a more difficult art than painting, music, or writing, which "have a direct following, generally from a class whose taste and understanding are pretty evenly balanced,—whereas a theater is divided into three and sometimes four classes." And all of those classes had to be addressed, as Jefferson also noted: "There must be no vagueness in acting. The suggestion should be unmistakable; it must be hurled at the whole audience, and reach with unerring aim the boys in the gallery and the statesmen in the stalls." Walt Whitman warmly recalled the Bowery Theatre around the year 1840, where he could look up to the first tier of boxes and see "the faces of the leading authors, poets, editors, of those times," while he sat in the pit surrounded by the "slang, wit, occasional shirt sleeves, and a picturesque freedom of looks and manners, with a rude, good-nature and restless movement" of cartmen, butchers, firemen, and mechanics. Others spoke of the mixed audience with less enthusiasm. Washington Irving wrote a series of letters to the *New York Morning Chronicle* in 1802 and 1803 describing his theater experiences. The noise in the gallery he found "is somewhat similar to that which prevailed in Noah's Ark; for we have an imitation of the whistles and yells of every kind of animal." When the "gallery gods" were roused for one reason or another, "they commenced a discharge of apples, nuts & ginger-bread, on the heads of the honest folks in the pit." Throughout the evening there was a chorus of "coughing and sneezing . . . *whistling and thumping* . . . The crackling of nuts and the craunching of apples saluted my ears on every side."[18]

Little had changed by 1832 when the English visitor Frances Trollope attended the theater in several American cities. In Cincinnati she observed coatless men with their sleeves rolled up, incessantly spitting, reeking "of onions and whiskey." She enjoyed the Shakespeare but abhorred the "perpetual" noises: "The applause is expressed by cries and thumping with the feet, instead of clapping; and when a patriotic fit seized them, and 'Yankee Doodle' was called for, every man seemed to think his reputation as a citizen depended on the noise he made." Things were no better in Philadelphia and, if anything, worse in New York theaters, where she witnessed "a lady performing the most maternal office possible . . . and a general air of contempt for the decencies of life." When he published his reminiscences in 1836, Tyrone Power tried to counter such accounts by praising the attentiveness and intelligence of his American audiences, but it appears that what differed was less the audience than Power's tolerance for it. For instance, in hailing the "degree of repose and gentility of demeanour" of the audience he performed for in New Orleans in 1835, he wrote:

> The least prolonged tumult of approbation even is stilled by a word to order: and when it is considered that here are assembled the wildest and rudest specimens of the Western population, men owning no control except the laws, and not viewing these over submissively, and who admit of no *arbiter elegantiarum* or standard of fine breeding, it confers infinite credit on their innate good feeling, and that sense of propriety which here forms the sole check on their naturally somewhat uproarious jollity.[19]

Evidence of this sort makes it clear that an understanding of the American theater in our own time is not adequate grounding for a comprehension of American theater in the nineteenth century. To envision nineteenth-century theater audiences correctly, one might do well to visit a contemporary sporting event in which the spectators not only are similarly heterogeneous but are also—in the manner of both the nineteenth century and the Elizabethan era—more than an audience; they are participants who can enter into the action on the field, who feel a sense of immediacy and at times even of control, who articulate their opinions and feelings vocally and unmistakably. Washington Irving wryly observed, "The good folks of the gallery have all the trouble of ordering the music." When the orchestra's selection displeased them, they stamped, hissed, roared, whistled, and groaned in cadence until the musicians played "*Moll in the wad, Tally ho the grinders*, and several other *airs* more suited to their tastes." In 1833 the *New York Mirror* reported that during a recent evening at the American Theatre the audience was unhappy with the overture, loudly called for "Yankee Doodle," "and its melting tones forthwith breathed forth in mellifluous harmony. The pit were gratified, and evinced their satisfaction by a gentle roar." The audience's vociferousness continued during the play itself, which was punctuated by expressions of disapproval in the form of hisses or groans and of approval in the form of applause, whistles, and stamping to the point that a Virginia editor felt called upon to remind his readers in 1829 that it was not "a duty to applaud at the conclusion of every sentence." A French reporter, attending a production of Shakespeare in California in 1851, was fascinated by the audience's enthusiasm: "The more they like a play, the louder they whistle, and when a San Francisco audience bursts into shrill whistles and savage yells, you may be sure they are in raptures of joy." Audiences frequently demanded—and got—instant encores from performers who particularly pleased them. "Perhaps," a New York editor wrote sarcastically in 1846, "we'll flatter Mr. Kean by making him take poison twice." As late as the 1870s an observer reported that while "the fashionable portion of the audience" in a small northeastern manufacturing city watched quietly as a dramatic troupe led by the great Italian actor Tommaso Salvini presented a "spiritless, dragging" version of *Hamlet*,

> the gallery made up in good humor and liveliness whatever was lacking of those qualities on the part of the actors themselves. When the ghost of Hamlet's father rose majestic from the underworld and caught his mosquito-net in the trap-door, they cheered him through all his frantic efforts to jerk himself loose; they manifested their sympathy with Hamlet's psychological difficulties by the groans with which they accompanied the immortal soliloquy; . . . and when, in the final act, the festal goblet was brought upon the stage, they called clamorously but good-naturedly upon the king to "set up the crowd."[20]

Like the Elizabethans, a substantial portion of nineteenth-century American audiences knew their Shakespeare well. Sol Smith reported that in 1839, when he wanted to put on an evening of acts from various Shakespearean plays in St. Louis, he had "no difficulty in finding Hamlets, Shylocks and Richards in abundance, very glad of the opportunity to exhibit their hidden powers." Constance Rourke has shown that as far west as

California, from miners' camps to the galleries of urban theaters, there were many who knew large parts of the plays by heart. This knowledge easily became an instrument of control, as more than one hapless actor found out. In the winter of 1856 Hugh F. McDermott's depiction of Richard III did not meet the critical expectations of his Sacramento audience. During the early scenes of Act I "a few carrots timidly thrown, had made their appearance," but the full ardor of the audience was roused only when Richard's killing of Henry included a "thrust, *a posteriori*, after Henry had fallen." Then, the *Sacramento Daily Union* reported, "Cabbages, carrots, pumpkins, potatoes, a wreath of vegetables, a sack of flour and one of soot, and a dead goose, with other articles, simultaneously fell upon the stage." The barrage woke the dead Henry, who fled followed by Richard, "his head enveloped in a halo of vegetable glory." Pleas from the manager induced the audience to allow the play to go on—but not for long. In Act II, McDermott's inept wooing of Lady Anne again exhausted the patience of the audience. "When Richard placed the sword in her hand," a reporter observed, "one half the house, at least, asked that it might be plunged in his body." This storm of shouts was followed by a renewal of the vegetable shower accompanied this time by Chinese firecrackers. As poor Richard fled for the second time, "a well directed pumpkin caused him to stagger, and with still truer aim, a potato relieved him of his cap, which was left upon the field of glory, among the cabbages."[21]

Scenes like this account for the frequent assurance on playbills that "proper officers are appointed who will rigidly enforce decorum." Proper officers or not, such incidents were common enough to prompt a nineteenth-century gentleman to note in his diary, "The egg as a vehicle of dramatic criticism came into early use in this Continent." Despondency over the use of such critical "vehicles" by audiences in Philadelphia's Chestnut Street Theatre led the actor Richard Fullerton to drown himself in the Delaware River in the winter of 1802. "He was annoyed by anonymous and cutting criticisms," a contemporary observed, "and by contemptible hissing and other open demonstrations directed to him personally when on the stage." Here was literal proof of the continued validity of Samuel Johnson's prologue:

> The drama's laws,
> the drama's patrons give,
> For we that live to please,
> must please to live.

"The public," an American critic agreed in 1805, "in the final resort, govern the stage." It was of course a two-edged sword; the same California audiences capable of driving King Richard from the stage could pay homage to a performance they recognized as superior. Irish-born Matilda Heron's portrayal of Juliet on New Year's night 1854 "so fascinated and entranced" the "walnut-cracking holiday audience," according to the *San Francisco Chronicle*, that "they sat motionless and silent for some moments after the scene was done; and then suddenly recovering themselves from the thraldom under which they had been placed, they came down in a shower of applause that shook the house."[22]

These frenetic displays of approval and disapproval were signs of engagement in what was happening on the stage—an engagement that on occasion could blur the line between audience and actors. At a performance of *Richard III* with Junius Brutus Booth at New York's Bowery Theatre in December 1832, the holiday audience was so large that some three hundred people overflowed onto the stage and entered into the spirit of things, the *New York Mirror* reported. They examined Richard's royal regalia with interest, hefted his sword, and tried on his crown; they moved up to get a close look at the ghosts of King Henry, Lady Anne, and the children when these characters appeared on stage; they mingled with the soldiers during the battle of Bosworth Field and responded to the roll of drums and blast of trumpets by racing across the stage. When Richard and Richmond began their fight, the audience "made a ring round the combatants to see fair play, and kept them at it for nearly a quarter of an hour by 'Shrewsbury's clock.' This was all done in perfect good humor, and with no intention to make a row." When Dan Rice came on to dance his famous Jim Crow, the on-stage audience made him repeat it some twenty times, "and in the afterpiece, where a supper-table [was] spread, some among the most hungry very leisurely helped themselves to the viands." Frequently, members of the audience became so involved in the action on stage that they interfered in order to dispense charity to the sick and destitute, advice to the indecisive, and, as one man did during a Baltimore production of *Coriolanus* and another during a New York production of *Othello*, protection to someone involved in an unfair fight. In a wonderful instance of how nineteenth century American audiences tended to see drama as both reality and representation simultaneously, a canal boatman screamed at Iago in a production of *Othello* in Albany, New York, "You damned-lying scoundrel, I would like to get hold of you after the show and wring your infernal neck."*[23]

T HE PLACE of Shakespearean drama in the nineteenth century American theater should make it clear how difficult it is to draw arbitrary lines between popular and folk culture. Here was professional entertainment containing numerous folkish elements, including a knowledgeable, participatory audience exerting important degrees of control. The integration of Shakespeare into the culture as a whole should bring into serious question our tendency to see culture on a vertical plane, neatly divided into a hierarchy of inclusive adjectival categories such as "high," "low," "pop," "mass," "folk," and the like. If the phenomenon of Shakespeare was not an aberration—and the diverse audiences for such art forms as Italian opera, such performers as the singer Jenny Lind, and such writers as Longfellow, Dickens, and Mark Twain would indicate that it was not—then the study of Shakespeare's relationship to the American people helps reveal the existence of a shared public culture to which we have not paid enough attention. It has been obscured by the practice of em-

---

*Constance Rourke has related another fine example: "On a small stage in a Kentucky village a gambler's family was pictured as starving and a countryman rose from one of the boxes. 'I propose we make up something for this woman,' he said. Some one whispered that it was all a sham, but he delivered a brief discourse on the worthlessness of the gambler, flung a bill on to the stage with his pocketbook, advised the woman not to let her husband know about it or he would spend it all on faro, and then with a divided mind sat down, saying, 'Now go on with the play.'"

ploying such categories as "popular" aesthetically rather than literally. That is, the adjective "popular" has been utilized to describe not only those creations of expressive culture that actually had a large audience (which is the way I have tried to use it), but also, and often primarily, those that had questionable artistic merit. Thus, a banal play or a poorly written romantic novel has been categorized as popular culture, even if it had a tiny audience, while the recognized artistic attributes of a Shakespearean play have prevented it from being included in popular culture, regardless of its high degree of popularity. The use of such arbitrary and imprecise cultural categories has helped obscure the dynamic complexity of American culture in the nineteenth century.

Our difficulty also proceeds from the historical fallacy of reading the present into the past. By the middle of the twentieth century, Shakespearean drama did not occupy the place it had in the nineteenth century. Although in the mid-twentieth century there was no more widely known, respected, or quoted dramatist in our culture than Shakespeare, the nature of his relationship to the American people had changed: he was no longer their familiar, no longer part of their culture, no longer at home in their theaters or on the movie and television screens that had become the twentieth-century equivalents of the stage. If Shakespeare had been an integral part of mainstream culture in the nineteenth century, in the twentieth he had become part of "polite" culture—an essential ingredient in a complex we call, significantly, "legitimate" theater. He had become the possession of the educated portions of society who disseminated his plays for the enlightenment of the average folk who were to swallow him not for their entertainment but for their education, as a respite from—not as a normal part of—their usual cultural diet. Recalling his youthful experiences with Shakespeare, the columnist Gerald Nachman wrote in 1979 that in the schools of America "Shakespeare becomes theatrical spinach: He's good for you. If you digest enough of his plays, you'll grow up big and strong intellectually like teacher." In 1955 Alfred Harbage characterized the mood prevailing at Shakespearean performances as "reverently unreceptive," containing "small sense of joy, small sense of sorrow; . . . rarely a moment of that hush of absorption which is the only sign-warrant of effectual drama." People attended Shakespeare the way they attended church: "gratified that they have come, and gratified that they now may go." The plays of Shakespeare, he reflected, "have ceased to be plays at all—they have become *classics.*" The efforts of such young producers and directors as Joseph Papp in the late 1950s and the 1960s to liberate Shakespeare from the genteel prison in which he had been confined, to restore his plays to their original vitality, and to disseminate them among what Papp called "a great dispossessed audience," is a testament to what had happened to Shakespearean drama since the mid-nineteenth century.[24]

Signs of this transformation appear throughout the twentieth century. In his 1957 treatise on how to organize community theaters, John Wray Young warned, "Most organizations will find it difficult to please with the classics . . . Shakespeare, Ibsen, Chekhov, the Greeks, and the other masters are hard to sell in the average community situation." Shakespeare had become not only a hard-to-sell classic to average members of the community but even an alienating force. In a 1929 episode of the popular comic strip *Bringing up Father*, the neighborhood bartender, Dinty Moore, suddenly goes "high hat" when he meets and courts a wealthy woman. The symbols of his attempt to enter "society," which separate him from his friends, are his fancy clothing, his poodle dog, his horseback riding and golf, his pretentious language, *and* his reading of Shakespeare's *Romeo and Juliet*, which so infuriates his friend Jiggs that he seizes the volume and throws it at Moore, whose having dared to read Shakespeare was portrayed as the ultimate put-down, the final sign of his class apostasy. In one of his wonderful monologues on politics, published in 1905, George Washington Plunkitt, ward boss of the fifteenth assembly district in New York City and one of the powers of Tammany Hall, admonished aspiring politicians:

> If you're makin' speeches in a campaign, talk the language the people talk. Don't try to show how the situation is by quoting Shakespeare. Shakespeare was all right in his way, but he didn't know anything about Fifteenth District politics . . . Go out and talk the language of the Fifteenth to the people. I know it's an awful temptation, the hankerin' to show off your learnin'. I've felt it myself, but I always resist it. I know the awful consequences.

In her account of her life as a worker, Dorothy Richardson deplored the maudlin yellowback novels that dominated the reading habits of working women at the turn of the century and pleaded for the wide dissemination of better literature:

> Only, please, Mr. or Mrs. Philanthropist, don't let it be Shakespere, or Ruskin, or Walter Pater. Philanthropists have tried before to reform degraded literary tastes with heroic treatment, and they have failed every time. That is sometimes the trouble with the college settlement folk. They forget that Shakespere, and Ruskin, and all the rest of the really true and great literary crew, are infinite bores to every-day people.[25]

Culture is a process, not a fixed condition; it is the product of unremitting interaction between the past and the present. Thus, Shakespeare's relationship to the American people was always in flux, always changing. Still, it is possible to isolate a period during which the increasing separation of Shakespeare from "every-day people" becomes more evident. The American Theatre in San Francisco advised those attending its May 29, 1855, production of *A Midsummer Night's Dream* that "owing to the length of the play there will be NO FARCE." Similarly, in 1869 the Varieties Theatre in New Orleans announced in its playbill advertising Mrs. Scott Siddons in *As You Like It*, "In consequence of the length of this comedy, it will constitute the Evening's Entertainment." In following decades it became less and less necessary for theaters to issue such explanations. In 1873 the California Theatre in San Francisco advertised *Coriolanus* with no promise of a farce or between-act entertainment—and no apologies. This became true in city after city. There is no precise date, but everywhere in the United States during the final decades of the nineteenth century the same transformation was evidently taking place; Shakespeare was being divorced from the broader world of everyday culture. Gone were the entr'acte diversions: the singers, jugglers, dancers, acrobats, orators. Gone, too, was the purple prose trumpeting the sensational events and pageantry that were part of the Shakespearean plays themselves. Those who wanted their Shakespeare had to take him alone, lured to his plays by stark playbills promising no frills or enhancements. In December 1890 Pittsburgh's Duquesne Theatre advertised productions of *The Merchant of Venice, Othello, Romeo and Juliet*, and *Julius Caesar* by announcing simply, "Engagment of Mr. Lawrence Barrett, supported by Miss Gale And a Competent Company of Players." Significantly, the frequent admonitions relating to audience behavior were now missing as well. By the early twentieth century, playbills of this type became the norm everywhere. William Shakespeare had become *Culture*.[26]

This change resulted in an inevitable decline in the frequency with which Shakespearean drama was produced. "Shakespeare was heard ten times in New York then [1840] for once that he is heard now," the critic Richard Grant White pointed out in 1882. What seemed to be the nadir to White appeared to be a golden age to Mark Twain who observed in 1908, "Thirty years ago Edwin Booth played 'Hamlet' a hundred nights in New York. With three times the population, how often is 'Hamlet' played now in a year? . . . What *has* come over us English-speaking people?" The question was still troubling a Shakespearean scholar who lamented in 1963, "the days when a Davenport and a Barry could open rival productions of *Hamlet* on the same night, as in 1875; when *Macbeth* could be seen at three different theatres in New York in 1849; when ten *Hamlets* could be produced in a single season, as in New York in 1857–58; . . . these days are unfortunately gone."[27]

It is easier to describe this transformation than to explain it, since the transformation itself has clouded our vision of the past. So completely have twentieth-century Americans learned to accept as natural and timeless Shakespeare's status as an elite, classic dramatist, to whose plays the bulk of the populace do not or cannot relate, that we have found it difficult to comprehend nineteenth-century conceptions of Shakespeare. Too frequently, modern historians of the theater have spent less time and energy understanding Shakespeare's nineteenth-century popularity than in explaining it away. The formula is simple and proceeds from an attempt to account for the indisputable popularity of a great master in a frontier society with an "overwhelmingly uneducated" public. The consensus seems to be that Shakespeare was popular for all the wrong reasons: because of the afterpieces and *divertissements* that surrounded his plays; because the people wanted to see great actors who in turn insisted on performing Shakespeare to demonstrate their abilities; because his plays were presented in altered, simplified versions; because of his bombast, crudities, and sexual allusions rather than his poetry or sophistication; because of almost anything but his dramatic genius. "Shakespeare," we are told in a conclusion that would not be important if it were not so typical, "could communicate with the unsophisticated at the level of action and oratory while appealing to the small refined element at the level of dramatic and poetic artistry." Esther Dunn studied the "indifferent and vulgar stuff" accompanying Shakespeare in the theater and concluded that, "if the public could stand for this sort of entertainment, night in and night out, they could not have derived the fullest pleasure from the Shakespearean portion of the programme." In 1926 Poet Laureate Robert Bridges spoke for many on both sides of the Atlantic when he attributed the "bad jokes and obscenities," "the mere foolish verbal trifling," and such sensationalism in Shakespeare's plays as the murder of Macduff's child or the blinding of Gloucester, to Shakespeare's need to make concessions "to the most vulgar stratum of his audience, . . . those wretched beings who can never be forgiven their share in preventing the greatest poet and dramatist of the world from being the best artist."[28]

Again and again, historians and critics have arbitrarily separated the "action and oratory" of Shakespeare's plays from the "dramatic and poetic artistry" with which they were, in reality, so intricately connected. We are asked to believe that the average member of the audience saw only violence, lewdness, and sensationalism in such plays as *Richard III*, *Hamlet*, *King Lear*, *Othello*, and *Macbeth* and was incapable of understanding the moral and ethical dilemmas, the generational strains between parents and children, the crude ambition of Richard III or Lady Macbeth, the haunting guilt of Macbeth, the paralyzing introspection and doubts of Hamlet, the envy of Iago, the insecurities of Othello. We have been asked to believe that such human conditions and situations were beyond the powers of most of the audience and touched only a "refined element" who understood the "subtleties of Shakespeare's art."

Certainly, the relationship of an audience to the object of its focus—be it a sermon, political speech, newspaper, musical composition, or play—is a complex one and constitutes a problem for the historian who would reconstruct it. But the problem cannot be resolved through the use of such ahistorical devices as dividing both the audience and the object into crude categories and then coming to conclusions that have more to do with the culture of the writer than that of the subject. In fact, the way to understand the popularity of Shakespeare is to enter into the spirit of the nineteenth century. Shakespeare was popular, first and foremost, because he was integrated into the culture and presented within its context. Nineteenth-century Americans were able to fit Shakespeare into their culture so easily because he *seemed* to fit—because so many of his values and tastes were, or at least appeared to be, close to their own, and were presented through figures that seemed real and came to matter to the audience. Shakespeare's characters, the lecturer Henry Norman Hudson insisted, were so vivid, so alive, that they assumed the shape "of actual persons, so that we know them as well and remember them as distinctly as we do our most intimate friends." A correspondent in *American Monthly* in 1836 declared that Shakespeare's characters "become as vivid and real as those which we encounter in life. They are the acting and moving beings in a world, into which we can expand ourselves with so complete a presence as to include them within our actual experience." For the teenaged William Dean Howells, who memorized great chunks of Shakespeare while working as an apprentice printer in his father's newspaper office in the 1850s, the world of Shakespeare was one in which he felt as much "at home," as much like "a citizen," as he did in his small Ohio town.[29]

Both worlds enshrined the art of oratory. The same Americans who found diversion and pleasure in lengthy political debates, who sought joy and God in the sermons of church and camp meeting, who had, in short, a seemingly inexhaustible appetite for the spoken word, thrilled to Shakespeare's eloquence, memorized his soliloquies, delighted in his dialogues. Although nineteenth-century Americans stressed the importance of literacy and built an impressive system of public education, theirs remained an oral world in which the spoken word was central. In such a world, Shakespeare had no difficulty finding a place. Nor was Shakespearean oratory confined to the professional stage; it often was a part of life. Walt Whitman recalled that as a young man he rode in the Broadway omnibuses "declaiming some stormy passage from Julius Caesar or Richard" to passersby. In the 1850s Mark Twain worked as an apprentice to the pilot-master George Ealer on the steamboat *Pennsylvania*: "He would read Shakespeare to me; not just casually, but by the hour, when it was his watch, and I was steering . . . He did not use the book, and did not need to; he knew his Shakespeare as well as Euclid ever knew his multiplication table." In Corpus Christi, Texas, in 1845, soldiers of the Fourth Infantry Regiment broke the monotony of waiting for the Mexican War to begin by staging plays, including a performance of *Othello* starring young Lieutenant Ulysses S. Grant as Desdemona. That the scene in Corpus Christi was not unusual is made clear by an entry George Templeton Strong made in his diary in 1850 after a stay at West Point: "Some of the officers got up a series of Shakespeare readings last winter by way of varying the routine of mess life." Many of Lincoln's aides and associates remember his tendency to recite long, relevant passages from Shakespeare during the troubling days of the Civil War. Lincoln was not alone; Shakespeare was part and parcel of nineteenth-century political discourse. Ex-Senator John B. Henderson of Missouri, for example, supported James G. Blaine's presidential aspirations by writing of him to Carl Schurz in 1884: "If he has been a Prince Hal in days gone by, when responsibility comes he will be a Henry V. The Falstaffs who have followed him . . . will not be recognized in shaping his policies nor be suffered to bring odium upon his Administration." Shakespearean allusions and quotations were a regular feature of nineteenth-century newspapers. In the antebellum New Orleans press, reports of thefts regularly featured such aphorisms as "who steals my purse steals trash," murder stories commonly compared the contemporary transgressor with such Shakespearean killers as Othello and Macbeth, and the kindest thing a critic could say of a local comedian was that he "would make the ghost of Hamlet's father laugh." Shakespeare was taught in nineteenth-century schools and colleges as declamation or rhetoric, not literature. For many youngsters Shakespeare was first encountered in schoolbooks as texts to be recited aloud and memorized. Through this impressive panoply of means, Shakespearean phrases, aphorisms, ideas, and language helped shape

American speech and became so integral a part of the nineteenth-century imagination that it is a futile exercise to separate Americans' love of Shakespeare's oratory from their appreciation for his subtle use of language.[30]

It was not merely Shakespeare's language but his style that recommended itself to nineteenth-century audiences. In a period when melodrama became one of the mainstays of the American stage, Shakespearean plays easily lent themselves to the melodramatic style. Shakespearean drama featured heroes and villains who communicated directly with the audience and left little doubt about the nature of their character or their intentions. In a series of asides during the opening scenes of the first act, Macbeth shares his "horrible imaginings" and "vaulting ambition" with the audience (I.iii–vii). Similarly, Iago confides to the audience "I hate the Moor," rehearses his schemes of "double knavery" to betray both Cassio and Othello, and confesses that his jealousy of Othello "Doth, like a poisonous mineral, gnaw my inwards; / And nothing can or shall content my soul / Till I am evened with him" (I.iii). As in melodrama, Shakespearean villains are aware not only of their own evil but also of the goodness of their adversaries. Thus Iago, even as he plots against Othello, admits that "The Moor—howbeit that I endure him not— / Is of a constant, loving, noble nature" (II.i).

Lines like these, which so easily fit the melodramatic mode, were delivered in appropriately melodramatic style. The actors who dominated the stage during the first half of the nineteenth century were vigorous, tempestuous, emotional. To describe these men, contemporaries reached for words like "hurricane," "maelstrom," "avalanche," "earthquake," "monsoon," and "whirlwind." Edmund Kean's acting, one of them noted, was "just on the edge, sometimes quite over the edge of madness." It "blinded and stunned the beholders, appalled the imagination, and chilled their blood." Walt Whitman, who saw Junius Brutus Booth perform in the late 1830s, wrote of him, "He illustrated Plato's rule that to the forming an artist of the very highest rank a dash of insanity or what the world calls insanity is indispensable." The first great American-born Shakespearean actor, Edwin Forrest, carried this romantic tradition to its logical culmination. William Rounseville Alger, who saw Forrest perform, described his portrayal of Lear after Goneril rebuffs him:

His eyes flashed and faded and reflashed. He beat his breast as if not knowing what he did. His hands clutched wildly at the air as though struggling with something invisible. Then, sinking on his knees, with upturned look and hands straight outstretched towards his unnatural daughter, he poured out, in frenzied tones of mingled shriek and sob, his withering curse, half adjuration, half malediction.[31]

As in melodrama itself, language and style in American productions of Shakespeare were not utilized randomly; they were used to inculcate values, to express ideas and attitudes. For all of the complaints of such as Whitman that the feudal plays of Shakespeare were not altogether fitting for a democratic age, Shakespeare's attraction for nineteenth-century audiences was due in no small part to the fact that he was—or at least was taken to be—in tune with much of nineteenth-century American consciousness. From the beginning, Shakespeare's American admirers and promoters maintained that he was preeminently a *moral* playwright. To overcome the general prejudice against the theater in the eighteenth century, Shakespeare's plays were frequently presented as "moral dialogues" or "moral lectures." In Newport, Rhode Island, in 1761 *Othello* was advertised as "Depicting the Evil Effects of Jealousy and other Bad Passions," and the example of Iago was utilized to warn, "The man that wrongs his master and his friend, / What can he come to but a shameful end?" For Thomas Jefferson, "A lively and lasting sense of filial duty is more effectually impressed on the mind of a son or daughter by reading *King Lear*, than by all the dry volumes of ethics and divinity that ever were written." For Abraham Lincoln, *Macbeth* stood as "the perfect illustration of the problems of tyranny and murder." And John Quincy Adams concluded, even as he was waging his heroic fight against the power of the slave South in the House of Representatives in 1836, that the moral of *Othello* was "that the intermarriage of black and white blood is a violation of the law of nature. *That* is the lesson to be learned from the play."[32]

Regardless of specific interpretations, writers of nineteenth-century schoolbooks and readers seemed to have agreed with Henry Norman Hudson that Shakespeare's works provided "a far better school of virtuous discipline than half the moral and religious books which are now put into the hands of youth" and reprinted lines from Shakespeare not only to illustrate the art of declamation but also to disseminate moral values and patriotic principles. As late as 1870 the playbill of a New Orleans theater spelled out the meaning of *Twelfth Night*: "MORAL: In this play Shakespeare has finely penciled the portraits of Folly and Vanity in the persons of Aguecheek and Malvolio; and with a not less masterly hand, he has exhibited the weakness of the human mind when Love has usurped the place of Reason." The affinity between Shakespeare and the American people went beyond moral homilies; it extended to the basic ideological underpinnings of nineteenth-century America. When Cassius proclaimed that "The fault, dear Brutus, is not in our stars, / But in ourselves, that we are underlings" (*Julius Caesar*, I.ii), and when Helena asserted that "Our remedies oft in ourselves do lie, / Which we ascribe to heaven: the fated sky / Gives us free scope" (*All's Well That Ends Well*, I.i), they articulated a belief that was central to the pervasive success ethos of the nineteenth century and that confirmed the developing American worldview.[33]

Whatever Shakespeare's own designs, philosophy, and concept of humanity were, his plays had meaning to a nation that placed the individual at the center of the universe and personalized the large questions of the day. The actor Joseph Jefferson held Shakespeare responsible for the star system that prevailed for so much of the nineteenth century since "his tragedies almost without exception contain one great character on whom the interest of the play turns, and upon whom the attention of the audience is centered." Shakespeare's characters—like the Davy Crocketts and Mike Finks that dominated American folklore and the Jacksons, Websters, Clays, and Calhouns who dominated American politics—were larger than life: their passions, appetites and dilemmas were of epic proportions. Here were forceful, meaningful people who faced, on a larger scale, the same questions as those that filled the pages of schoolbooks: the duties of children and parents, husbands and wives, governed and governors to one another. In their lives the problems of jealousy, morality, and ambition were all writ large. However flawed some of Shakespeare's central figures were, they at least acted—even the indecisive Hamlet—and bore responsibility for their own fate. If they failed, they did so because ultimately they lacked sufficient inner control.

Thus Othello was undone by his jealousy and gullibility, Coriolanus by his pride, Macbeth and Richard III by their ambition. All of them could be seen as the architects of their own fortune, the masters of their own fate. All of them, Henry Norman Hudson taught his audiences, "contain within themselves the reason why they are there and not elsewhere, why they are so and not otherwise." In 1906 Martha Baker Dunn looked back on her long-standing relationship with Shakespeare, whom she first met through his plays when she was a young girl ill with measles, and recalled how attracted she always was to the "moral of individual responsibility" in his work: "Shakespeare's message is the message of a robust manhood and womanhood: Brace up, pay for what you have, do good if you wish to get good; good or bad, shoulder the burden of your moral responsibility, and never forget that cowardice is the most fatal and most futile crime in the calendar of crimes."[34]

How important this quality of individual will was can be seen in the fate of Sophocles' *Oedipus* in nineteenth-century America. The play was introduced twice in the century to New York audiences and failed both times, largely because of its subject matter. The *New York Tribune*'s reaction, after *Oedipus* opened in January 1882, was typical: "King Oedipus certainly carries more woe to the square inch than anybody else that ever walked upon the stage. And it is woe of the very worst kind—without solace, and without hope." Sophocles seemed guilty of determinism—an ideological stance nineteenth-century Americans rejected out of hand. "The overmastering fates that broke men and women upon the wheel of torture that destiny might be fulfilled are far away from us, the gods that lived and cast deep shadows over men's lives are turned to stone," the *New York Herald*'s reviewer wrote. "The helpful human being—who pays his way through the world finds it hard to imagine the creature kicking helpless in the traps of the gods." Similarly, critics attacked the bloodshed and immorality in *Oedipus*. The *New York Mirror* denounced "a plot like this, crammed full of murder, suicide, self-mutilation, incest, and dark deeds of a similar character."[35] Shakespearean drama, of course, was no less laced through with gore. But, while this quality in Sophocles seemed to Americans to be an end in itself, Shakespeare's thought patterns were either close enough or were made to seem close enough so that the violence had a point, and that point appeared to buttress American values and confirm American expectations.

This ideological equation, this ability of Shakespeare to connect with Americans' underlying beliefs, is crucial to an understanding of his role in nineteenth-century America. Much has been made of the adaptations of Shakespeare as instruments that made him somehow more understandable to American audiences. Certainly, the adaptations did work this way—not primarily, as has been so widely claimed, by vulgarizing or simplifying him to the point of utter distortion but rather by heightening those qualities in Shakespeare that American audiences were particularly drawn to. The liberties taken with Shakespeare in nineteenth-century America were often similar to liberties taken with folklore: Shakespeare was frequently seen as common property to be treated as the user saw fit. Thus many small changes were made for practical and moral reasons without much fanfare or fuss: minor roles were consolidated to create richer acting parts; speeches and scenes, considered overly long or extraneous, were shortened or omitted; sexual references were rendered more palatable by shifting such words as "whores" to "wenches," having Othello refer to "stolen hours of unfaithfulness" rather than "stolen hours of lust," and changing the phrase "happiness to their sheets" to "happiness be theirs"; contemporary sensibilities were catered to by making Juliet eighteen rather than thirteen, by softening some of Hamlet's angriest diatribes against Ophelia and his mother, or by preventing Othello from overtly manhandling Desdemona before he finally strangles her. Some of the alterations bordered on the spectacular, such as the flying, singing witches in *Macbeth* and the elaborate funeral procession that accompanied Juliet's body to the tomb of the Capulets in *Romeo and Juliet*. On the whole, such limited changes were made with respect for—and sensitivity to—Shakespeare's purposes.[36]

It is important to realize that, while some of the alterations were imported from England and others were made in America, none were adopted indiscriminately. Of the many drastically revised editions of Shakespeare that originated in England, only those by David Garrick, Nahum Tate, and Colley Cibber held sway in the United States during the nineteenth century. David Garrick's *Catharine and Petruchio* (1756), a three-act condensation of *The Taming of the Shrew* that retained the basic thrust of Shakespeare's original, won considerable popularity as an afterpiece and was not superseded until Augustin Daly produced the full version of Shakespeare's play in 1887. The popularity of Garrick's revision of *Romeo and Juliet*, which allowed Juliet to awaken from her sleep moments before Romeo's poison took effect so that the the two lovers could enjoy a final farewell, was further proof that Shakespeare was viewed as a human playwright whose dramatic effects were often imperfect and could be improved upon. For our purposes, however, Nahum Tate's revision of *King Lear* (1681), and Colley Cibber's revision of *Richard III* (1700), are the most interesting. If brevity and enhanced dramatic effect were the chief virtues of Garrick's revisions, the attractions of Cibber's *Richard* and Tate's *Lear* were more complex and suggest that those alterations of Shakespeare that became most prevalent in the United States were those that best fit the values and ideology of the period and the people.

For most of the nineteenth century Colley Cibber's *Richard III* held sway everywhere.* Cibber's revision, by cutting onethird of the lines, eliminating half of the characters, adding scenes from other Shakespearean plays and from Cibber's own pen, succeeded in muting the ambiguities of the original and focusing all of the evil in the person of Richard. Thus, although Cibber retained Shakespeare's essential plot and much of his poetry, he refashioned the play in such a way that, while his work was done in the England of 1700, it could have been written a hundred years later in the United States, so closely did it agree with American sensibilities concerning the centrality of the individual,

---

*Its popularity continued well into the twentieth century. In 1909 Alice Wood reported that Cibber's version of *Richard III* "is still holding the stage and is still preferred by a large part of the community," and thus "the struggle for the 'Richard the Third' of Shakespeare is still 'on.'" In 1930, Arthur Colby Sprague attended a performance of *Richard III* in Boston and was treated to "the Cibber text, practically in its entirety" although Cibber's name was nowhere mentioned. As late as 1955, Laurence Olivier, in his film version of *Richard III*, continued to recite Cibber's as well as Shakespeare's lines.

the dichotomy between good and evil, and the importance of personal responsibility. Richmond's speech over the body of the vanquished Richard mirrored perfectly America's moral sense and melodramatic taste:

> Farewel, Richard, and from thy dreadful end
> May future Kings from Tyranny be warn'd;
> Had thy aspiring Soul but stir'd in Vertue
> With half the Spirit it has dar'd in Evil,
> How might thy Fame have grac'd our English Annals:
> But as thou art, how fair a Page thou'st blotted.

If Cibber added lines making clear the fate of villains, he was no less explicit concerning the destiny of heroes. After defeating Richard, Richmond is informed that "the Queen and fair Elizabeth, / Her beauteous Daughter, some few miles off, are / On their way to Gratulate your Victory." His reply must have warmed America's melodramatic heart as much as it confirmed its ideological underpinnings: "Ay, there indeed my toil's rewarded."[37]

Tate's altered *King Lear*, like Cibber's *Richard III*, virtually displaced Shakespeare's own version for almost two centuries.* Tate, who distorted Shakespeare far more than Cibber did, devised a happy ending for what was one of the most tragic of all of Shakespeare's plays: he created a love affair between Edgar and Cordelia and allowed Cordelia and Lear to live. Although there were certainly critics of this fundamental alteration, it proved popular with theatergoers. When in 1826 James H. Hackett chided his fellow actor Edmund Kean about his choice of Tate's ending rather than Shakespeare's, Kean replied that he had attempted to restore the original, "but when I had ascertained that a large majority of the publlic—whom we live to please, and must please to be popular—liked Tate better than Shakespeare, I fell back upon his corruption; though in my soul I was ashamed of the prevailing taste, and of my professional condition that required me to minister unto it." Still, many Americans defended the Tate version on ideological grounds.

---

*It was not until November 16, 1875, when Edwin Booth presented his "restored" version of *Lear*, that an important American actor performed the play without benefit of Tate.

"The moral's now more complete," wrote a contemporary, "for although Goneril, Regan, and Edmond were deservedly punished for their crimes, yet Lear and Cordelia were killed without reason and without fault. But now they survive their enemies and virture is crowned with happiness." That virtue be "crowned with happiness" was essential to the beliefs of nineteenth-century Americans. Thus audiences had the pleasure of having their expectations confirmed when Edgar concludes the play by declaring to "Divine Cordelia":

> Thy bright Example shall convince the World
> (Whatever Storms of Fortune are decreed)
> That Truth and Vertue shall at last succeed.[38]

T HE PROFOUND and longstanding nineteenth-century American experience with Shakespeare, then, was neither accidental nor aberrant. It was based upon the language and eloquence, the artistry and humor, the excitement and action, the moral sense and worldview that Americans found in Shakespearean drama. The more firmly based Shakespeare was in nineteenth-century culture, the more difficult it is to understand why he lost so much of his audience so quickly; why as early as 1890 A. C. Wheeler could announce "The Extinction of Shakespeare," and ask rhetorically, "Does anyone suppose that the theatre will ever be able to reawaken in the public the interest in Shakespeare's work that attended its earlier productions?"[39]

Certainly some of the factors underlying Shakespeare's transformation were intricately connected to the internal history of the theater. So long as the theater was under attack on moral grounds, as it was in the eighteenth and early nineteenth centuries, Shakespeare, because of his immense reputation, could be presented more easily and could be used to help make the theater itself legitimate. Shakespearean drama also lent itself to the prevalent star system. Only the existence of a small repertory of well-known plays, in which Shakespeare's were central, made it feasible for the towering stars of England and America to travel throughout the United States acting with resident stock companies wherever they went. The relative dearth of native dramatists and the relative scarcity of competing forms of theatrical entertainment also figured in Shakespeare's popularity. As these conditions were altered, Shakespeare's popularity and centrality were affected. As important as factors peculiar to the theater were, and I will return to them at the end of this chapter, the theater did not exist in a vacuum; it was an integral part of American culture—of interest to the historian precisely because it so frequently and so accurately revealed the conditions surrounding it. A fuller explanation must therefore be sought in the larger culture itself.

Among the salient cultural changes at the turn of the century were those in language and rhetorical style. The oratorical mode, which so dominated the nineteenth century and which helped make Shakespeare popular, hardly survived into the twentieth century. In 1838 Philip Hone heard Senator John Crittenden of Kentucky denounce the sub-treasury bill and pronounced it "the greatest speech I ever heard. . . . He spoke just three hours, and when he concluded, and the Senate adjourned, the audience lingered in their seats, as if loath to leave the spot of their enchantment." By the close of the century no longer would Americans tolerate speeches of such duration; no longer was their attention riveted upon such political debates as that between Webster and Hayne in 1830, which consumed several days. It is true that in the closing years of the century William Jennings Bryan could still rise to national political leadership through his superb oratorical skills, but it is equally true that well before his death in 1925 he lived to see himself become an anachronism, the bearer of a style redolent of an earlier culture. What was true of politics was true of the theater. "Philosophy in action, not in words, represents the ideal of what is best and most desirable in the drama of these times," the *New York Times* declared in 1909 in an attempt to understand why "no large and steady portion of the regular theatregoing public will be diverted from its pursuit of the things which really interest it" to attend Shakespearean drama. The reason, the *Times* concluded, was that Shakespeare had catered more to the ear than the eye; had provided more of a rostrum for the speaker than a visual arena for acting out human drama.[40]

The surprisingly rapid decline of oratory as a force in national life, which deserves more intensive study, certainly was affected by the influx of millions of non-English-speaking people. The more than one thousand foreign-language newspapers and magazines published in the United States by 1910 testify graphically to the existence of a substantial group for whom Shakespeare, at least in his original language, was less familiar and less accessible. Many immigrant groups, of course, created their own theaters, which, Louise Taylor has argued, helped to keep Shakespeare alive in Chicago during the closing decades of the nineteenth century. One certainly could make the same argument for New York City on whose Yiddish stages a number of Shakespearean plays became familiar in unique versions. Here, for example, is Hutchins Hapgood's summary of the Yiddish *Hamlet* (1899):

> The uncle is a rabbi in a small village in Russia. He did not poison Hamlet's father but broke the latter's heart by wooing and winning his queen. Hamlet is off somewhere getting educated as a rabbi. While he is gone his father dies. Six weeks afterwards the son returns in the midst of the wedding feast, and turns the feast into a funeral. Scenes of rant follow between mother and son, Ophelia and Hamlet, interspersed with jokes and sneers at the sect of rabbis who think they communicate with the angels. The wicked rabbi conspires against Hamlet, trying to make him out a nihilist. The plot is discovered and the wicked rabbi is sent to Siberia. The last act is the graveyard scene . . . Ophelia is brought in on the bier. Hamlet mourns by her side and is married, according to the Jewish custom, to the dead woman. Then he dies of a broken heart.

In similar fashion, Romeo and Juliet (Raphael and Shaindele) were depicted as the children of antithetical religious factions with Friar Lawrence cast as a Reform rabbi. In Jacob Gordin's popular *The Jewish King Lear*, Lear is transformed into a Russian Jewish merchant who ignores the lesson of Shakespeare's *King Lear*, which a friend reads to him, and prematurely divides his wealth among his grasping daughters only to end up blind, poor, and broken. The existence of such productions does not preclude the fact that these immigrant folk were a vital factor in the creation of a ready constituency for the rise of the more visual entertainments such as baseball, boxing, vaudeville, burlesque, and especially the new silent movies, which could be enjoyed by a larger and often more marginal audience less steeped in the language and the culture.[41]

If what Reuel Denney called the "deverbalization of the

forum" weakened Shakespeare among some segments of the population, the parallel growth of literacy among other groups also undermined some of the props that had sustained Shakespeare's popularity. Literacy encroached upon the pervasive oral culture that had created in nineteenth-century America an audience more comfortable with listening than reading. The "men who move and lead the world," Professor Melvil Dewey declared in 1876, "are using the press more and the platform less." Thus the generations of people accustomed to hearing and reciting things out loud—the generations for whom oral recitation of the King James version of the Bible could well have formed a bridge to the English of Shakespeare—were being depleted as America entered a new century.[42]

These language-related changes were accompanied by changes in taste and style. John Higham has argued that from the 1860s through the 1880s romantic idealism declined in the United States. The melodramatic mode, to which Shakespeare lent himself so well and in which he was performed so frequently, went into a related decline. "The grand days of histrionics," Olive Logan declared as early as 1879, were "now forever past." No longer would critics advise actors, as they had counseled Tyrone Power earlier in the century, "You must not be so quiet: give them more bustle . . . You must paint a little broader, my dear fellow, you're too natural for them; they don't feel it." Edwin Booth, the most influential Shakespearean actor in America during the closing decades of the nineteenth century, played his roles in a less ferocious, more subtle and intellectualized fashion than his father and most of the other leading actors of the first half of the century had. When asked how his acting compared to his father's, Booth replied simply, "I think I must be somewhat quieter."* The younger Booth's quietness became the paradigm.[43]

When Robert Bruce Mantell opened in *Richard III* in 1904,

---

*The questioner was the young actor Otis Skinner. As he was preparing for his first portrayal of Shylock in 1893—the year of Booth's death—Skinner discovered the extent of Booth's influence: "I found myself reading speeches with the Booth cadence, using the Booth gestures, attitudes and facial expressions, in short, giving a rank imitation. The ghost of the dead actor rose between me and the part."

the critic for the *New York Journal* praised him by writing, "There were none of the mouthings and rantings of your old school; there were none of the noise and incoherency of the bumptious barnstormer." "We cannot abide Shakespeare spouted after the manner of the old days," the Boston drama critic H. T. Parker proclaimed in 1914, while the critic-scholar Brander Matthews observed that same year, "Our actors are now less rhetorical and more pictorial—as they must be on the stage of our modern theater." Conceptions of what was "natural" and tasteful on the stage changed so rapidly that by the end of their careers actors like Booth and Mantell were considered by many to be vestiges of the old school.* The visceral, thunderous style fell into such disfavor that by 1920 the critic Francis Hackett not only berated John Barrymore for his emotional portrayal of Richard III but also took Shakespeare himself to task for the "unsophisticated" manner in which he had crafted the play that nineteenth-century audiences had enjoyed above all others: "The plot, the psychology, the history, seem to me infantile . . . Are we led to understand Richard? No, only to moralize over him. Thus platitude makes cowards of us all."[44]

These gradual and decisive changes in language, style, and taste are important but by themselves do not constitute a totally satisfying explanation for the diminished popularity of Shakespeare. As important as changes in language and the decline of oratory were, they did not prevent the development of radio as a central entertainment medium at the beginning of the 1920s or the emergence of talking movies at the end of that decade. Nor was there anything inherent in the new popular media that necessarily relegated Shakespeare to a smaller, elite audience; on the contrary, he was quite well suited to the new forms of presentation that came to dominance. His comedies had an abundance of slapstick and contrived happy endings, his tragedies and historical plays had more than their share of action. Most im-

---

*In the 1920s Alan Downer saw Mantell—then in his seventies—act *Macbeth* in a Syracuse theater: "As he huddled through his part for the thousandth time, he was plainly an actor who had lived too long, worked too hard. The theatre had disowned him, he was acting in a dead tradition, living in a dead repertory."

Edwin Forrest as Macbeth.

The transformation in Shakespeare's role in American culture was partly reflected in the transition from such American Shakespeareans as Edwin Forrest, whose emotional style dominated the first half of the nineteenth century, to Edwin Booth, whose more restrained cerebral style won increasing favor in the second half of the century.

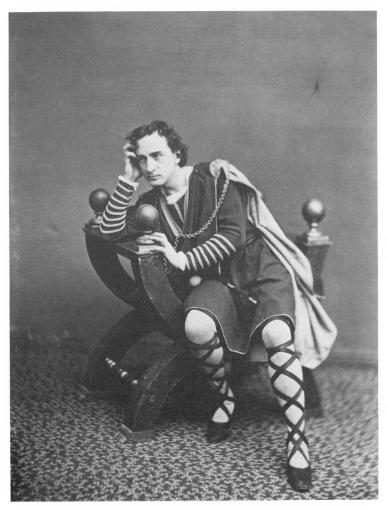

Edwin Booth as Hamlet.

portant, having written for a stage devoid of scenery, Shakespeare could and did incorporate as much spatial mobility as he desired into his plays: twenty-five scene changes in *Macbeth*, one of his shortest plays, and forty-two in *Antony and Cleopatra*, where the action gravitated from Alexandria to such locales as Rome, Messina, Athens, and Syria. This fluidity—which caused innumerable problems for the stagecraft of the nineteenth century—was particularly appropriate to the movies, which could visually reproduce whatever Shakespeare had in mind, and to radio, which, like the Elizabethan stage itself, could rely upon the imagination of its audience. In 1927 the film director Abel Gance was full of hope. "Shakespeare, Rembrandt, Beethoven will make films," he exclaimed, "all legends, all mythologies and all myths, all founders of religion, and the very religions . . . await their exposed resurrection, and the heroes crowd each other at the gate." A few years later an American critic declared that only Hollywood could rescue Shakespeare from the confines of the intellectuals and of Broadway and make him available once again to Main Street. That these hopes went unrealized, that the new media did not take full advantage of so recently a popular source of entertainment as Shakespearean drama, demands further explanation.[45]

Shakespeare of course remained—and remains—a presence in American society. In the 1895 edition of Montgomery Ward's catalogue, for example, one could purchase the complete works of Shakespeare in many forms for a variety of relatively reasonable prices. In one volume for $1.23; in three volumes for $1.85; in four volumes for $1.50 (cloth) or $3.98 (half calf); in eight volumes for $4.00 (cloth) or $6.75 (French morocco with gilt edges); in thirteen volumes for $3.98; in forty volumes with five hundred illustrations for $11.00. In this and related forms, Shakespeare remained readily and easily accessible but less and less as a living playwright and more and more as a literary classic.[46]

Even when Shakespeare penetrated to the very heart of mass culture in the form of films and radio and television programs, it was almost always as a means of gaining prestige for the producer, director, and actors as in Max Reinhardt's 1935 film *A Midsummer Night's Dream*—featuring such improbable but interesting casting as James Cagney and Joe E. Brown playing

Bottom and Flute respectively—which captured the attention of the intellectual and artistic communities but not of the general populace. The *New York Times* reviewer was typical in praising it not as a film but as "a work of high ambitions," and "a credit to Warner Brothers and to the motion picture industry." *A Midsummer Night's Dream*, *Time* magazine announced, "will be exhibited throughout the U.S. in theatres usually used for legitimate productions rather than in cinemansions, impressively brought to the attention of schools, women's clubs and Shakespeare societies." "Culture groups will be as happy as bees," the *New Yorker* declared, and the *New Republic* predicted that "at its many screenings there will be no lack of Ah's and Oh's, culture clubs will have discussions, newspaper critics will put on their Sunday adjectives; but . . . there is going to be a powerful minority of American husbands who will get one load of the elves and pixies, and feel betrayed." In 1937 when CBS announced a summer Shakespearean radio series featuring such popular actors as Burgess Meredith as Hamlet, Walter Huston as Henry IV, and Edward G. Robinson as Petruchio, its main rival, NBC, immediately resurrected the celebrated John Barrymore, then in a state of decline, and put him in a "Streamlined Shakespeare" series on Monday nights at eight o'clock directly opposite the CBS show so that listeners had to choose between the two.[47]

Shakespeare had become a cultural deity to whom even some of the most commercially minded producers and directors occasionally paid homage. Nevertheless, the conventional wisdom among radio, movie, and ultimately television executives, was that Shakespeare was for show not for profit. As early as 1890, A. C. Wheeler declared that any astute theater manager "will tell you that the intrinsic Shakespeare 'spells failure.' You must make a contemporaneous event of him with a notorious actor or an affluent backer." Shortly before his death in 1984, the actor Richard Burton—who had once had to pay for the chance to do a film version of *The Taming of the Shrew*—summed up a longstanding attitude when he commented: "Generally if you mention the word Shakespeare in Hollywood, everybody leaves the room, because they think he's box-office poison." When in the late 1970s the Public Broadcasting System prepared to show the

television productions of the Shakespearean dramatic corpus produced by BBC-TV and Time-Life Television, it treated its task
as one of education more than entertainment, arranging for
college and university credit for the programs and preparing
instructional kits for junior and senior high schools throughout
the nation.[48]

Certain Shakespearean plays, scenes, and soliloquies retained
sufficient familiarity to encourage the continuation of parody.
One favorite bit of newspaper verse turned Hamlet into a tor-
tured poker player:

> To draw or not to draw, that is the question.
> Whether it is safer in the player to take
> The awful risk of skinning for a straight,
> Or, standing pat, to raise 'em all the limit,
> And thus, by bluffing, get it . . .

A firm in Savannah used the same soliloquy to sell its fruit, hay,
grain, and peanuts:

> TO BE
> Or not to be—gin to save money
> For your future maintenance . . .
> Whether 'tis more sagacious in you
> To handle poor goods at high prices,
> Or by patronizing the Only Depot,
> Get the best at bottom prices . . .

Shakespeare proved equally adept at selling canned meat and
soap. In one advertisement Caesar's complaint, "Yon Cassius has
a lean and hungry look," prompted Brutus to respond, "Feed
him on Libby, McNeill & Libby's Cooked Corned beef." An ad
in *Youth's Companion* had the rustic Uncle Josh ask his neighbor
at the theater why Lady Macbeth was wringing her hands so:

> "It's Duncan's blood," the man replied,
> "She strives the fearful stains to hide."
> "Why don't she wash her hands, b'gosh!
> With Ivory Soap?" cried Uncle Josh.[49]

Though such references were common well into the twentieth
century, they seem to have become increasingly limited to the

handful of Shakespearean scenes and characters that remained well known in the society and were as emblematic of change as of continuity. Film parodies, for example, were largely confined not merely to *Romeo and Juliet* but primarily to the balcony and funeral scenes from that play. In Hal Roach's 1926 film *Bromo and Juliet*, the humor derived less from true parody of Shakespeare's plot or language than from the fact that the actor playing Romeo came to the theater drunk and turned the balcony scene into chaos. *Hamlet and Eggs* (1937), which dealt with an exhausted Shakespearean director who tries to find rest on an isolated ranch in Arizona only to be forced to put on an amateur production of *Romeo and Juliet*, came closer to nineteenth century parody when Juliet awakens in her tomb and sings, "O Bury Me Not on the Lone Prairie." But for the most part its humor derived from the contrast between the rough Western audience and the overcivilized Shakespearean director, who by the end of the film returns to his effete New York crowd converted to cowboy dress and speech. In the 1940 cartoon *Shakespearean Spinach*, Popeye as Romeo and Olive Oyl as Juliet sing their lines to the tunes of operatic arias, presumably on the assumption that one form of high culture is indistinguishable from another. The notion that Shakespearean drama was elevated above the cultural fare of everyday life was fundamental to all of these parodies. In the spring of 1939, a radio version of *Romeo and Juliet,* starring the heavyweight boxer Tony Galento (Two Ton Tony) as Romeo, attempted to induce laughter through the contrast created by filtering Shakespeare's glorious language through a pugilist's accent and phrasing. The announcer Milton Cross introduced the show by musing in his elevated tones, "These are days of contrasts.—When Tchaikovsky invades Tin Pan Alley." Referring sarcastically to Galento, he promised, "Theatrical history is about to be made!" In a real sense, the parody was less of Shakespeare than of Galento and the culture he presumably represented.[50]

"Whin Shakespere was played I often had a seat in th' gal'ry, . . . because I'd heerd me frind Hogan speak iv Shakespere. He was a good man, that Shakespere," the bartender Mr. Dooley told his friend Mr. Hennessy shortly after the new century had begun. "Why don't they play Shakespere any more?" Hennessy wondered. The answer of course was that they were still playing Shakespeare but in a different manner and to a different clientele, which a leading magazine characterized in 1900 as that "refined minority which still finds pleasure in Shakespeare and in all the dramas of the old-time school." Had Shakespeare largely vanished from or become a negligible force in American culture, as let us say Henry Wadsworth Longfellow has, we might be less hard pressed for an explanation of the changes, since many genres of culture regularly wax and wane. The problem that requires thoughtful attention is not why Shakespeare disappeared from American culture at the turn of the century, since he did not; but rather why he was *transformed* from a playwright for the general public into one for a specific audience. This metamorphosis of Shakespearean drama from popular culture to polite culture, from entertainment to erudition, from the property of "Everyman" to the possession of a more elite circle, needs to be seen within the perspective of other transformations that took place in nineteenth-century America.[51]

AT THE BEGINNING of the nineteenth century, the theater was a microcosm; it housed both the entire spectrum of the population and the complete range of entertainment from tragedy to farce, juggling to ballet, opera to minstrelsy. The theater drew all ranks of people to one place where they constituted what Erving Goffman has called a "focused gathering"—a set of people who relate to one another through the medium of a common activity. The term is useful in reminding us that in the theater people not only sat under one roof, they interacted. In this sense, the theater in the first half of the nineteenth century constituted a microcosm of still another sort: a microcosm of the relations between the various socioeconomic groups in America. The descriptions of such observers as Washington Irving and Mrs. Trollope make it clear that those relations were beset by tensions and conflicts. In 1830 the Tremont Theatre Investigating Committee worried about the "mass of vulgarity" that was being attracted to Boston's theaters, which were rapidly ceasing to be "fashionable" places of resort. Even so convinced a democrat as Walt Whitman complained by 1847 that the New York theaters were becoming "'low' places where vulgarity (not only on the stage, but in front of it) is in the ascendant, and bad-taste carries the day with hardly a pleasant point to mitigate its coarseness." Whitman excepted only the Park Theatre "because the audiences there are always intelligent, and there is a dash of superiority thrown over the Performances." Earlier in the century the Park Theatre had received the patronage of the entire public; by the 1830s it had become more exclusive, while the Bowery, Chatham, and other theaters became the preserves of gallery gods and groundlings. After visiting the New York theaters, Mrs. Trollope wrote in 1832, "The Park Theatre is the only one licensed by fashion, but the Bowery is infinitely superior in beauty; it is indeed as pretty a theatre as I ever entered, perfect as to size and proportion . . . but it is not the fashion. The Chatham is so utterly condemned by *bon ton*, that it requires some courage to decide upon going there." This development was not exclusive to New York. "I have discovered the *people* are with *us*," Tyrone Power reported from Baltimore in 1833, since the Front Theatre, at which he was performing, drew "the sturdy democracy of the good city," while its rival, the Holiday Theatre, was "considered the aristocratic house."[52]

There was an increasing segregation not only of audiences but ultimately of actors and styles as well. On a winter evening in 1863, George William Curtis, the editor of *Harper's*, took a "rustic friend" to two New York theaters. First they went to see Edwin Forrest at Niblo's Gardens. "It was crammed with people. All the seats were full, and the aisles, and the steps. And the people sat upon the stairs that ascend to the second tier, and they hung upon the balustrade, and they peeped over shoulders and between heads." Forrest's acting, Curtis noted, was "a boundless exaggeration of all the traditional conventions of the stage." Theatrically, he wrote, Forrest represented "the muscular school; the brawny art; the biceps aesthetics; the tragic calves; the bovine drama; rant, roar, and rigmarole." Still, he conceded that Forrest "move[d] his world nightly . . . There were a great many young women around us crying . . . They were not refined nor intellectual women. They were, perhaps, rather coarse. But they cried good hearty tears." After one act his friend whispered,

The Park Theatre in November 1822, as depicted in a watercolor by John Searle featuring the portraits of more than eighty contemporaries. Searle himself is in the front row center of the orchestra, facing away from the stage with one eye on us as we peruse his painting. The Park was to become the most fashionable of New York's theaters.

The Bowery Theatre in 1856, from whose stage the mass of New Yorkers enjoyed Shakespeare and other popular dramatic productions.

"I have had as much as I can hold," and they went up the street to the Winter Garden, where Edwin Booth was portraying Iago. "The difference of the spectacle was striking. The house was comfortably full, not crowded. The air of the audience was that of refined attention rather than of eager interest. Plainly it was a more cultivated and intellectual audience." And just as plainly they were seeing a very different type of acting. "Pale, thin, intellectual, with long black hair and dark eyes, Shakespeare's Iago was perhaps never more articulately represented . . . ; all that we saw of Booth was admirable."[53]

In 1810 John Howard Payne complained, "The judicious few are very few indeed. They are always to be found in a Theatre, like flowers in a desert, but they are nowhere sufficiently numerous to *fill* one." By the second half of the century this was evidently no longer the case. Separate theaters, catering to the "judicious," appeared in city after city, leaving the other theaters to those whom Payne called "the idle, profligate, and vulgar." The psychologist Robert Somer has shown the connections between space and status and has argued that "society compensates for blurred social distinctions by clear spatial ones." Such scholars as Burton J. Bledstein and William R. Taylor have noted the Victorian urge to structure or rationalize space. As the traditional spatial distinctions among pit, gallery, and boxes within the theater were undermined by the aggressive behavior of audiences caught up in the egalitarian exuberance of the period and freed in the atmosphere of the theater from many of the demands of normative behavior, this urge gradually led to the creation of separate theaters catering to distinct audiences and shattered for good the phenomenon of theater as a social microcosm of the entire society.[54]

This dramatic split in the American theater was part of more extensive bifurcations that were taking place in American culture and society. How closely the theater registered societal dissonance can be seen in the audiences' volatile reaction to anything they considered condescending behavior, out of keeping with the unique nature of American society. Anything even bordering on unpatriotic or aristocratic behavior was anathema. Joseph Jefferson told of the time in the early 1840s when he was asked to sing a patriotic anthem in a St. Louis theater, forgot the words, and was hissed off the stage. A performance of *Henry V* in Philadelphia's Chestnut Street Theatre in 1808 resulted in a riot because Henry's declaration "I thought upon one pair of English legs did march three Frenchmen," was interpreted as propaganda in favor of aristocratic England against revolutionary France. Having learned his lesson, William Wood, the theater's manager, insisted in 1825 that the actor Francis Wemyss change the line "Herbert stuck to his commander to the last, and died as every Englishman should," to read "as every brave man should." Wemyss insisted on delivering the line as it was written and, as he later reported, "I was saluted by such a general hiss as is seldom heard within the walls of a theatre."[55]

Not only was obeisance to the republic required, but allegiance to the *democratic* nature of the republic was demanded as well. As early as 1772 the manager David Douglass offered a reward for information leading to the arrest of vandals who "broke open the gallery door of the theatre, tore off and carried away the iron spikes which divide the galleries from the upper boxes." The tension created by hierarchical seating arrangements helps explain the periodic rain of objects that the gallery unleashed upon those in more privileged parts of the theater. When Washington Irving was "saluted aside [his] head with a rotten pippen" and rose to shake his cane at the gallery gods, he was restrained by a man behind him who warned that this would bring down upon him the full wrath of the people; the only course of action, he was advised, was to "sit down quietly and bend your back to it."[56]

English actors, who were *ipso facto* suspected of unpatriotic and undemocratic leanings, had to tread with particular caution. Edmund Kean failed to do so in 1821 when he canceled his performance of *Richard III* in Boston because only twenty people were in the audience. The next day's papers denounced him for insulting and dishonoring the American people and suggested that he be taken "by the nose, and dragged . . . before the curtain to make his excuses for his conduct." Four years later, when Kean returned to Boston, he attempted to make those excuses, but it was too late. The all-male audience that packed the theater and overflowed onto the streets allowed him neither to perform *Richard III* nor to apologize for what he admitted were his "indiscretions." A barrage of nuts, foodstuffs, and bottles of odorous drugs drove him weeping from the stage and the theater, after which the anti-Keanites in the pit and gallery turned on his supporters in the boxes and did grievous damage to the theater. Kean performed in Philadelphia, New York, and Charleston without serious incident but on the opening night of *Richard III* in Baltimore he faced what an observer called "a violent opposition" that "rendered all [his] attempts to be heard hopeless." He was finally escorted from the theater "safely, but in extreme terror," and never again appeared in the United States.[57]

In 1834 the Irishman Tyrone Power committed exactly the same error—he canceled a performance in Albany, New York, when the audience numbered less than ten—and found that even his outspoken democratic sympathies could not save him from a similar fate. When he next performed two days later, he reported, "the house was filled with men, and everything foreboded a violent outbreak . . . On my appearance the din was mighty deafening; . . . every invention for making the voice of humanity bestial was present and in full use. The boxes I observed to be occupied by well-dressed men, who generally either remained neutral, or by signs sought that I should be heard." Upon the intervention of the manager, Power was allowed to explain himself, after which "the row was resumed with added fierceness: not a word of either play or farce was heard."[58]

Scenes like this could take place suddenly upon the slightest of provocations. In the fall of 1831 J. R. Anderson, an English actor and singer, arrived in New York City accompanied by stories that he had spoken abusively of Americans on board ship and that he continued his abuse after landing in America. The aristocratic Philip Hone attended Anderson's debut at the Park Theatre on Thursday, October 13, and found him "standing in the front of the stage, with the most imperturbable self-posses-sion, amidst deafening shouts of 'Off! Off! Go back to England! Tell them the Yankees sent you back!'" The play went on in a dumb show: "The songs were sung, and the dialogue was spo-ken," but every time Anderson appeared "the clamorous uproar was renewed, and the curtain fell midst . . . disorder." Despite his contrite letter of apology in the newspapers, when Anderson next appeared two nights later he faced more than noise. Apples, oranges, eggs, "and other like missiles," descended upon the stage. An alarmed manager held an impromptu town meeting, asked his patrons—a group of whom had come to support An-derson—what they desired and responded to the dominant cries of "let him be withdrawn!" "off with him!" "send him home!" by "bowing in token of compliance" and removing Anderson from the play. Although the *Evening Post* concluded that "the audience, for a riotous one, behaved with singular decorum," the people were not yet pacified. The following day, Sunday, large groups gathered in front of the theater, shouting, cheering, breaking windows, and battering doors. The American and tri-colored flags were exhibited from the Park's upper windows, which appeared to appease the people, who were further pro-pitiated on Monday when the front of the theater was "covered with transparencies of patriotic subjects, flags and eagles in abun-dance." On Tuesday, the Park Theatre's main rival cautiously preceded its announcement of that evening's play—*The Glory of Columbia*—by declaring: "BOWERY THEATRE—The Manager announces that this Theatre will heareafter be called the 'American Theatre, Bowery.'"[59]

The full extent of class feeling and divisions existing in egalitarian America was revealed on a bloody Thursday in May 1849 at and around the Astor Place Opera House in New York City. The immediate catalyst was a long-standing feud between two leading actors, the Englishman William Charles Macready and the American Edwin Forrest, who had become symbols of antithetical values. Forrest's vigorous acting style, his militant love of his country, his outspoken belief in its citizenry, and his frequent articulation of the possibilities of self-improvement and social mobility endeared him to the American people, while Macready's cerebral acting style, his aristocratic demeanor, and his identification with the wealthy gentry made him appear Forrest's diametric opposite. On May 7, Macready and Forrest appeared against one another in separate productions of *Macbeth*. Forrest's performance, at the Broadway Theatre, was a triumph both dramatically and politically. When Forrest spoke Macbeth's lines, "What rhubarb, senna or what purgative drug will scour these English hence?" the entire audience, according to the actor Lester Wallack, "rose and cheered for many minutes." Macready's performance, at the Astor Place Opera House, was never heard—he was silenced by a storm of boos and cries of "Three groans for the codfish aristocracy," which drowned out appeals for order from those in the boxes, and by an avalanche of eggs, apples, potatoes, lemons, and, ultimately, chairs hurled from the gallery, which forced him to leave the stage in the third act. For hours after the theater was forcibly closed, Macready's opponents triumphantly paraded through the streets chanting snatches of the witches' chorus:

> When shall we three meet again
> In thunder, lightening, or in rain?
> When the hurlyburly's done,
> When the battles lost and won.

"This cannot end here," Philip Hone correctly predicted in his diary the next day; "the respectable part of our citizens will never consent to be put down by a mob raised to serve the purpose of

The Astor Place Riot, 1849.

such a fellow as Forrest." Though Macready was prepared to leave the country, he was dissuaded by persons of "highest respectability," including Washington Irving and Herman Melville, who urged him not to encourage the mob by giving in to it and assured him "that the good sense and respect for order prevailing in this community will sustain you."* Eighteen hundred people filled the Astor Place Opera House on the evening of May 10, with some ten thousand more on the streets outside. Assisted by the quick arrest of the most voluble opponents inside the theater, Macready completed his performance of *Macbeth*, but only under great duress. Those outside—stirred by orators' shouts of "Burn the damned den of the aristocracy!" and "You can't go in there without . . . kid gloves and a white vest, damn 'em!"—bom-

---

*The signers of the letter to Macready included twenty-two lawyers, six merchants, five editors, three authors, two physicians, one banker, one broker, one shipowner, one hotel proprietor, and several other assorted businessmen.

barded the theater with paving stones, attempted to storm the entrances, and were stopped only after detachments of militia fired point blank into the crowd. In the end at least twenty-two people were killed, and over one hundred and fifty were wounded or injured.* "Although the lesson has been dearly bought," Philip Hone noted in his diary, "it is of great value, inasmuch as the fact has been established that law and order can be maintained under a Republican form of government."[60]

If the eighty-six men arrested were at all typical, the crowd had been composed of workingmen—coopers, printers, butchers, carpenters, servants, sailmakers, machinists, clerks, masons, bakers, plumbers, laborers—whose feelings were probably reflected in a speech given at a rally in City Hall Park the next day: "Fellow citizens, for what—for whom was this murder committed? . . . Was it done for the sake of justice and the object of preserving order? (Loud cries of 'No, no.') I think not. For what, then, was it done? To please the aristocracy of the city, at the expense of the lives of inoffending citizens—to please an aristocratic Englishman, backed by a few sycophantic Americans . . . to revenge the aristocrats of this city against the working classes." Mingling with the crowd gathered at Astor Place the day after the riot, a journalist reported, "There was evidently a strong feeling excited, but it was not so much against the military whom all parties exonerate from blame, as against the committee of the Opera House, and those who signed the requisition to Mr. Macready to appear again, in the face of the organised opposition against him. It would seem as if Macready and Forrest were now lost sight of, and 'the d——d aristocracy,' as the crowd call them, are the obnoxious party."[61]

Although such observers as the *New York Tribune* and the *Boston Traveller* saw the riot as the "absurd and incredible" result of a "paltry quarrel, of two actors jealous of each other's reputation," the role of class was not ignored. The *Home Journal*

---

*Richard Moody sets the number killed at thirty-one: twenty-two during the riot itself and nine more as a result of wounds received during the riot. In his more recent research, Peter Buckley has only been able to account for a total of twenty-two dead: eighteen during the riot and four more as a result of wounds received.

viewed the riot as a protest against "aristocratizing the pit" in such new and exclusive theaters as the Astor Place Opera House and warned that in the future the republic's rich would have to "be mindful where its luxuries offend." The *New York Herald* asserted that the riot had introduced a "new aspect in the minds of many . . . nothing short of a controversy and collision between those who have been styled the 'exclusives,' or 'upper ten,' and the great popular masses." The New York correspondent for the *Philadelphia Public Ledger* lamented a few days after the riot, "It leaves behind a feeling to which this community has hitherto been a stranger—an opposition of classes—the rich and poor . . . a feeling that there is now in our country, in New York City, what every good patriot hitherto has considered it his duty to deny—*a high and a low class.*"[62]

From the rhetoric used both during and after the riot, it is clear that many of those who engaged in it understood that to term the altercation between Forrest and Macready a personal one was only a partial truth; that in a larger and truer sense it was a clash over questions of cultural values, over the role of the people in culture. "I was not hostile to Mr. Macready because he was an Englishman," a speaker proclaimed on May 11, "but because he was full of his country's prejudices from the top of his head to his feet." Macready's first encounter with Forrest, whom he saw perform in New York in 1826, produced a criticism not of Forrest so much as of his relationship with his audience and of the culture that enveloped both the actor and his admirers: "I said then," Macready later wrote of Forrest, "if he would cultivate those powers and really study, where, as in England, his taste could be formed, he would make one of the very first actors of this or any day. But I thought he would not do so, as his countrymen were, by their extravagant applause, possessing him with the idea and with the fact, as far as remuneration was concerned, that it was unnecessary." Through the years, Macready's critique of Forrest continued to be coupled to his distaste for Forrest's audience, whom he termed "vulgar," "coarse," "underbred," "ruffianly," "disagreeable," "ignorant." Following Forrest's portrayal of King Lear in 1843, Macready wrote privately, "I did not think it the performance of an artist . . . But the state of society here and the condition of the fine arts are in themselves evidences of the improbability of an artist being formed by them." Though the two actors maintained civil relations, Macready's deepening obsession with the disruptive environment of the theater and Forrest's growing sense of ideological identification with his audience to the point where, as Peter Buckley has remarked, he began to see it as his constituency, created inevitable tensions. The break came on March 2, 1846, in Edinburgh while Macready, waving his handkerchief, was performing the brisk pirouette he had long ago introduced into his portrayal of Hamlet. In the audience, Forrest, who considered what he called Macready's "fancy dance" an effete "desecration of the scene," broke the dark silence with a loud hiss. Macready was first stunned, then enraged by the impropriety. "I do not think that such an action has its parallel in all theatrical history! The low minded ruffian!" he wrote in his diary two days later. In a letter to the *Times* of London, Forrest defended himself and the right of audiences everywhere to exercise and articulate their independent cultural judgment:

> As well-timed and hearty applause is the just meed of an actor who deserves well, so also is hissing a salutary and wholesome corrective of the abuses of the stage; and it was against one of these abuses that dissent was expressed . . . That a man may manifest his pleasure or displeasure after the recognized mode, according to the best of his judgement, actuated by proper motives, and for justifiable ends, is a right which until now I have never heard questioned.

Forrest here anticipated the defense summation of the attorney John Van Buren in the trial of the Astor Place rioters:

> The right to hiss an actor off the stage is an undisputed right of anyone who goes into a theatre of his own will and there is no pretence of saying he ought to be indicted for conspiracy . . . The right of hissing an actor has been exercised from time immemorial. It has been exercised in this country towards Mr. Kean, towards the Woods, towards Cook, and Anderson, towards other Englishmen, towards Power, and towards Macready himself, by the general judgement of the people.[63]

The purpose of acting, Shakespeare had Hamlet say in his charge to the players, "was and is, to hold, as 'twere, the mirror up to nature; to show virtue her own feature, scorn her own image, and the very age and body of the time his form and pressure" (III.ii). The functions of the nineteenth-century American stage were even broader. As a central institution, the theater not only mirrored the sweep of events in the larger society but presented an arena in which those events could unfold. When in *The Confidence Man* Herman Melville turned to the reader and observed that "in real life, the proprieties will not allow people to act out themselves with that unreserve permitted to the stage," he was enunciating merely part of the case.[64] "Unreserve," in fact, characterized not only the actors on the stage but the audiences in front of it. The theater was one of those houses of refuge in the nineteenth century where the normative restrictions of the society were relaxed and both players and audience were allowed "to act out themselves" with much less inner and outer restraint than prevailed in society. Both were permitted a degree of tolerance not generally experienced outside of the theater, a degree of tolerance that soon proved to be greater than many desired inside the theater as well.

The Astor Place Riot, which in essence was a struggle for power and cultural authority within theatrical space, was simultaneously an indication of and a catalyst for the cultural changes that came to characterize the United States at the end of the century. Theater no longer functioned as an expressive form that embodied all classes within a shared public space, nor did Shakespeare much longer remain the common property of all Americans. The changes were not cataclysmic; they were gradual and took place in rough stages: physical or spatial bifurcation, with different socioeconomic groups becoming associated with different theaters in large urban centers, was followed inevitably by the stylistic bifurcation described by George William Curtis, and ultimately culminated in a bifurcation of content, which saw a growing chasm between "serious" and "popular" culture.

These developments help explain the transformation of Shakespeare, who fit the new cultural equation so well. His plays had survived the test of time and were therefore immortal; his language was archaic and therefore too difficult for ordinary people; his poetry was sublime and therefore elevating—especially if his plays could be seen in a theater and a style of one's own choice, devoid of constant reminders that they contained earthier elements and more universal appeals as well. The nineteenth century had harbored two Shakespeares: the humble, everyday poet who sprang from the people and found his strength and inspiration among them, and the towering genius who in 1838 was depicted on the curtain of Richmond's Marshall Theatre as rising above a storm of fanaticism while the figure of Fame points and the figure of History records this "Never-dying Truth": "We ne'er shall look upon his like again."[65] The happy symbiosis between the two began to wear thin by the end of the century when the sacred Shakespeare emerged triumphant.

In HONOR of Shakespeare's three hundredth birthday on April 23, 1864, Barnum's American Museum helped to raise funds for a proposed statue by announcing benefit performances of *Catharine and Petruchio*, concluding with the farce, *Dumb Belle* and featuring "MR. HARRISON, the Comic and Impromptu Singer, and MR. STOEPEL, with his WOOD AND STRAW INSTRUMENTS," between the acts. This was in addition to Barnum's "COLOSSAL GIANTS," "INFANT DRUMMER," "THREE ALBINO CHILDREN," "TABLEAUX OF MOVING WAX FIGURES," "MONSTER SERPENT," and "MUSICALLY-EDUCATED SEAL." Barnum's mode of honoring Shakespeare proved to be a throwback to the past. More typical of the developing mood was the tercentenary celebration at which the actor James H. Hackett spoke of "this reverent act," described "the reverence of those gathered round" as "too deeply awakened to admit of applause," and proclaimed Shakespeare's greatness to be "so transcendant and far-reaching that it may command not merely our admiration and our gratitude, but our homage as well." Eight years later, at the dedication of the monument to Shakespeare in Central Park, the poet William Cullen Bryant could hardly find superlatives adequate to his subject. He hailed Shakespeare as "a genius far beyond all ordinary greatness," compared him to the giant Sequoia trees and "the cataract of Niagara," spoke of "an imagination so creative, a reason so vigorous, a wisdom so clear and comprehensive," that his life afforded us "a glimpse of what . . . the immortal part of man shall be," and voiced his conviction that Shakespeare was one of those great minds "the Maker of all sometimes sends upon the earth and among mankind, as if to show us of what vast enlargement the faculties of the human intellect are capable."[66]

Such rhetoric was far removed from the attitude manifested by Herman Melville in his 1850 review of Hawthorne, in which he predicted that "if Shakespeare has not been equalled, he is sure to be surpassed, and surpassed by an American born now or yet to be born." As early as 1846, Edgar Allan Poe attacked those who went beyond respect for genius to stand in awe of it: "Your Shakspeare worshippers, for example—what do they know about Shakspeare? They worship him—rant about him—lecture about him—about *him*, *him*, and nothing else . . . They have arrived at an idea of his greatness from the pertinacity with which men have called him great. As for their own opinion about him— they really have none at all." By 1884 Richard Grant White was asserting that "Shakespereanism" had become "a cult, a religion, with priests and professional incense-burners, who lived . . . by his worship." Although Shakespeare had written "to please a miscellaneous and uncultivated public," these "shrine-makers" were dedicated to the proposition "that the reading of Shakespeare is an art, and the editing of him a mystery." The "new literary religion" of which White complained was to win increasing numbers of adherents in the coming decades.[67]

Even in the first half of the nineteenth century there were those who felt that Shakespeare was not meant for the masses. As one bard put it:

> Throw not the pearl of Shakespeare's wit,
> Before the swine of the Bowery pit.

The conviction that Shakespearean drama no longer be compromised by mingling it with lesser forms of entertainment—and thus with lesser forms of people—deepened. In 1892 the Polish actress Helena Modjeska wrote that when she had first arrived in the United States she was surprised to see plastered on walls "posters, lithographs, pictures of Shakespeare standing side by side with advertisements of patent medicines and dog-shows." More shocking were the newspapers which listed theatrical notices under the heading "Amusements," where she discovered "just beneath an elaborate criticism on the performance of 'Julius Caesar,' an account of a show of trained monkeys." Where, she asked, "is art then? Art has covered her face and flown away, ashamed of those who cease thus to be priests at her altar and simply become commercial travellers in art, changing the stage to a sample-room where the public has only a vague idea what the article might have been if it had been shown under the best conditions." The playwright Israel Zangwill spoke of "the barbarousness of cutting up a play with vaudeville items," and compared people who mixed Shakespeare and other genres of amusement to "people who enjoy impartially the cheapest wine and the choicest vintages." In 1910 a committee examining Boston's amusement situation was disturbed that the new Shubert Theatre followed two weeks of Shakespeare with a "commonplace" musical and recommended that in the future theaters try to establish greater symmetry between their offerings and their clientele by creating a more homogeneous cultural atmosphere so that the Shubert would devote itself to "first-class serious attractions," the Majestic to musical comedies, and the Globe to "farces and other light performances." In such an atmosphere, T. R. Sullivan promised, it would be possible to perform Shakespeare "not in a modern, mutilated acting version, but played with a full text."[68]

It was necessary to confine Shakespeare to certain theaters catering to a discreet clientele because he was simply too complex for untrained minds. Mark Liddell examined seventeen lines from Polonius's farewell to his son and discovered nineteen forms of expression which even an average educated man would fail to understand. We were in danger of losing "the supreme poet of the whole world," Liddell insisted, if we continued to deceive ourselves that all one needed to digest Shakespeare "is a knowledge of every-day English." A writer in *World's Work* began his analysis "Why Shakspere Is Not Understood," by asserting that "not one in ten thousand of us can really read common passages of Shakspere intelligently," and so convinced himself of the fact that Shakespeare wrote in what amounted to a foreign language, that in his conclusion he doubled the bad news: "Not one man in twenty thousand can read Shakspere intelligently." James Russell Lowell confessed, "I never open my Shakespeare but I find myself wishing that there might be professorships established for the expounding of his works as there used to be for those of Dante in Italy." Those still courageous enough to tackle Shakespeare on their own were advised that they had best be willing and able to work at it. In 1903 the University Society advertised its thirteen-volume *New International Shakespeare* as "the only edition published that gives two full sets of Notes in connection with each play—Explanatory Notes for the average reader and Critical Notes for the critical student or scholar." Shakespeare, billed as the "supreme teacher," who "shows the way—more clearly than any other author—to the higher intellectual and moral life," and who "uses a larger vocabulary than any other writer," was obviously not to be approached lightly. "This edition," the ad promised, "contains a complete Method of Study for each play, . . . the idea of the editors being to give in the set a college course in Shakespeare Study." The *Review of Reviews* promoted its eleven-volume *Eversley Shakespeare* edition by featuring an endorsement attributed to Mark Twain:

> I am of the unlearned and to me the Notes and Introduction are invaluable; they translate Shakespeare to me and bring him within the limits of my understanding. Most people have limits similar to mine, and need these generous helps; here they have their opportunity to supply their lack.[69]

By the turn of the century Shakespeare had been converted from a popular playwright whose dramas were the property of those who flocked to see them, into a sacred author who had to be protected from ignorant audiences and overbearing actors threatening the integrity of his creations. On April 23, 1879—Shakespeare's three hundred and fifteenth birthday—Edwin Booth was playing the lead role in *Richard II* at McVicker's Theatre in Chicago while in the dress circle a dry good's clerk named Mark Gray sat comparing Booth's performance with the text of Shakespeare's play. By Act V, apparently infuriated at the alterations Booth was introducing, Gray drew his pistol and fired two shots at Booth in an attempt, as one eye witness put it, "to kill the man that could, as he thought, so murder Shakespeare." Gray's action was obviously extreme, but his concern for what actors and their audiences were doing to Shakespeare was widely shared. The attitudes of such as John Quincy Adams, who distinguished in 1836 between "the true Shakespeare" he read in his study and "the spurious Shakespeare often exhibited upon the stage," gained an increasing number of adherents in the second half of the century. The Englishman Charles Lamb found a warm reception in the United States when he asserted that Shakespeare's finest creations were reduced to mere caricatures on the stage. How, he asked, could Hamlet's inner musings "be represented by a gesticulating actor, who comes and mouths them out before an audience, making four hundred people his confidants at once?" The love dialogues of Romeo and Juliet or Othello and Desdemona were "sullied and turned from their very nature by being exposed to a large assembly." Actors only reduced Shakespeare's "fine vision" to the mundane standard of flesh and blood: "We have let go a dream, in quest of an unattainable substance." Shakespeare's plays, Lamb insisted, were suited neither for performance on a stage nor for exposure to the multitudes since they were "so deep that the depth of them lies out of the reach of most of us." The American critic A. C. Wheeler was in essential agreement, arguing that the theater "materializes Shakespeare, and in doing so vulgarizes him. Intellectual good taste outside of the theatre spiritualizes him." A. A. Lipscomb announced in 1882 that Shakespeare "has ascended to a new and higher sphere in the firmament of intellect." Increasingly, men had come to understand both that "Shakespeare off the stage is far superior to Shakespeare on the stage," and that to comprehend the "special worth" of Shakespeare required "rigid mechanical training," without which "Shakespeare is not of much use." Shakespeare, Lipscomb predicted "is destined to become the Shakespeare of the college and university, and even more the Shakespeare of private and select culture. Nor will he ever be perfectly himself and perfectly at home anywhere else."*[70]

---

*The essential validity of Lipscomb's prediction—the extent to which it became impossible to conceive of Shakespeare apart from higher education—is illustrated in a poster displayed on Metro subways in Washington, D.C., in

The human Shakespeare who existed for most of the nineteenth century could be parodied with pleasure and impunity; the sacred Shakespeare who displaced him at its close posed greater problems. For years Mark Twain found himself ambivalent about—and unable to complete—a parody of *Hamlet* featuring Hamlet's foster brother, Basil, a traveling book agent who tries to sell books to Hamlet, the Queen, and the Ghost, saying of the last, "I reckon I begin to see what he was chasing me around like that for . . . he wanted to *subscribe*. I'll just set him down for a couple of copies, anyway." Burlesquing Shakespeare's language, Twain has Basil complain of the way people around him speak:

> Why it ain't *human* talk; nobody that ever lived, ever talked the way they do. Even the flunkies can't say the simplest thing the way a human being would say it. "Me lord hath given commandment, sirrah, that the vehicle wherein he doth of ancient custom, his daily recreation take, shall unto the portal of the palace be straight conveyed; the which commandment, mark ye well, admitteth not of wasteful dalliance, like to the tranquil mark of yon gilded moon atwart the dappled fields of space, but, even as the molten meteor cleaves the skies, or the red-tongued bolts of heaven, charged with death, to their dread office speed, let this, me lord's commandment, have instant consummation!"

Though Edwin Booth encouraged Twain to complete his parody, other friends advised him that "it would be a sort of sacrilege."[71]

It is hardly coincidental that in this atmosphere there was a blossoming of books and articles maintaining that Shakespeare's plays were the product of another writer. The loftier Shakespeare's position became, the more untenable it was that a man of his low social standing and dubious education—whom the American teacher and author Delia Bacon dismissed as "a stupid, ignorant, illiterate, third-rate play-actor"—could have risen to the heights of his drama, which must have been the creation of someone better trained, better born, more nobly situated: Sir

---

1986. A worried Shakespeare is depicted pleading with the Metro's riders: "Help our colleges cope with inflation. The money you give may decide whether I'm to be or not to be."

Francis Bacon, Sir Walter Raleigh, Edmund Spenser, the Earls of Oxford, or Rutland, or Derby, *anyone* more fit to play the new role assigned to the former bard of Avon. Though the arguments in this prolonged debate were often detailed and intricate, they revolved around questions of culture and suitability. Appleton Morgan challenged his readers to truly conceive "of the man who gave the wife of his youth an old bedstead, and sued a neighbor for corn delivered, penning Antony's oration above Caesar, or the soliloquy of Macbeth debating the murder of Duncan . . ." Ignatius Donnelly had only to compare William Shakespeare, "the guzzling, beer-drinking, poaching, lying play-actor, of whom tradition does not record a single generous expression, or a single lovable act," with the scholar and statesman Francis Bacon, "founder of the school of philosophy which has done so much to produce our modern advancement and civilization," to understand who was the more likely author of the plays.[72]

The inspired plays of the noble playwright—whoever he turned out to be—required an appropriate setting. In 1867 George Henry Lewes had warned of the drift in American plays toward cheap diversion and declared that unless there was "a decided separation of the drama which aims at art from those theatrical performances which only aim at amusement of a lower kind," and unless one or more theaters were devoted to what he called "poetic drama," then "the final disappearance of the art is near at hand." By the end of the century the separation Lewes had called for was clearly becoming manifest and terms were being shaped to describe it. "So out of vogue is the classic drama in America," Norman Hapgood observed in 1899, "that in theatrical circles it is frequently called 'the legitimate,' to distinguish it from contemporary plays." The term Hapgood referred to was not entirely novel. In England the terms "legitimate" or "regular" had long distinguished plays with spoken dialogue from those in which the dialogue had to be accompanied by music. In 1832 Douglas Jerrold helped to redefine the term when he told a parliamentary committee investigating the state of the drama that a play was legitimate "when the interest of the piece is mental rather than physical." In his testimony, the actor William Macready agreed, defining a legitimate play as one possessing poetic quality or superior literary worth. It was in this sense that the term was imported and used in America. Thus by the turn of the century "legitimate," or its slang variant "legit," came to be defined as "concerned with . . . stage plays, or serious art; classical; semi-classical; other than popular." In the twentieth century the term also came to refer to the increasing separation that was taking place between drama and such elements as slapstick, acrobatics, and equestrian acts, which had been integral appendages of drama in nineteenth-century theater and were now divorced into such distinct entertainment genres as vaudeville, burlesque, and the circus.[73]

Legitimate plays needed to be housed in legitimate theaters and performed before discrete audiences, Hapgood insisted, because "the more ignorant spectators, who formerly followed the lead of the educated, now read, have opinions and enforce them. Caliban is in power and sits in judgment at the theatre." This denigration of popular audiences and propensity to blame them for the low state of the drama was common. For James Ford the decline of Shakespeare was directly attributable to the period's commercial activity, which exhausted Americans and left little room for higher endeavors: "The fact that the men who are doing the real work of the world should find themselves in a mood for melodious tomfoolery, rather than for such an intellectual diversion as the representation of *Hamlet*, argues not that their brains are defective, but that business is brisk." Whatever the cause, the results were the same. "Our audiences do not want ideas in their plays," the *Dial* complained in 1898; "they want costumes, and tricks of stage-carpentry, and farcial situations; they are hugely delighted by a catchy song or an utterly irrelevant dance; they will tolerate sentiment if not too delicate, and even passion if its origin be not too deep within the soul; but ideas they will not have on any terms." Consequently, American theatrical productions were lavish and impressively dazzling to the senses, "but they do not make art their foremost consideration." Nor would they so long as a heterogeneous audience dominated the stage.[74]

This fear of the masses and their effect on "legitimate" theater was paralleled by the existence of increasingly attractive mass surrogates for the theater. The new movie industry in particular provided alternatives not merely to the content presented on the stage but, even more significantly perhaps, to the atmosphere that increasingly pervaded the theater in the new century. In 1915 Walter Prichard Eaton contemplated the profound changes that had taken place in the theater audience. Whereas in the past "the galleries were always packed with a proletarian audience," this was no longer true. Now a worker could take his wife and three children to the movies for the price of one gallery seat at the regular theater. But Eaton was quick to recognize that the problem was not a simple one of economics. He related the attempt of a group of wealthy men in a New England industrial town to attract a wide audience by purchasing the best theater, installing an excellent stock company and reducing the cost of gallery seats to compete with movie prices. "But the theatre was on the 'fashionable' side of town, it was looked upon by the six thousand mill operatives and their families . . . as something that belonged to the other class—and they would not go near it." In the movie house the worker

> will not be segregated from the rest of the audience, the "shirt-front" contingent below stairs, the class which employs him by day. He will sit on the ground floor, with his own kind, feeling as it were a kind of proprietorship in the playhouse. Here he is apart from his daytime distinctions of class; he is in an atmosphere of independence. He is paying as much as anybody else, and getting as good a seat. It will require a tremendous deal of "educating" before you can persuade such a man to invest a dollar and a quarter instead of twenty-five cents, out of a yearly wage of $500, on a single evening's entertainment, and to invest it in a theatre where he enters by the back stairs.

Vaudeville houses established a similarly egalitarian atmosphere. At the opening of Keith's New Boston Theatre in 1894, a vaudeville actress recited a dedicatory poem in which she promised the audience that, "all are equal here," and assured them that Keith's recognized "no favorites, no class." Behavior patterns that had once characterized playhouses were increasingly transferred to other types of theaters. Rollin Lynde Hartt's description of the "low-browed men and boys" at New York's Gaiety Theatre, a burlesque house, in 1908 sounds very much like Mrs. Trollope's depiction of a Shakespearean theater seventy years earlier: "If heat annoys, men shed their coats. Always they smoke . . . they indulge in audible dramatic criticism . . . Whistling, stamping, and hand-clapping rage in gallery and balcony." The process of divorcing popular entertainment from the legitimate stage, which had been gradually at work throughout the second half of the nineteenth century, came to fruition in the twentieth.[75]

The point, then, is not that there was a conspiracy to remove Shakespeare from the American people but that cultural developments occurred which produced the same result—a result compounded by the fact that during these years American entertainment was shaped by many of the same forces of consolidation and centralization that molded other businesses. For the first two-thirds of the nineteenth century, the American theater was characterized by local stock companies, permanently attached to a specific theater, whose performances were frequently augmented by the prestigious star actresses and actors who roamed the country. After the Civil War these independent, decentralized stock companies began to be replaced by what were called combination companies, which generally were organized in New York City and spent the season touring local theaters with a single play. The rapidity of the change was impressive: the fifty permanent stock companies operating in the larger cities from Portland, Maine, to San Francisco in 1871 had declined to less than ten by the end of the decade. By 1886 almost three hundred combination companies were touring the country. As they became increasingly dependent upon traveling combination companies, theaters in an area attempted to increase the efficiency of the booking process by banding together in theatrical circuits. In 1896 a half dozen important theater owners and booking agents from New York, Philadelphia, and Boston forged these local circuits into a centralized national booking system which ultimately functioned as a national theatrical monopoly. "We decided," one of the participants later wrote, "that the betterment of the whole theatrical business would be achieved if the bookings of all the theatres could be centered in one office." The Theatrical Trust, commonly known as the Syndicate, which at its inception comprised thirty-three theaters, soon controlled bookings in some five hundred to seven hundred theaters throughout the nation. The Syndicate, along with the new rival organization controlled by the Shuberts, with which it alternately warred and collaborated, and which itself came to control upward of one thousand theaters and employ more than three thousand entertainers by 1921, increasingly determined the nation's theatrical repertory. The actor-managers who had dominated the nineteenth-century theater were replaced in the twentieth century by the producer–booking agents centered in New York City. Broadway and the American theater became more and more inseparable, the repertory of the former becoming the standard fare of the latter.[76]

Philistines were now in the saddle, Norman Hapgood complained in 1899; "the control of our theatres by speculators suits the tendencies of a mercenary age." Writing in a more positive vein, Robert Grau made the same point in 1910. During the last "forty years of progress," he observed, "the amusement purveyor has advanced to a position, which places him on a level with the great magnates and financiers of the commercial and industrial world."[77] If it is true—as I believe it is—that the businessmen who managed the new theater chains and huge booking agencies approached their tasks with a hierarchical concept of culture, with the conviction that an unbridgeable gulf separated the tastes and predilections of the various socioeconomic groups, and with the belief that Shakespeare was "highbrow" culture of little interest to the masses and therefore of slight potential profit to producers, then we have isolated another decisive factor in Shakespeare's transformation from popular to elite culture.

Whatever the causes, the results of the transformation were clearly illustrated in the Twentieth Century Club's assessment of Boston theaters in 1909 and 1910. The club's Drama Committee found that Boston vaudeville, burlesque, and movie houses combined could accommodate an audience of 608,000 people weekly (with the movies alone accommodating 402,000), while the city's legitimate theaters could accommodate only 151,000. When the committee broke down the figures more discretely it found that theaters featuring Shakespearean drama could accommodate less than one percent of the Boston theaters' potential weekly audience. What the committee found in 1910 had already been experienced by Edwin Booth two decades earlier when in Sep-

tember 1890 he and his fellow Shakespearean actor Lawrence
Barrett were asked to give up their two week engagement at the
Boston Theatre in favor of a highly successful melodrama since,
as the management informed him, it would be "a pity to interrupt
a run that pays so well." In Boston, as in the nation, the centrality
of Shakespeare in theaters that catered to the widest possible
diversity of genres and people was a thing of the past.[78]

It was appropriate then, as Charles Shattuck has reminded us,
that the major event in celebration of the three hundredth anniversary of Shakespeare's death be commemorated in New York
City in 1916 by a ten-day run of an extravaganza entitled *Caliban
by the Yellow Sands*, written by the poet Percy MacKaye, and
performed by a cast of over 1,500 actors, singers, and dancers
in Lewisohn Stadium before a total audience of 135,000. This
Tempest-like allegory concluded with Caliban, who has yearned
to usurp Prospero and rape Miranda, kneeling in penance at the
feet of a God-like Shakespeare. The language throughout was
larded with the proper "thees" and "werts" and "cansts" and
"wouldsts." "Wist where the sea-bull / Flap-flappeth his fin and
walloweth there his cow / And snoreth the rainbow from his
nostrils," Caliban exclaims to Miranda. No one objected to this,
Professor Shattuck concludes, "for it was the sound of 'poetry';
it was 'Shakespeare.' The huge audience knew, for the most part,
that Shakespeare talked like that."[79] It was, after all, archaic and
inaccessible—precisely what Shakespeare had become to the vast
majority of Americans.*

In 1868 Kate Field created an imaginary dialogue concerning
the decline of the theater, concluding with the declaration of her
most optimistic debater that the elevation of the theater would
come "with culture; culture will come with the lapse of a hundred
years . . . Meanwhile calm your ardor, and rest assured that the
elevation of the stage is as inevitable as the elevation of humanity."[80] Whatever the merit of Field's prediction, her insistence

---

*When he was visiting San Francisco with his one-man show, *Acting Shake-
speare*, in 1987, Ian McKellen was asked what he did if he forgot a soliloquy.
He smiled and replied: "You can usually say some rubbish or other. It's Shakespeare and nobody will ever know."

that the theater could not be seen apart from the rest of what she called "culture" was correct. Similarly, the transformation of Shakespeare cannot be understood without placing it alongside the nineteenth-century history of opera, symphonic music, and the fine arts—the other central components of the high culture that was to emerge at the turn of the century. What Shakespeare's career in nineteenth-century America signifies will remain murky until it is examined in the context of the broader phenomenon of cultural bifurcation of which it was only a part.

Two

The Sacralization
of Culture

IN THE FINAL YEAR of his life, Walt Whitman, commenting on his youthful days from 1835 to 1860, wrote that he "should like well" if the contralto Marietta Alboni or the tenor Alessandro Bettini or "the old composer" Giuseppe Verdi "could know how much noble pleasure and happiness they gave me, and how deeply I always remember them and thank them to this day . . . I was fed and bred under the Italian dispensation, and absorb'd it, and doubtless show it."[1] Whitman was not alone. Many of his fellow Americans in those years were "fed and bred under the Italian dispensation."*

The parallels between Italian opera and Shakespeare's plays in nineteenth-century America are striking. They both were performed in a variety of settings, enjoyed great popularity, and were shared by a broad segment of the population. "The people are *Sonnambula*-mad," George Templeton Strong wrote in his diary after attending a performance of Bellini's *La Sonnambula* at New York's Castle Garden in the summer of 1851. "Everybody goes, and nob and snob, Fifth Avenue and Chatham Street, sit side by side fraternally on the hard benches." Indeed, for someone with Strong's aristocratic predilections, the heterogeneity of opera audiences and the popularity of opera could be trying. Following a performance of Bellini's *Norma*, he wrote condescendingly of the audience and the soprano: "The house was crowded and enthusiastic; the louder this lady screamed, the

---

*Italian opera did not become important in the United States until the early nineteenth century. From the American premier of John Hippesley's ballad opera *Flora* in Charleston in 1735 and the introduction of John Gay's immensely popular *The Beggar's Opera* in the 1740s until the turn of the century, most operas in America were of English origin, although a few like Andrew Barton's *The Disappointment* (1767) were created by Americans themselves.

more uproariously they applauded, and her solitary windpipe was a fair match for the vociferous bravos of her 5,000 admirers . . . Norma holloed so . . . and so made the fur fly, that the exaltation of the audience knew no bounds." He noted with amused interest the "vociferous bellowings" of the "frowzy" throngs of "Teutonic" immigrants who attended Wagnerian operas, cheered the German singers in the cast, and washed cakes down with lager beer during the intermissions. Condescension could turn to contempt, as it did after an 1852 performance of *Don Giovanni*:

> House crowded but cold . . . It would be strange if a miscellaneous mob of operatic New Yorkers should appreciate Mozart. They have taken it for granted that Verdi's sustaining unisons and Donizetti's stilted commonplaces of languid sentiment are good, and *Don Giovanni* must, therefore, be to them something far from good. I should as soon expect people whose reading has been chiefly in Eugene Sue to become excited over the *Vicar of Wakefield*.

Like Shakespearean drama, then, opera was an art form that was *simultaneously* popular and elite. That is, it was attended both by large numbers of people who derived great pleasure from it and experienced it in the context of their normal everyday culture, *and* by smaller socially and economically elite groups who derived both pleasure and social confirmation from it.[2]

In his poem, "Proud Music of the Storm," Whitman celebrated the aesthetic wonders of opera and its importance in his life, but treated it as part and parcel of the musical world that surrounded and sustained him:

> All songs of current lands come sounding round me,
> The German airs of friendship, wine and love,
> Irish ballads, merry jigs and dances, English warbles,
> Chansons of France, Scotch tunes, and o'er the rest,
> Italia's peerless compositions.

Here too Whitman spoke for many of his fellow Americans who experienced opera as part of the world around them. Just as some nineteenth century Americans domesticated Shakespeare by claiming him as their own countryman, so the *New York Times* asserted in 1859: "It is not, we trust, too boastful to say that

New York is the American parent of Italian opera." Whitman's testimony makes it clear how available opera was. In his column in the *Brooklyn Daily Eagle* on February 24, 1847, Whitman informed his readers of their many opportunities to enjoy opera: the Olympic Theatre, was "giving a run" of popular operas, "very neatly got up on a small scale; Miss Taylor appears tonight as Zorlina in 'Fra Diavolo.'" At the opera house on Chambers street, they were offering a series, of Italian operas: "tonight 'Lucrezia Borgia.' On Wednesday night it will be pleasanter to go, for then they give 'Lombardi.'" At the Park Theatre a musical corps "late from Havana," was presenting opera two evenings a week. The entertainment pages of the city's other newspapers tell the same story. Advertisements in the *New York Times*, for example, indicate that four days before Christmas 1854, New Yorkers could attend the Academy of Music, where the great singers Giulia Grisi and Giovanni Mario were performing Donizetti's *Lucia di Lammermoor* and the first act of Bellini's *Norma*.

An opera being performed in Niblo's Theatre, New York City, 1854.

At Niblo's Gardens, Donizetti's opera was being presented in English as *Lucy of Lammermoor*; Auber's *Fra Diavolo* was at the Broadway Theatre, and von Flotow's *Martha* was being sung at the Stadt Theatre on the Bowery. In addition, at 663 Broadway Perham's Troupe offered "The Laughable Operatic Extravaganza of DON GIOVANNI; or, The Spectre On Horseback," along with "AN UNEQUALED PROGRAMME OF ETHIOPIAN SONGS, CHORUSES, SOLOS, DUETS, JIGS, FANCY DANCES, &c."[3]

This operatic variety was not confined to a handful of Northeastern cities. New Orleans was one of the centers of opera in nineteenth-century America and had the nation's first permanent opera company. During the spring of 1836 four separate opera companies were in residence offering such an array that in the third week of April the citizens of New Orleans could choose between fourteen performances of nine different operas. Despite the sophistication of its presentations and the opulence of its opera houses, New Orleans opera never became merely the possession of the affluent. Opera became an integral part of New Orleans culture, shared by audiences across a spectrum of social and economic classes.* "Operas," proclaimed the *New Orleans Bee* in 1836, "appear to amuse our citizens more than any other form of public amusement—except balls."[4]

Nor was American opera dependent upon such established cultural and population centers as New Orleans. Katherine Preston's important research reveals the variety and ubiquity of the traveling opera companies that traversed America during the first half of the nineteenth century performing opera in both Italian and English. Troupes like that of Manuel Garcia, which first appeared in New York in 1825, the Montressor Company, which arrived in 1832, the Havana Opera Company, which began

---

*Henry Kmen, the leading student of nineteenth-century New Orleans music, has concluded that "early New Orleans opera [was] much more a real part of the community than has been true of most of our latter-day opera . . . The fact that the opera in New Orleans had to function as entertainment for as wide an audience as possible brought it closer to the average citizen . . . In a sense the opera in New Orleans did just what many critics argue that our television and other entertainment media should do today: people were offered the artistically good along with the popular."

touring the United States in the mid-1830s and by the late 1840s numbered over one hundred musicians, and the many English opera companies, journeyed through wide areas of the country bringing opera to Americans in the populous cities of the Eastern Seaboard and the interior river cities not far removed from the frontier. Thus the Pyne and Harrison English Opera Company— which like all the English opera companies did not confine its offerings to *English* operas but most often featured foreign-language operas in English translation—first performed in New York, Philadelphia, and Boston in 1854 and in the fall of 1855 left on a six-month tour that took it to Baltimore, Pittsburgh, Cincinnati, Louisville, New Orleans, Mobile, St. Louis, Indianapolis, Washington, D.C., and Richmond. After a brief return to New York the company took off again on tours to Chicago, Detroit, Madison, Wisconsin, and other interior cities and towns. During the three years the Pyne and Harrison Company spent in America, it performed complete operas more than five hundred times and gave over one hundred operatic concerts. That it was but one of scores of similar Italian and English companies touring the country in the mid-nineteenth century allows us to begin to appreciate the accessibility and popularity of opera in the United States.[5]

The great European opera singers did exactly what the great English Shakespearean actors did: they journeyed to America, where lucrative tours awaited them. Theodore Thomas, who as a young man in the 1850s played violin in opera orchestras, has written that the "most brilliant, finished, and mature vocalists of the world, such as Jenny Lind and Sontag . . . Mario, Grisi, Bosio, Alboni, and others" appeared in the United States in those years. "I doubt if there were ever brought together in any part of the world a larger number of talented vocalists than were gathered in New York between 1850 and the early sixties." In 1883 the *New York Times* boasted that New York opera audiences "are likely to be favored with some of the most brilliant performances of the age. A traveler abroad would have to journey over the whole Continent to hear in a single season the song-birds who are to be imported all at once for the entertainment of local amusement-seekers."[6]

Opera in America, like Shakespeare in America, was not presented as a sacred text; it was performed by artists who felt free to embellish and alter, add and subtract. When, in 1825, the Garcia family brought New York its first *Barber of Seville* in its original language, one reviewer lamented, "For ourselves (ignoramuses that we are!) we do not relish the music, because we do not understand the Italian." He was gratified to note that during the performance of December 10, the young Maria Garcia, who as Maria Malibran was later to become one of the nineteenth century's greatest singers, incorporated into Act II a "favourite Scotch Song," which she sang with such feeling that "'encore' was sounded from every part of the house." Garcia complied by singing "Home Sweet Home" "with more science and effect than we ever heard it before."[7]

It was common on the American stage for opera companies to insert popular airs of the day either as a supplement to, or as a replacement for, certain arias. In New Orleans in the 1830s the leading soprano, Madam Feron, injected songs like "The Arab Steed" and "An Old Man Would Be a Wooing," into Rossini's *Barber of Seville* and "The Light Guitar" and "Bright Eyes" into Mozart's *Marriage of Figaro*.* It was common too for opera to be presented along with other forms of popular entertainment, often being preceded or followed by comic plays. Mozart's *Figaro* was presented in English at the Park Theatre in 1825 followed by the farce *Presumption; or, The Fate of Frankenstein*. Auber's opera *Gustavas III; or, The Masked Ball* was preceded by the comedy *Petticoat Government* in 1834 and followed by the farce *My Young Wife and an Old Umbrella* in 1839. Throughout these years audiences enjoyed the operas of Donizetti, Rossini, and Bellini alongside plays like *More Blunders than One, Sam Patch in France*, and *Shocking Events* as well as entertainment with such strong contemporary flavor as the "new grand military spectacle, *Napoleon Buonaparte*." In 1835 Meyerbeer's French opera *Robert le Diable* had its New Orleans premiere accompanied by the minstrel Dan Rice dancing his acclaimed Jump Jim Crow, while other operas in that city regularly

---

*This was not unique to the United States, of course. Indeed, such composers as Rossini would leave places in their operas for such intrusions.

shared the bill with light musical comedies called "vaudevilles," and still others featured strong men, jugglers, animal acts, a "Trestigiator, Mimic and Angostemith," and the tightrope artist Herr Cline who danced a *pas de deux* with his grandmother on the high wire.[8]

Flexibility seems to have been one of the few laws governing the production of opera for most of the nineteenth century. When, in December 1834, the proprietors of the Richmond Hill Theatre wanted to premiere the overture to Mercadante's opera *La Donna Caritea*, they simply fit it in between the first and second acts of Bellini's *Il Pirata*. Similarly, the overture to Spontini's *Fernand Cortez* was performed between acts of Rossini's *La Donna del Lago* at the Italian Opera House in 1833. In 1855 the fourth act of Verdi's *Rigoletto* was followed by the final act of Vaccai's *Giulietta e Romeo*, which in turn was followed by the second and fourth acts of Verdi's *Il Trovatore*.[9]

Though they were accustomed to a good deal of alteration and flexibility, opera audiences, like audiences for Shakespearean drama, were frequently knowledgeable enough to insist upon getting what had been promised. When a visiting Italian troupe cut the final scene from an 1837 performance of Rossini's *Semiramide*, with no prior announcement and no explanation, the *New Orleans Picayune* reported that "those who had paid . . . to witness *Semiramide* entire" created a final scene of their own: "the pit became uproarious . . . Such a din we have rarely heard. Hissing, howling, whistling, kicking and screaming reigned in that temple where, but a few moments before, all was harmony." When the management tried to drive the audience out by darkening the hall,

> t'was the signal for the demolition of everything they could lay their hands on. Chairs and canes were thrown toward the splendid chandalier [*sic*]—the pride of the St. Charles [Theatre]—and for some time its destruction appeared inevitable . . . The drapery around the boxes was torn, the cushions in the pit ripped open, the seats broken, and chairs were flying in all directions.

When *Semiramide* was performed the next night, after proper apologies were made to the audience, the *Picayune* reported that "the last note that ever Rossini composed was played and sung to the full extent, and every thing passed off without further commotion."[10]

Again as with Shakespeare, the familiarity of opera also was manifest by the large number of burlesques and parodies it stimulated. Only six years after Bellini's *La Sonnambula* received its first performance in Milan in 1831, it appeared in New York as a ballet pantomime, then opened as a parody called *The Roof Scrambler* in 1839, and found its most widespread burlesque form as the Ethiopian opera, *Lo, Som am de Beauties* in 1845. Rossini's *La Gazza Ladra* was given in a version called *The Cats in the Larder* in 1840; Donizetti's *Lucia di Lammermoor* added to its popularity in a burlesque version, *Lucy-did-Sham-Amour* first presented in 1848; Verdi's *Ernani* was presented as *Herr Nanny* from the stage of the Burton Theatre in 1849; and Buckley's Serenaders Hall presented a string of opera burlesques preceded by blackface minstrelsy throughout these years. In Philadelphia in November 1849 the New Orleans Serenaders promised an evening of "several new overtures, choruses, quartettes, duets and burlesque operatic pieces from Linda, Norma, Lucretia Borgia, La Fille du Regiment, &c., &c." In the same city in 1850, the National Circus on Chestnut Street advertised "WALLET, the great English clown" who would conclude his performance with "the Pantomime entitled IL DON GIOVANNI, or The Libertine of Madrid." Though such performances diminished as the century wore on, they never disappeared. In 1873 Bryant's Minstrels presented *Cinderella in Black* and in 1876 New York's Chickering Hall announced a night of "AMATEUR MINSTREL ENTERTAINMENT (FOR THE BENEFIT OF A COUNTRY CHURCH) . . . To conclude with a grand selection from THE RING OF THE NIBELUNGEN" conducted by "Herr Wagner, of drawing-room car fame."[11]

Clearly, opera was not encased in a framework too rigidly respectable to allow for an emphasis upon violence and spectacle. The announcement of the Lafayette Theatre's performance of Cherubini's *Lodoïska*, which enjoyed great popularity in the first half of the century, promised that "In the 3rd act, Mr. Burroughs & Mr. Wallack, will fight a broad-sword combat, to the music of the Overture of Lodoiska." Similarly, an advertisement for a production of *Il Trovatore* in 1858 revealed that Act I, Scene 1, would feature "The duel—Outside of Count Di Luna's castle"; Act III, "The camp of the Knights—Exterior of the castle by moonlight"; and Act IV, "The catastrophe—The dungeon." A New Orleans production of *Robert le Diable* was advertised as containing "a scene embodying Martin's masterly picture of Pandemonium . . . likely to prove one of the most splendid scenic effects ever witnessed." In addition to scenic spectacles and violent action, the promise of ballet extravaganzas was an important part of nineteenth-century opera advertisements.[12]

As the century progressed, a dichotomy widened between opera given in English translation and opera performed in the original tongue. In English translation, opera, and especially arias from opera, became popular culture. Whatever problems many Americans may have had with *Il Barbiere di Siviglia* when the Garcias first performed it in Italian in New York in 1825, they had little but admiration for *The Barber of Seville*, which was performed initially at the Park Theatre in the Englishman Henry Rowley Bishop's translation on May 3, 1819, and repeated every season through 1824.* Rossini's *La Cenerentola*, which was first performed in America by the Garcias in 1826, won great popularity only in 1831 when it was performed, in Michael Rophino Lacy's translation, as *Cinderella; or, the Fairy-Queen and the Glass Slipper*. It played for more than fifty performances during the first season alone, remained a regular feature of American theaters for decades, and became in the judgment of one music historian "one of the most popular works of musical theater in the history of the American stage." The same story was repeated with such operas as *The Libertine*, an English version of Mozart's *Don Giovanni*, Bellini's *La Sonnambula* and *Norma*, Donizetti's *Daughter of the Regiment* and *Lucia di Lammermoor*, and Verdi's *Rigoletto* and *La Traviata*, all of which—along with the bulk of the other operas that constituted the basic repertory of the Italian opera companies—won great popularity and frequent financial success in English translations before the Civil War.[13]

For many Americans the preference for opera in English over

---

*Between the English and Italian premiers of Rossini's opera, it was presented in French in New Orleans in 1823.

opera in foreign tongues was primarily a question of comprehension. Even the aristocratic Philip Hone wrote in his diary after a performance of *La Gazza Ladra* in 1833: "The performance occupied four hours—much too long, according to my notion, to listen to a language one does not understand." Two years later he was still frustrated at his inability to comprehend Italian opera more fully: "We want to understand the language; we cannot endure to sit by and see the performers splitting their sides with laughter, and we not take the joke; dissolved in 'briny tears,' and we not permitted to sympathize with them; or running each other through the body, and we devoid of the means of condemning or justifying the act." But Hone understood that the question was more complex than language alone. The sale of exclusive private boxes at the Italian opera house, which cost $6,000 each, he wrote in 1835, "forms a sort of aristocratical distinction. Many people do not choose to occupy seats . . . while others recline upon satin cushions, and rest their elbows upon arm-chairs." Opera in Italian came to signify the Old World pretensions and effete snobberies that so frequently angered playgoers and served as a catalyst for the numerous theater riots of the first half of the century.* When the "Italian singing birds" of a visiting opera troupe had "warbled their last notes and flown" from Chicago in 1859, the *Daily Journal* worried about the effects of the Italian opera "with its fashionable toilets," and reminded its readers that "the high spiced esculents will do now and then, but they hurt the digestion; the plain, everyday dish administers to our nutriment." In contrast, a critic for the *Mobile Daily Advertiser* hailed the Pyne and Harrison Company's English

---

*Walt Whitman harbored the same fears about the influence of opera, with its "anti-republican spirit," as he did about the feudal overtones of Shakespearean drama. In editorials he wrote in the mid- and late 1840s, Whitman insisted that we had long enough received Europe's "tenors and her buffos, her operatic troupers and her vocalists, . . . listened to and applauded the songs made for a different state of society . . . made for royal ears . . . and it is time that such listening and receiving should cease." In fact, Whitman was no more successful in shaking his operatic habits than he was in cutting his ties to Shakespeare, and in the 1850s he was still writing about opera, urging his readers to attend it, and hailing it as the "sublimist and most spiritual of the arts."

rendition of Bellini's *La Sonnambula*: "There was no attempt at display, no assumptions of foreign manners or style—but we had the good old English all the way through." A New Orleans critic complained that after a local singer had journeyed to Italy his style "became completely vitiated by artifice as well as art. But when he chooses to give sweetly and simply a song of his native Scotland . . . there are few who excel him." In what was apparently an attempt to render foreign-language opera less exotic, audiences in New Orleans often demanded that overtures to Italian operas be augmented by such familiar patriotic tunes as "Yankee Doodle" and "Hail Columbia." When one conductor chose to ignore these entreaties "the audience began to tear up chairs and benches."[14]

Although some English-language versions, such as Rophino Lacy's rendering of Auber's *Fra Diavolo*, remained largely faithful to the original, in general English-language versions of Italian opera were more than mere translations; they were thorough adaptations in the spirit of the ethos prevailing in both Europe and America during the first half of the nineteenth century, an ethos that did not consider opera—or most other forms of music, for that matter—to be finished, inalterable works of art. Thus Lacy's version of *La Cenerentola*, which was far more popular in the United States than Rossini's original, restored the fairy tale's familiar fairy godmother and glass slipper motifs, which Rossini had omitted, and, to accompany the altered text, incorporated arias from three other Rossini operas. Henry Rowley Bishop, who created English versions of some twenty-five operas, injected ten songs and six dances of his own into his translation of Mozart's *Marriage of Figaro* along with a character he imported from Rossini's *Barber of Seville*. Even before mid-century there were American critics who condemned these altered versions as "lawless outrages . . . the decapitation, scalping, maiming, and mangling of musical compositions . . . [which] should be considered sacred," but Katherine Preston has shown that the new versions were more commonly hailed as "opera for the people," with such popular adapters as Bishop winning praise for "cultivating the national taste, and opening our ears to the beauties of foreign authors."[15]

It was not necessary to frequent the opera to become familiar with the music. Popular songs in English based on operatic arias could be encountered everywhere in nineteenth-century America. As early as the 1790s the popular song "Away with Melancholy" was derived from an aria in Mozart's *Magic Flute*. In 1820 "La ci darem la mano," from *Don Giovanni* took the country by storm as "Now place your hand in mine, dear." And so it continued for decades. Years before Rossini's opera *Tancredi* was performed in America, its aria "Di tanti palpiti" won fame as "Here we meet too soon to part." Bellini's "Casta diva" became "Chaste goddess" while other arias from his *Norma* won popularity as "Hear me, Norma," and "Where are now the hopes I cherished." The well-known songs "Over the Summer Sea," "Ah! I Have Sighed to Rest Me," and "Gaily through Life I Wander" came from arias in Verdi's *Rigoletto, Il Trovatore,* and *La Traviata*. Even Wagner contributed his Bridal Chorus from *Lohengrin* and his "Song of the Evening Star" from *Tannhäuser* to America's popular music. In 1882 the critic Richard Grant White recalled that when he was a schoolboy some fifty years earlier, the English version of *La Sonnambula* "was the delight of all music-loving people, cultivated and uncultivated, from North to South, from East to . . . West. Nothing but 'Still so gently o'er me stealing,' or 'Hear me swear now,' was heard from the throats of singers, the fingers of piano-forte thrummers, and even the lips of whis-tlers." Thus, as Charles Hamm has demonstrated, not only were parlor songs sung in the opera house but operatic songs were sung in the parlor, the *bel canto* style adapting itself easily to the intimacy of the home. Sheet music of songs by Bellini, Rossini, Donizetti, and others sold side by side with the music of such perennial favorites as Henry Russell, the Hutchinsons, and Ste-phen Foster, and it is clear from the copies of this sheet music that have been preserved that the people who performed it in their parlors felt as free to pencil in alterations to the music of Mozart and Verdi as they did to the music of Stephen Foster, still one more indication that the distinctions we have learned to make were for the most part foreign to the nineteenth century.[16]

There was a consciousness in mid-nineteenth-century America of the significance of this shared culture. The triumphant Amer-ican tour of the operatic soprano Jenny Lind from 1850 to 1852 became an occasion for self-congratulation. A letter to the *New*

York Tribune proudly proclaimed that "this great people, so intent on acquisition, so bewildered at times by the rapidity of their own progress, have not forfeited the capacity of appreciating excellence . . . on such a scale as the world has never before seen." In a nation recently rocked by the Astor Place Riot with its divisive tone of class warfare, the tumultuous and almost universally positive reception accorded Lind was perceived as evidence that the spirit of equality not only prevailed but was no threat to the nurturing of distinction in all endeavors. Nathanial Parker Willis, the editor of the *New York Home Journal*, proclaimed Lind's tour "a very republican operation," and referred to "the quiet ease with which the luxury of the exclusives—Italian music—has passed into the hands of the people . . . Now it is as much theirs as anybody's! . . . Opera music has . . . become a popular taste." This could never have happened in a country like England, Willis asserted. "The hardened crusts between the different strata of society, would never let a taste pass, with this marvelous facility, from one class to another." In the United States, by contrast, the Swedish soprano's widespread popularity was "proof of the slightness of separation between the upper and middle classes of our country—of the ease with which the privileges of a higher class pass to the use of the class nominally below—and marks how essentially, as well as in form and name, this is a land of equality." As late as 1883 the *New York Times* praised Italian opera "as an efficient popularizing medium for good music," and editorialized that while there was as yet no American school of music, "when the American composer does appear, he will find a great people filled with a genuine love for all that is noble in music, ready to receive and appreciate him." That same year *Frank Leslie's Illustrated Newspaper* boasted that in contrast to England, where "the gentry and aristocracy attend the opera as a fashionable duty," musical taste and education were so widely diffused in the United States that "*prima donnas* like Patti and Nilsson return to the country where popular demonstrations are dearer to them than a nod from the royal box or the neatly turned compliments of dukes and peers."[17]

It is hard to exaggerate the ubiquity of operatic music in nineteenth-century America. In 1861 a band played music from *Rigoletto* to accompany the inauguration of President Lincoln.

THE OPERA OF

JENNY LIND, IN

LA SOMNAMBULA.

Although Jenny Lind had given up performing in complete operas before coming to the United States, Americans were familiar enough with her repertory to be able to picture her, in their minds and their lithographs, directly in the opera whose well-known arias she sang for them. In this New York lithograph of 1850, Lind is portrayed in one of the period's most popular operas. Her angelic visage was typical of the idealized way she was depicted throughout her stay.

THE SECOND DELUGE.

First appearance of Jenny Lind in America.

An 1850 cartoon gently satirizing the mass excitement generated by Lind's tour of the United States.

In the midst of the Civil War a soldier in the Twenty-fourth Massachusetts Volunteer Regiment wrote home: "I don't know what we should have done without our band. Every night about sun down [bandmaster Patrick S.] Gilmore gives us a splendid concert, playing selections from the operas and some very pretty marches, quicksteps, waltzes and the like." In the mining town of Virginia City, Nevada, a singer had to include in her repertory not only popular ballads and familiar old favorites but also "several operatic arias which might exhibit the flexibility and range of her voice." When George Makepeace Towle returned from his tour of duty as American Consul in England shortly after the Civil War and set about rediscovering his native land, he recorded the extent to which opera was part of the public domain: "*Lucretia Borgia* and *Faust*, *The Barber of Seville* and *Don Giovanni* are everywhere popular; you may hear their airs in the drawing rooms and concert halls, as well as whistled by the street boys and ground out on the hand organs." A friend of the Boston music critic John Sullivan Dwight wrote him from Newport in the 1870s, "To-day I have heard '*Casta Diva*' seven times; four times with the monkey [played on the hand organ], and three times without (i.e., sung in houses); on the whole I prefer it with the monkey."[18]

While testifying to the popularity and availability of opera in America, Dwight's friend's final ironic observation also revealed a growing impatience with the fruits of such popularity, an impatience that we witnessed earlier in the attitudes of George Templeton Strong. Dwight himself manifested the same impatience in 1878 when he struck out at those operatic managers who insisted upon presenting Italian operas in English. He admitted that the Germans regularly performed operas in translation but insisted that while the German language lent itself especially well to translation—"An English opera might sound even better in the German than in the original!"—Anglicizing Italian operas was an entirely different matter:

> The musical, sonorous and expressive words, the rich vowel sounds, . . . lose almost all their charm in English; lose their flavor, forfeit their individuality in fact. It ceases to be the same thing. Think how clumsy and uncouth the English syllables must sound, which try to render that mellifluous language! And what is still worse, think how flat and commonplace, how stilted and inflated, all the dialogue, and even the Arias sound in such an English parody.

Following an 1862 concert in Lockport, New York, the *Lockport Daily Journal and Courier* regretted "that the Anglo-Saxon tongue is not better adapted to the real spirit and soul of vocal music" and observed that "music is never quite so witching as when it takes on a 'foreign air.'"[19]

By the turn of the century such attitudes had themselves borne fruit and the picture I have been sketching had changed. In 1853 *Putnam's Magazine* had proposed that P. T. Barnum, who was responsible for Jenny Lind's tour of the United States, be named the manager of New York's Opera. "He understands what our public wants, and how to gratify that want. He has no foreign antecedents. He is not bullied by the remembrance that they manage so in London, and so in Naples, and so in St. Petersburg. He comprehends that, with us, the opera need not necessarily be the luxury of the few, but the recreation of the many." *Putnam's* described the realities of the mid-nineteenth century as Thomas Whitney Surette described those of the early twentieth when he observed in 1916: "Opera is controlled by a few rich men who think it a part of the life of a great city that there should be an opera house with a fine orchestra, fine scenery, and the greatest singers obtainable. It does not exist for the good of the whole city, but rather for those of plethoric purses. It does not make any attempt to become a sociological force; it does not even dimly see what possibilities it possesses in that direction." Opera houses, he continued, "surround themselves with an exotic atmosphere in which the normal person finds difficulty in breathing . . . they are too little related to the community."[20]

Increasingly, then, as with Shakespeare before it, opera was performed in isolation from other forms of entertainment to an audience that was far more homogeneous than those which had gathered earlier. The tendency to describe audiences at Italian and other foreign language operas as "the galaxy of fashion and beauty," the "beauty, taste, and fashion of the city," the "better class, the most refined and intelligent of our citizens," the "high minded, the pure and virtuous," accelerated as the century progressed.* In 1885 the *San Francisco Chronicle* described the audience that greeted the visiting Mapleson Opera Company at the Grand Opera House as "a bright representation of San Francisco society, comprising the beauty, youth and elegance of its fair sex . . . [and] almost all the leading men who had made a mark in their various professions," while it criticized the minority who in "apparent disregard of the mandates of fashion" had "the very poor taste" to combine "a decollete dress with a hat" or "a light walking dress and a hat of the Valois form."[21]

---

*There were of course exceptions. As late as 1897 the *Los Angeles Herald* noted that a visiting opera company "did not attract the people of wealth. Italian and Mexican citizens were conspicuous in the audience throughout the engagement, but the bon-ton of American society sought its pleasure elsewhere."

Although opera was not, then or now, totally divorced from popular culture—as witness the great popularity of such singers as Caruso at the turn of the century and Pavarotti in our own day—by the end of the nineteenth century it, like Shakespearean drama, was no longer part and parcel of the eclectic blend of culture that had characterized the United States. More and more, opera in America meant foreign-language opera performed in opera houses like the Academy of Music and the Metropolitan Opera House, which were deeply influenced if not controlled by wealthy patrons whose impresarios and conductors strove to keep the opera they presented free from the influence of other genres and other groups. Matilda Despard congratulated New York operagoers on their improving tastes and urged them to keep progressing along the neat evolutionary path she laid out, which had thus far taken them "through quaint old English operettas, English versions of Italian and German operas, pure Italian and German compositions of Rossini, Bellini, Verdi, Spohr, Weber, and Mendelssohn, up to the present high development of taste for and appreciation of Meyerbeer, Gounod, Schumann, and colossal Richard Wagner, at last—giant destroyer of ancient opera traditions." Wagner's distinction between "serious" and "frivolous" opera found a growing number of adherents in the United States. After attending his first performance of Verdi's *Macbeth*, George Templeton Strong noted the absurdity of attempting "to marry Northern legend to modern Italian music," especially when the mode was "Verdiesque. Screaming unisons everywhere, and all the melodies of that peculiar style the parallel whereof is rope-dancing." In 1884 *Harper's New Monthly Magazine* announced the appearance of "another audience of the highest cultivation and of another taste," which harbored "a significant disposition to regard Italian opera itself as a kind of Mother Goose melodies, good enough for a childish musical taste, but ludicrous for the developed and trained taste of to-day." It is, *Harper's* decreed, "a far cry from *Rigoletto* to the *Götterdämmerung* and from the *Sonnambula* to *Parsifal*."[22]

Although *Harper's* announcement of "the decline and fall of the Italian opera" proved to be premature, all forms of opera were deeply affected by the growing insistence that opera was a "higher" form of art demanding a cultivated audience. For such critics as W. J. Henderson of the *New York Times*, the important issue was not whether one preferred Verdi or Wagner but whether one insisted that both composers be performed with what Henderson considered to be taste and discrimination. Thus he praised the graceful melody and sentimental force of the aria "Ah, si ben mio," in Verdi's *Il Trovatore*, even while he condemned "the stupid bawling of the high C" in a second aria, "De quella pira" as "a piece of throat acrobatics designed for the evocation of delirious bravi from the Italian waiters who occupy the standing room behind the orchestra rail." The behavior that had once surrounded operatic productions was increasingly rejected and censured. In 1900 the Metropolitan Opera concluded its season by presenting four acts from four separate operas—an arrangement common enough not long before. Now the Metropolitan earned the reprimand of the *Times'* Henderson who had no kind words to say of anybody or anything associated with the evening. The audience was ignorant: "There were people who had never heard 'Carmen' before. There were people who had never heard of 'Il Flauto Magico.' There were people who had never heard 'Lucia' . . . There were people who did not know any one of the three ladies in 'The Magic Flute,' and who had no way of finding out which was which." Such people he was convinced could have come only "to hear most of the famous singers of the company at once and for one price of admission." He was still more critical of management for it had thrown away "all semblance of art in the opera house" and had put together "a hotch-potch continuous performance of extracts from operas" in order to "draw more money than the best vaudeville entertainment in the city," and had deliberately lured these ignorant people there by offering them "a program of broken candy." Opera, Henderson was insisting, was too important, too exalted an art form to present itself to an uninformed, eclectic audience, many of whom cared more for the performers than the art being performed. To present excerpts rather than entire operas was to demean the very integrity of opera as an art form.[23]

In repudiating quite precisely many of the ways in which opera had been presented for much of the nineteenth century, Henderson was not an aberrant crank; on the contrary, he represented accurately the direction in which such forms of expressive culture as opera were traveling. He symbolized a transition that, in Ronald Davis's terms, saw opera becoming "more a *symbol* of culture than a real cultural force," and the opera house becoming less a center of entertainment than a sacred source of cultural enlightenment, less a living theater than, as Herbert Lindenberger has put it, "a museum displaying masterpieces in many period styles."[24]

IF SYMPHONIC MUSIC was never as popular or as accessible to the people at large as opera, its history in the nineteenth century nevertheless tells us much about the general development of American culture and helps us to understand the structural transition both it and opera went through.

It is important to recognize that the most popular and ubiquitous instrumental organization in nineteenth-century America was the band, over 3,000 of which, containing more than 60,000 musicians, existed on the eve of the Civil War. It is equally essential to understand that the clear distinction we tend to make today between bands and orchestras did not obtain for much of the nineteenth century. For most Americans the distinction, in so far as it existed at all, was more a functional than an aesthetic one. In the 1830s, and 1840s, William Robyn, a German immigrant living in St. Louis, composed marches, vespers, a mass, and chamber music, and helped to found the aptly named Philharmonic Band, which performed as both an orchestra and a marching band. Nineteenth-century bands and orchestras shared musicians, who moved easily and regularly between the two, often earning money by belonging to both types of organization simultaneously. They also shared repertories: overtures, operatic arias, waltzes, polkas, fantasies, and of course marches were the common fare of both. Numbers like "La Traviata Quickstep," which Union soldiers marched to during the Civil War, or "The Bandit Quickstep," derived from Verdi's opera *Ernani*, might cause us some problems of categorization today, but in the nineteenth century they were widely disseminated and easily accepted blends of two of the most popular musical genres.[25]

One of the period's first and most eminent band directors,

Harvey B. Dodworth, also functioned as a violinist in the New York Philharmonic Orchestra, which he had helped to found. A typical band concert he led in New York in February 1852 interspersed marches, polkas, and songs with music by Mendelssohn, Verdi, Rossini, and Bellini, and featured violin solos by the future symphonic conductor Theodore Thomas. During the late 1840s and early 1850s, the teenage Thomas earned his living as a violinist in bands, chamber groups, and opera and theater orchestras. "Better music was played in the theatres then, however, than at the present time," he recalled in 1904. "It was in a theatre orchestra that I first made the acquaintance of Beethoven's 'Coriolanus Overture,' which was played before the curtain rose for Shakespeare's tragedy." When Boston's famous bandmaster, Patrick S. Gilmore, staged his grandiose five-day National Peace Jubilee in 1869—featuring ten thousand singers and an orchestra of a thousand musicians, and advertising a performance of the Anvil Chorus from *Il Trovatore* that would include a hundred firemen beating anvils with sledge hammers and close with the firing of a hundred cannons—he performed not only popular and patriotic airs but the overture from Wagner's *Tannhäuser*, liberal excerpts from Rossini's *Stabat Mater* featuring the operatic soprano Euphrosyne Parepa-Rosa, as well as instrumental and choral pieces by Bach, Mozart, Schubert, Haydn, Handel, Mendelssohn, Beethoven, and Meyerbeer. It is a testament to the nineteenth century's acceptance of musical eclecticism that, with the predictable exception of John Sullivan Dwight, Gilmore received the full cooperation of Boston's musical establishment: Eben Tourjée, director of the New England Conservatory, assembled and rehearsed the chorus; Julius Eichberg, director of the Boston Conservatory, created a chorus of thousands of Boston's schoolchildren; Carl Zerrahn, conductor of the Handel and Haydn Society, put together the huge orchestra.* In the final

*Dwight adamantly refused to aid Gilmore on the grounds that his "grandiloquent pretension" was "as uncongenial as possible to the whole sphere of Art" and would merely inflame "the imagination of the ignorant or only sentimentally and vaguely musical." In retrospect, Dwight admitted that whether Gilmore's jubilee "considered musically, was very good or not, it musically *did* good."

The three thousand singers of the Mammoth Oratorio Chorus rehearsing for Boston's National Peace Jubilee in 1869.

One hundred Boston firemen rehearsing their role in the Anvil Chorus to be performed at the National Peace Jubilee.

These illustrations manifest the eclectic nature of the musical festivals of the nineteenth century as well as the high degree of participation of large numbers of amateurs.

year of his life, Gilmore acknowledged his propensity for the sensational: "I have fired the public beast through *cannon* and *anvil*," he admitted, but quickly added, "I gave them great music *withal*."[26]

John Philip Sousa, Gilmore's successor as America's preeminent bandmaster, agreed, writing of Gilmore after his death in 1892, "He had gone into the highways and byways of the land, playing Wagner and Liszt, and other great composers, in places where their music was absolutely unknown, and their names scarcely more than a twice-repeated sound." Sousa himself wrote symphonic poems, cantatas, and operettas as well as military marches, and emulated the eclectic repertories of Dodworth and Gilmore. When the twenty-five year old Sousa took over the U.S. Marine Band in 1880, he found that its library contained "not a sheet of Wagner, Berlioz, Grieg or Tschaikowsky or any other of the modern composers who were attracting attention throughout the musical world," and quickly rectified the situation. He saw no inconsistency in such programming: "I have no hesitation in combining in my programme tinkling comedy with symphonic tragedy or rhythmic march with classic tone-picture." The pianist William Mason made a practice of closing his concerts by improvising upon any themes suggested by the audience. "All sorts of themes were put into the hat," he has written, "from Mozart, Beethoven, 'Jordan is a hard road to travel,' 'We won't go home till morning,' and many negro melodies." The possible mixtures of music and instruments was hard to predict. At a Boston concert in the 1860s, the audience was treated to a fantasia on themes from William Vincent Wallace's opera *Maritana* played as a duet for mouth harmonica and the music hall's new Great Organ—a combination, the program announced, "never before attempted in the history of music!" In the world of instrumental music as in the world of theatrical performance, then, the nineteenth century was much more fluid, much less rigidly hierarchical than the century that was to follow.[27]

This musical flexibility flowed naturally from the dominant practices and attitudes of eighteenth-century America. A concert given in Baltimore on September 12, 1796, attests to the prevalence of a musical ethos quite divergent from the one we have come to know; an ethos that thought it quite proper to follow a Haydn overture with the song "And All for My Pretty Brunette," and a Bach overture with the song "Oh, None Can Love Like an Irish Man." Concerts featured not only a blend of musical styles but a mixture of entertainment genres. Charlestonians who attended a concert featuring a Mr. Humphreys on the French horn in 1773, were promised the *"grand deception,"* of a Mr. Saunders who "will let any number of ladies or gentlemen think of as many cards as they please, and the same will be found in a roasted leg of mutton, hot from the fire, which will be placed on the table."[28]

It should hardly surprise us then that three of the most popular European visitors to the United States in the first half of the nineteenth century—the Viennese ballerina Fanny Elssler, the Norwegian violinist Ole Bull, and the Swedish soprano Jenny Lind—along with many less well-known foreign stars, symbolized the best of European culture without an aura of exclusiveness. Bull would gladly play "Yankee Doodle," "The Arkansas Traveller," or "The Last Rose of Summer" in the midst of his dazzling classical solos; Lind regularly mixed Swedish folk songs and such popular American songs as "Home Sweet Home" with her operatic arias; Ellsler combined classical ballet with English hornpipes and Spanish folk dances. All three were able to assume a place in a cultural lexicon that cut through class and income; they were welcomed and admired by people from all segments of the society and "owned" by none; they represented the norm in mid-nineteenth-century America. Ellsler, the ballerina whose successful and profitable tour in the United States between 1840 and 1842 established the model for Bull and Lind, is a good example of how popularity could penetrate an entire society. Enthusiastic crowds mobbed her wherever she appeared, and she had difficulty making her way through admiring throngs between her hotel and the theaters she performed at. Young men detached the horses from her carriage and pulled it through the streets themselves. Shops peddled Fanny Ellsler brand boots, garters, stockings, corsets, parasols, cigars, shoe polish, shaving soap, and champagne. Boats, horses, and children were named in her honor. Burlesques of her ballets appeared with surprising speed following her first appearances. On the days she performed in Washington, D.C., Congress had difficulty mustering a quorum.

None of this hullabaloo was sufficient to diminish her in the eyes of the elite. An admiring Philip Hone watched her at the Park Theatre in New York and noted, "a more respectable audience never greeted the fair *danseuse* in any country she has charmed." During her performance in Boston Margaret Fuller supposedly whispered to Emerson, "this is poetry," and was told, "No, Margaret. It is religion."[29]

The note of extravagance that the nineteenth century added to this traditional eclecticism was shaped by the "jumbo" concerts of another visitor from Europe, the French conductor Louis Antoine Jullien, who toured the United States in 1853 and 1854. Augmenting the orchestra he brought with him with enough American musicians to create an ensemble of one hundred—one of the largest orchestras Americans had yet heard—Jullien gave two months of concerts in New York City and then toured the country from New England to New Orleans giving well over two hundred concerts in ten months. In order to attract audiences to the music—particularly movements from Beethoven's symphonies—he felt it was his mission to bring to the general public, Jullien included popular dance music, waltzes, and quadrilles featuring such numbers as the "Katy-did Polka" and the "Prima Donna Waltz," and led his musicians in a flamboyant manner. In June 1854 he presented a "Grand Musical Congress"—the first of what were to become known throughout America as musical "festivals"—featuring fifteen hundred instrumentalists and sixteen choral societies performing oratorios and symphonic numbers, as well as such novelties as the *Fireman's Quadrille*, which included fireworks and a simulated fire so realistic that it induced hysterical screaming and fainting spells among some in the audience. In the midst of this musical mix, Jullien exhibited a symbolic reverence for Beethoven's music, which he conducted with white kid gloves and a jeweled baton handed to him on a silver tray by a servant. All of this extravaganza was not quite enough to bury a level of musical quality new to many auditors. "His fiddles all bowed together," marveled one reviewer, "he attained a *pianissimo*, while the New York Philharmonic could not even achieve a *piano*, much less a *pianissimo*." Theodore Thomas, who was one of Jullien's violinists and considered him "the musical charlatan of all ages," nevertheless admitted that "New York has never had, before or since, the like of his wood-wind players." The Boston critic John Sullivan Dwight, who normally had little tolerance for showmanship, urged "all who have any music in their souls" to flock to the French conductor's concerts: "Never have we had such a chance to learn what a great orchestra can be and is . . . It cannot but open many ears and souls to the grandeur of a Beethoven's conceptions to hear one of his masterpieces from this orchestra."[30]

Such gargantuan attempts to reach out to the general public with the wonders of symphonic music affected even so serious a musician as the German-born friend of Wagner Leopold Damrosch, who in 1881 treated New York City to a festival featuring a chorus of 1,200 voices accompanied by an orchestra numbering 250 performing the music of Berlioz, Handel, and Beethoven. According to Damrosch's son Walter, who had helped to train part of the chorus, the Seventh Regiment Armory was filled with an audience of 10,000 for every performance. And, for all of his criticism of Jullien, Theodore Thomas evidently had learned a few things from him. In his New York Festival of 1882, Thomas conducted an orchestra of nearly 300 musicians and a chorus of 3,200 singers. In October 1892, at the inaugural ceremonies of the Columbian Exposition in Chicago, Thomas outdid even this, presiding over a chorus of 5,500 voices, an orchestra of 200 musicians, 2 large military bands, and 2 drum corps of 50 drummers each. These musical extravaganzas, which through their use of hundreds of amateur singers and musicians (choruses of 500–600 voices were considered normal for ordinary festivals) encouraged a good deal of local participation and blurred the line between performers and audience, became common throughout the nation, reaching as far into the interior as Boise, Idaho, which in 1873 staged a jubilee conducted by a violinist who earned his living as a miner and featuring the Anvil Chorus concluding with the obligatory cannon fusillade.[31]

There were musical groups in nineteenth-century America that struggled against allowing their music to be affected by such spectacles, that strove to concentrate on the *music* rather than the *performance*. In the fall of 1848, twenty-five young German musicians, calling themselves the Germania Musical Society, arrived in the United States in order, as they declared, "to further in the hearts of this politically free people the love of the fine art of music through performance of masterpieces of the greatest German composers as Bach, Haydn, Mozart, Beethoven, Spohr, Schubert, Mendelssohn, Schumann; also, Liszt, Berlioz, and Wagner." Though New York had enjoyed the Philharmonic Society since 1842, the Germans brought with them a standard of musicianship not yet regularly experienced in America. After one of their early concerts in the Broadway Tabernacle, a reviewer for the *New York Herald* wrote, "The audience appeared as though awed through the whole performance by the sublimity of sounds too sensitively expressed to admit of more rapture than those created by supernatural agency." For the next six years they traveled through America, as far west as Minneapolis, performing some nine hundred concerts before approximately one million people. While they accomplished many firsts, such as playing the very first full symphony—Beethoven's Sixth—ever heard in Pittsburgh, and brought lasting changes to the American musical scene, they were forced to perform an eclectic repertory in order to survive and had to play before audiences that frequently behaved as they would have in beer halls; the musicians complained of people arriving and leaving as they pleased and of loud conversation that time and again compelled the conductor to halt his performance until order was restored. They also performed in settings for which their European background probably had not fully prepared them. Their two-week series of concerts in Brown's Building in Baltimore, for instance, was followed by, as one advertisement proclaimed:

GRAND CONCERT OF MUSIC . . .
An African Monkey
and several
CHINESE DOGS
Come One Come All*

*The constant intrusion of the surrounding culture was something symphonic conductors had to contend with for many years. Walter Damrosch recalled conducting in Oklahoma City for the first time in 1904. He had just completed the Prelude to Wagner's *Parsifal* and was about to lift his baton to begin orchestral excerpts from the first act when the theater manager ran up onto the

And, if the critic William Apthorp is to be believed, they also learned to engage in novel tactics to win the attention of their audiences. At one Boston performance, during a number entitled "The Railway Galop," "a little mock steam-engine kept scooting about (by clockwork?) on the floor of the hall, with black cotton wool smoke coming out of the funnel."³²

The difficulties confronting nineteenth-century American champions and practitioners of European symphonic music are manifest in the career of Theodore Thomas, a figure of enormous importance in the development of American culture. Born in Germany and brought to the United States at the age of ten in 1845, Thomas became a precocious and effective force for introducing large numbers of Americans to classical and modern currents of European music. He traveled with his orchestra so frequently and so widely from New England to San Francisco, that his routes were popularly known as the "Thomas Highway." There is abundant testimony of Thomas's success in exposing large numbers of people to new musical experiences. Charles Edward Russell, for example, never forgot that in 1877, when he was a young man living in a Mississippi River town, Thomas and his orchestra visited and performed a program of Mendelssohn, Gounod, Saint-Saëns, Schumann, Berlioz, and Liszt. For those in the audience, Russell wrote many years later, "life was never the same afterward . . . There had been shown to them things and potentialities they had never suspected. So then there really existed as a fact, and not as something heard of and unattainable, this world of beauty, wholly apart from everyday experiences. Anybody could go into it at any time; . . . the door was open; this man had opened it." James Gibbons Huneker, one of the many who attributed to Thomas their introduction to "the enchanted realm of symphonic music," maintained in 1917 that Thomas "literally taught us how to listen to beautiful music from Bach to Richard Strauss." ³³

---

stage and called out: "Ladies and gentlemen: I am proud to see so many of you here to-night and take this opportunity of announcing to you that I have already made arrangements for next season for a course which will be in every respect better than the one I am giving you this year! I also would like to announce that Stewart's Oyster Saloon wll be open after the concert . . ."

While still in his early twenties, Thomas became well known in New York City as a solo violinist, as a member of the Mason-Thomas Quartette, and as concertmaster and later conductor of an operatic orchestra. But for Thomas the opera was not where the action was. "A symphony orchestra shows the culture of a community, not opera," he wrote. "The man who does not know Shakespeare is to be pitied; and the man who does not understand Beethoven and has not been under his spell has not half lived his life. The master works of instrumental music are the language of the soul and express more than those of any other art." In 1862 Thomas decided that what this country most needed musically "was a good orchestra, and plenty of concerts within reach of the people." At the time, New York's Philharmonic Society, with an orchestra of sixty players, presented only five yearly subscription concerts, which it supplemented by selling seats to its rehearsals as well.* Since the Philharmonic could not guarantee full-time work, if an orchestra member had another engagement he would go to it rather than to the rehearsal. "A clarinet or oboe part would be played on a violin, or a bassoon part on the 'cello, etc.," Thomas reported. "The conductor therefore could not rehearse as he ought, and the audience talked at pleasure . . . Such conditions debarred all progress." A member of the Philharmonic succinctly described the situation Thomas was determined to reverse:

> Nearly all the members of the Philharmonic play at balls and dances during the greater part of the year. They then get together to play a half dozen doubled up programs during the year, rush through old scores during five hour rehearsals preceding a concert and are then expected to play their programs artistically. Take into additional consideration that some of them never play at all except at the few Philharmonic concerts, and the tale of woe and disheartening anguish is soon told.[34]

When Thomas established his orchestra, he was able to guarantee his own musicians full-time work only by incessantly traveling with them to cities that had no orchestra of their own and

---

*The New York Philharmonic, founded in 1842, gave four concerts each season through 1858, five through 1868, and six through 1892.

by giving summer concerts in New York. These summer concerts—which were inaugurated tentatively in 1865, found a permanent home in Central Park Garden in 1868, and continued until 1875, after which Thomas took them to other cities throughout the United States—illustrate the conditions under which musicians with Thomas's aspirations were forced to operate. Thomas's successes were considerable. When the celebrated pianist Anton Rubinstein came to the United States in 1872, he wrote, "I have found in America something which I least expected to find. I had no idea that such a new country had an orchestra like Theodore Thomas'." At a time when the Philharmonic Society and Thomas's own orchestra were able to sustain less than a dozen concerts between them during New York's regular winter season, Thomas presented 1,126 concerts in Central Park Garden. To put it more dramatically, in its summer series between 1868 and 1875, the Theodore Thomas Orchestra gave more than four times as many concerts as the New York Philharmonic did in its first fifty years. In his autobiography Thomas claimed that musically his summer concerts "exerted a greater educational influence than any institution in America; for the first time, the people enjoyed a good orchestra and good music." This great achievement was due in part to the manner in which Thomas was willing to present his music. Central Park Garden consisted of a restaurant on the corner of Fifty-ninth Street, south of which was a partly covered auditorium, featuring an elevated platform for an orchestra, fronted by several hundred seats and surrounded by open garden spaces with tables "at which beer and light refreshments were served. The air was redolent of tobacco smoke."[35]

Thus, to expose the American people to the music he loved and to keep his orchestra together, Thomas was willing to perform the compositions of the great classical and contemporary composers to an audience that was drinking, smoking, and often chatting. Thomas, who could be adamant on questions of propriety, as we shall see in the next chapter, would also indulge in what he called "little extravagances" to delight his audiences. "On one occasion," he tells us,

> while playing the "Linnet Polka," I requested the piccolo players to climb up into the trees before the piece began. When they

commenced playing from their exalted position in the branches, it made a sensation. I remember another funny incident which happened about this time. In the "Carnival of Venice" the tuba player had been sent, not up the trees, but back of the audience into the shrubbery. When he began to play the police mistook him for a practical joker who was disturbing the music, and tried to arrest him! I shall never forget the comical scene, as the poor man fled toward the stage, pursued by the irate policeman, and trying to get in a note here and there as he ran.[36]

Doubtless, such scenes were more amusing in retrospect than in practice. The fact is that the need to tour constantly, to intersperse the music he admired with polkas, waltzes, and other "light" pieces, to engage in the practices just described in order to pay his musicians and preserve his orchestra, took their toll on Thomas. "Circumstances," he finally complained in the fall of 1889, "force me to prostitute my art and my talents." In 1874 Thomas had written the directors of the Brooklyn Philharmonic Society, "Throughout my life my aim has been to make good music popular and it now appears that I have only done the public justice in believing . . . that the people would enjoy and support the best in art when continually set before them in a clear and intelligent manner." Though he continued to pursue this end, through summer concerts, young people's concerts, and workingmen's concerts, he less and less considered it his life's work. "A little experience," his wife has written, "taught him that neither children nor what are called 'wage-workers' were sufficiently advanced intellectually to be able to appreciate the class of music which was his specialty." Thomas himself came to argue that as the "highest flower of art," symphonic music could be understood only by "the most cultivated persons." The music suitable for "the ignorant or immature mind" had very clearly defined melodic and rhythmic patterns such as that played by the best bands. He continued to believe that there should be concerts for "these classes" which would prepare them for "a higher grade of musical performances," but such work could be accomplished by smaller and less costly organizations and need not waste the time of a great symphony orchestra. The problem was that for a great symphony orchestra to devote itself to suitable music and appropriate audiences, it needed the kind of guaranteed financing that would make it as independent of the market place as possible. Thus, when in 1889 C. Norman Fay, a Chicago businessman, asked Thomas, "Would you come to Chicago if we could give you a permanent orchestra?" Thomas answered without hesitation, "I would go to hell if they gave me a permanent orchestra."[37]

Though hardly hell, Chicago proved not to be paradise either. Thomas has described the difficulties he faced in building the Chicago Symphony Orchestra, the most serious of which was "the indifference of the mass of the people to the higher forms of music." He complained that the very announcement of a symphony was enough to keep many from attending a concert. He had difficulties even with his more knowledgeable audiences, for Wagner had "accustomed them to strong doses of excitement, and contrast, and everything without these tonic properties was regarded with indifference." In resisting the general desire for "music of a lighter character," Thomas was aided by the fact that before agreeing to come to Chicago he had demanded a guarantee against deficits of $50,000 per annum for three years. Fay has admitted that he and his fellow businessmen "almost laughed" at what they considered Thomas's hypercautiousness in demanding this guarantee. They remembered the packed houses for the summer concerts that Thomas had conducted in Chicago throughout the 1880s. "But," Fay has written, "we reckoned without the drawing power of that vast airy Expositon Building down by the Lake, the only cool place in town, the palms and the little tables, the dim sequestered reaches at the sides and back of the floor, where quietly glowed the cigar and foamed the beer, where melted the ice and the glance of its fair consumer, while from afar came the refrain of the 'Spring Song' or the noble melody of the 'Ave Maria.' We were not so musical,

---

Facing page

The popular, accessible atmosphere of Central Park Garden, contrasted with the more restricted, hallowed precincts of Steinway Hall, graphically represent the didactic and sacred aspects of Thomas's career.

A contemporary cartoon portraying Theodore Thomas and his audience at the summer concerts in New York's Central Park Garden.

The Theodore Thomas Orchestra in Steinway Hall, New York City, 1890, on the eve of Thomas's move to Chicago to create the Chicago Symphony Orchestra.

after all." Thomas had something more demanding in mind for his regular season concerts. "The great works of the great composers greatly performed, the best and profoundest art, these and these alone," he insisted, would form the core of his repertory. He was willing to make some compromises. "To those who cannot enjoy the great music, poor fellows, I do not grudge that they can enjoy . . . I will play for them now and then, but it is not for Tell Overture and Handel Largo that Chicago supports my orchestra. One does not buy a Krupp cannon to shoot sparrows."[38]

Thomas knew what Fay was to learn: such a program meant inevitable deficits. Several years after Thomas's death, Fay estimated that in its first eighteen years the Chicago Symphony took in about $1,800,000 at the box office. The additional $1,000,000 necessary for the orchestra's existence was provided by what Fay called "one hundred modest and generous men and women." This group included some of the most important and most affluent families in Chicago: names like Field, McCormick, Armour, Otis, Sprague, Swift, and Pullman were prominent, and their funds enabled Thomas for the first time in his career to rise above the exigencies of the box office, above the immediate demands of his audiences, and implement his belief that "a first-rank orchestra can be maintained only by preserving the highest standard." Never did Thomas doubt what that standard was. In 1876, during the Philadelphia Centennial Exposition, Thomas had been the first conductor of a major American orchestra to present an "American Night" consisting exclusively of works by American composers. He continued to present such programs in New York and Chicago for the rest of his career. Though he was also active in introducing the music of such contemporary European composers as Wagner and Brahms, he resented the notion that they or any other modern composers represented the music of the future. As far as he was concerned, the pantheon was already established: "Bach, Handel, Mozart and Beethoven were sons of God!" he proclaimed in 1898. "There are three epochs in the history of art; (1) the Greek; (2) the period which produced Shakespeare; (3) the period which gave the world Beethoven." Thus at the end of his life, after fourteen years in Chicago, Thomas had a permanent orchestra with a guaranteed budget, and the right to concentrate on what he considered the highest forms of musical expression to be performed for those he judged to be cultivated. "He longed to play to an audience which could understand his best, without any more preparatory effort . . . missionary work did not appeal to him as it had in former years," Mrs. Thomas has written of her husband's final years. "The object for which I have worked all my life is accomplished," Thomas wrote shortly before his death in January 1905, forgetting perhaps that his original goal—to spread the great symphonic music to as large a segment of the people as possible, to, as he put it, "make good music popular"—had been a bit more expansive.[39]

It is not surprising that in his struggle to mold the Chicago Orchestra to his liking, Thomas often pointed to the example of the Boston Symphony Orchestra, which had been established in 1881. "Do you wish our programmes to be inferior in standard to those of the Boston Orchestra?" he asked his trustees when he felt pressure to dilute his repertory. When they replied in the negative, Thomas was quick to point out that the Boston Orchestra never gave a concert without a symphony. "That helped! I was able to keep up the standard of my programmes, not withstanding all opposition, until finally the intelligent and influential minority were ready to give up their musical trifles for broader forms, carrying with them the rest of our musical world, and at last I risked arranging programmes for a cultivated audience."[40]

The establishment of the nation's first permanent symphonic orchestra in Boston in 1881, which created such a potent model for and gave so much hope to Thomas and others, owed a great deal to John Sullivan Dwight the Boston critic, journalist, and editor who had mounted an enduring struggle for such an institution for decades. Dwight, who in addition to being preoccupied with music had been a Transcendentalist, a Unitarian minister, a member of the Brook Farm community, a student of German literature, and a translator of Goethe, was seeking not just an orchestra, for Bostonians benefited from the periodic visits of such artists as Theodore Thomas and his orchestra, and Dwight himself had helped to found the Harvard Musical Association, which, beginning in the winter of 1865–66, put on an annual series of concerts. What he longed for was a *permanent*, independent orchestra that would epitomize and disseminate the highest musical standards. As early as 1840, Dwight had praised a concert given by The Amateur Orchestra and speculated that if it could only be induced to stay together and practice sufficiently, "We might even hope to hear one day the 'Sinfonia Eroica,' and the 'Pastorale' of Beethoven." Such an orchestra "might be but a labor of love at the outset; but it would create in time the taste which would patronize and reward it." So adamant was Dwight on the subjects of standards and taste that when, four years after the Civil War, the citizens of Boston were treated to Patrick Gilmore's sensational National Peace Jubilee, Dwight's instinct was to leave the city for the duration rather than be complicit in what he considered to be mass musical vulgarity.* The wag who listed him as John Sebastian Dwight was doubtless making a point rather than a mistake.[41]

Dwight used the pages of *Dwight's Journal of Music*, which he published from 1852 until 1881, to articulate tirelessly the conception of a sacralized art: an art that makes no compromises with the "temporal" world; an art that remains spiritually pure and never becomes secondary to the performer or to the audience; an art that is uncompromising in its devotion to cultural perfection. It was this aim that Dwight enunciated when he asserted in 1873 that Boston possessed a public for "concerts pledged to nothing but to standard music of the highest order . . . caring more for such chances of keeping alive their acquaintances with the great unquestioned masterworks, than for any novelty, more for the music than for the performer, more for the matter than the manner, more for Art than for the personality

---

*Dwight's ethereal, lofty approach to culture is illustrated in an incident related by one of his associates in the Harvard Musical Association. During a committee meeting, James T. Fields mentioned a newly published song entitled "Give My Chewing-Gum to Gerty," and wondered "what on earth the next line can be." Everyone laughed, but Dwight remained perplexed and finally exclaimed, "Strange, very strange, indeed. Chewing gum,—yes, I can understand chewing gum being made the subject of a popular song nowadays. People make songs on pretty much everything. But what bothers me is the other part,—why especially to Goethe?"

of any artist," and when he insisted, "While all else in our musical life is changing, blown this way and that by the caprices of fashion and the tricks of advertisement, we want one series of concerts, permanent itself, devoted to the permanent; one to which we may *always* look for opportunities of refreshing our knowledge and our feeling of the great masterworks of men of genius, grouped in programmes which shall have symmetry and harmony of tone . . . and a pervading spirit of pure art; for in this only is there any lasting satisfaction, any charm that will survive the mere excitements of the moment; and in this only is there real culture."[42]

Dwight would countenance nothing that stood in the way of this ideal. He was deeply suspicious of virtuoso soloists who placed more emphasis upon their technique than upon the faithful transmission of the great music they performed. He worried that concerts featuring such talents as the soprano Christine Nilsson or the pianist Anton Rubinstein became *ipso facto* "a Rubinstein or Nilsson concert . . . Beethoven and Mozart lose the place of honor" and the audience was led to forget that "the first end and aim" was "to make the master compositions, the sublime or exquisite tone-poems, Symphonies, Concertos, Overtures, &c., of such rare spirits as Bach, Haydn, Beethoven, Schubert, paramount in interest, so that the music shall be of more consequence than the interpreter, the poem than the reader."* He had contempt for those who attended concerts to *see* as well as to hear and went so far as to suggest that "it would be better if the performer were invisible." The function of a concert was not "rendition"—a word he fairly spit out—but conservation: "to keep the standard master works from falling into disregard, to make Bach and Handel, Haydn and Mozart and Beethoven, Schubert, Mendelssohn, and Schumann, and others worthy of such high companionship, continually felt as living presences and blessed influences among us." He was a

---

*It was typical of Dwight that the greatest praise he could bestow upon the Germania Musical Society was that "music is religion to these men," whose "spirit of devotion, the merging of the individual in the common interest," he found even more admirable than their musical skills.

relentless opponent of anything that diluted or detracted from the great masterworks, and years before the organization of the Boston Pops Concerts in the spring of 1885 he supported the creation of popular orchestral concerts that would present "light, bright, sentimental" music to those who craved it and thus presumably free classical concerts from this obligation.[43]

Dwight understood that a permanent orchestra devoted to the standard works of the great composers could not live on what he called "gate money"; it must "rest upon a *foundation*, in every sense of the term." The question, he asked in the fall of 1880, "is: Can our moneyed men, our merchant princes and millionaires, be got to give their money, and give it freely for this object?" Dwight did not have long to wait for his answer. In his issue of April 9, 1881, he reprinted "A WORD IN THE INTEREST OF GOOD MUSIC," which had been placed in the local papers the week before by the Boston stockbroker Henry Lee Higginson, who announced his intention of filling the void left by the lack of "a full and permanent orchestra, offering the best music at low prices, such as may be found in all the large European cities." Higginson's note was concrete: the Boston Symphony Orchestra would consist of sixty musicians led by the German-born English baritone and composer Georg Henschel, would give twenty concerts during its premier season, and would charge five to ten dollars for season tickets and twenty-five to seventy-five cents for single admissions. Although the note said nothing about finances, an ecstatic Dwight revealed that Higginson "is prepared and willing, if need be, to sustain large losses in the enterprise, in which artistic excellence, completeness, and the elevation of the public taste are evidently of more account to him than any saving of expense, pecuniary profit being wholly out of the question."[44]

The person who solved "the orchestra question" by what Dwight called "one-man power, a *coup-d'etat*, with no pretence of any *plebiscite*," had as a young man spent four years in Europe studying music. To his father's constant demand that he end his Continental idyll and return to join the family's State Street firm, he replied, "If you . . . remember that I enjoy in the depths of my soul music as nothing else, you'll easily comprehend my stay." His father never did come to understand, and the younger Higginson, bowing finally to the inevitable, returned to serve in the Civil War, made an unsuccessful attempt at an independent commercial career as an oil speculator in Ohio and a cotton planter in Georgia, and then, after what his friend Henry Adams characterized as a "desperate struggle," Higginson in 1868 took his place in Lee, Higginson and Company, where he was to remain until his death in 1919, lamenting in later years that he "never walked into 44 State Street without wanting to sit down on the doorstep and cry."[45]

Though Higginson adjusted to his commercial career more fully than this rhetoric suggests, it is clear that he never could conceive of Lee, Higginson and Company, as his destiny; he preferred the role of philanthropist and musical benefactor. By 1881 he felt financially secure enough to make his bold announcement but he did not make it precipitately. He had devoted much time to planning for the new orchestra and had a set of definite goals. These he could put into effect at his own pace because of his decision to be the sole financial sustainer for the Boston Symphony Orchestra—which was to be *his* orchestra to a much greater extent than he ever was willing to admit. Writing in *Century Magazine* some years later, Richard Aldrich made a remark that he attributed to Higginson himself: "The Boston Symphony Orchestra is Mr. Henry L. Higginson's yacht, his racing-stable, his library, and his art gallery, or it takes the place of what these things are to other men of wealth with other tastes." Higginson gave the members of his orchestra permanent positions and ultimately even a pension system, but at no time did he attempt to disguise the price of this security: the acceptance of his paternalistic rule. In 1918, in an address to his musicians from the stage of Symphony Hall in Boston, he revealed what his relationship to them had been from the very beginning:

> Do not suppose that I am ignorant about the various members of the Orchestra. At one time I knew every man; and if that is not the case now, I know many of you, and listen carefully to the playing of this or that man; know well when Witek is doing his best, hear Ferir, hear Warnke, never miss a note of Longy or Marquarre or Grisez or Wendler or Sardony; I know very well what the trumpets are doing, and the trombones, and watch the

drummer, and listen for the tuba; I watch with pleasure the double basses as they stand behind you all. We lost Schuecker last year, and have in his place an admirable artist whose skill gives us much pleasure. In short, I watch the musicians almost too much, for it often interferes with my pleasure, thinking whether they are playing their best, and listening to the various points instead of listening for the whole. Whenever I go to a concert, there is always a sense of responsibility on my mind, and there is always a great joy.[46]

Higginson had wasted little time in establishing his sovereignty over his musicians. In the midst of the symphony's first season Higginson, against the urgent advice of his conductor (who had been reared in the European system where musicians enjoyed a great deal of freedom), sent the members of his orchestra a new contract which stipulated that from Wednesday through Saturday, "you will neither play in any other orchestra nor under any other conductor than Mr. Henschel, except if wanted in your leisure hours by the Handel and Haydn Society, nor will you play for dancing." Mixed musical genres were out; his men were to be devoted to great music and to his orchestra exclusively. All but four of his musicians refused his terms, but Higginson remained adamant. As he recalled it in 1911, he told the delegate that was sent to negotiate with him "that the concerts would go on and that it was only a question of who would play." The implied threat of replacing his musicians with others brought over from Europe was sufficient: "During the next few days almost every man came to me and asked to be engaged." Higginson, who refused throughout his career to deal with any union or association representing his musicians and insisted on personally signing an individual contract with each player annually, admitted in 1888, "My contracts, are very strong, indeed much stronger than European contracts usually are."* The web

---

*Section 12 of the orchestra contract read: "If said musician fails to play to the satisfaction of said Higginson, said Higginson may dismiss said musician from the Orchestra, paying his salary to the time of dismissal, and shall not be liable to pay him any compensation or damages for such dismissal." Higginson's contracts with his conductors were no less strong. The contract with his third conductor, Arthur Nikisch, in 1889 gave Nikisch "sole artistic direction" of the

of authority which Higginson wove so quickly around his musicians brought charges of monopoly against him. By binding
his musicians to him for four consecutive days a week, the *Boston
Transcript* charged, "He thus 'makes a corner' in orchestral players, and monopolizes them for his own concerts and those of
the Handel and Haydn Society . . . Mr. Higginson's gift become
an imposition, it is something that we *must* receive, or else look
musical starvation in the face." At no time did Higginson consider compromising an arrangement that to him seemed an absolute prerequisite to the kind of orchestra and the type of music
he had in mind for Boston.[47]

Higginson moved to control not only his musicians but also
the repertory they performed. Although his first conductor,
Georg Henschel, was criticized frequently for the severity of his
programs and in 1884 received a valentine poem that began,
"Oh, Henschel, cease thy higher flight! / And give the public
something light," he in fact took pains to reach out to a variety
of tastes. Higginson's second conductor, Wilhelm Gericke, was
less willing to bend. When he arrived in the fall of 1884, Gericke
has testified, the audience had become accustomed to "some light
music in the second part of every concert . . . But, as Mr.
Higginson wanted to bring the concerts to a higher standard,
and as the name of the Orchestra was 'The Boston Symphony
Orchestra,' I did not see the reason why the programme should
not be put throughout on a classical basis and have the character
of a real Symphony Concert." Higginson approved of Gericke's
programming and helped him withstand the initial complaints
of the public. During the inaugural performance of Brahms's
Third Symphony, Gericke reported, "the audience left the hall
in hundreds." In 1887, during the first performance of Anton
Bruckner's Symphony No. 7 the defection was more complete;
according to Gericke, by the final movement "we were more
people on the stage than in the audience." Gericke's observations
were corroborated by a critic for the *Gazette* who attributed the

---

orchestra "subject only to the approval of said Higginson," and stipulated that
"it shall rest with the said Henry L. Higginson to decide whether any member
or members of said orchestra shall be engaged, retained or dismissed."

"general exodus" to the fact that Bruckner's symphony was "a prolonged moan and groan, varied now and then with a gloomy and soul-depressing bellow;—Wagner in a prolonged attack of sea-sickness." The next year Richard Strauss's *In Italy* received a similar reception. "The auditors marched out by platoons during the pauses between the movements," a critic recorded, "and some of the bolder ones even made a dash for the doors during the performance." It was, this same critic commented, "the old story of the instruction of the unwilling—the gradual and difficult direction of desire."[48]

In fact, the missionary urge never received top priority in Higginson's complex agenda. He saw himself less as a proselytizer to the masses than as a preserver of the faith: a builder of the temple and a keeper of the flame. Though he supported his conductors' penchant for occasional experimentation—always with the caveat that "of course anything *unworthy* is to be shut out"—Higginson, like Thomas and Dwight, never lost his strong preference for the work of the classic Austro-German composers, especially Beethoven, who had first captivated him as a youth and who he remained convinced were ethically and aesthetically superior. "I do not like Wagner's music, and take little interest in the newer composers," he wrote in 1881. During World War I, when he was under pressure to fire his German conductor Karl Muck, he shared with his friend Charles W. Eliot his worries about the implications of hiring a conductor from France. "I do not want the modern men, that is, the men who believe in the modern music only and have little respect for the old music; and that is the tendency of the [French] conductors."[49]

"Ever since my boyhood," Higginson told his musicians when he was eighty years old, "I have longed to have a part in some good work which would leave a lasting mark in the world. Today we have a noble orchestra—the work of our hands—which gives joy and comfort to many people." But not too many. From the beginning, Higginson seems to have had a conviction that Theodore Thomas arrived at only gradually: that great music, indeed, great culture, had a limited audience and could be spread to large numbers only by diluting it, a tendency Higginson battled against all of his life. Higginson agreed with Dwight that the concert hall was a classroom but not an unlimited one. The highest type of music, Dwight had argued, appeals to the highest type of individual. Thus, the "bond of union" supplied by chamber music "only reaches the few; coarse, meaner, more prosaic natures are not drawn to it." For his part, Dwight doubtless would have approved of the question Higginson asked when he was criticized for not reaching out more directly to the masses in his programming and ticket prices: "If a series of concerts were offered at low prices only to the 'truly poor,' do you suppose that any one but the truly rich would frequent them?"[50]

When, during his 1889 farewell address to Wilhelm Gericke, Higginson asserted, "I alone am responsible for the concerts of the Symphony Orchestra," he was ostensibly referring to finances, but those who had watched his career carefully understood that the accuracy of his statement went beyond money. It was, after all, Higginson who chose the conductors, Higginson who had ultimate authority for hiring and firing the members of the orchestra, Higginson who insisted that the musicians devote themselves exclusively to the orchestra and eschew such vulgar activities as performing for dances, Higginson who persisted in segregating the musical fare so that "light" music was increasingly relegated to summer performances by the Boston Pops Orchestra while the Symphony Orchestra "purified" its programs, presenting music that he and his conductors considered worthy, whether or not it was popular with the audiences. In a speech to his orchestra in 1914, Higginson accurately defined his role and his purpose as "to pay the bills, to be satisfied with nothing short of perfection, and always to remember that we were seeking high art and not money: art came first, then the good of the public, and the money must be an after consideration." Higginson's goal was costly; in his 1914 address he revealed that during the thirty-three years of the Boston Symphony's existence the deficit, which he insisted on meeting himself, had come to $900,000. This considerable sum, coupled with his determination, allowed Higginson to accomplish what others had only dreamed of: the creation of the nation's first permanent, independent, disciplined orchestra, which commanded the full services of its musicians and had the freedom and power to present European art music on its own terms.[51]

The *New York Times* absorbed the lessons of the experiments in Boston and Chicago, which it followed with close attention: there could be no true orchestral permanence without the ability to command the full time of the best musicians and this in turn was impossible without "a pecuniary guarantee that amounts to an endowment." Permanence, in short, required the intervention of the wealthy. The *Times* challenged "the rich music lovers of New York" by reminding them that they could have "a permanent orchestra of the first class," any time they wanted it. When the editors of a San Francisco newspaper read the announcement of Higginson's intention to fund a symphony orchestra in Boston, they commented, "Oh! for a few such men in our midst!" In fact, it turned out that there were indeed "a few such men" in the midst of a number of American cities. Not men who could or would take the sole responsibility as Higginson did, but men who would, along the lines of Fay and his wealthy associates in Chicago, band together in a private association to guarantee the financial stability, and thus the existence, of a symphony orchestra. Not incidentally, they also guaranteed their own influence within the orchestra. When Joseph Pulitzer, who had been a major contributor to the New York Philharmonic for years, died in 1911 he left the orchestra $900,000 on the condition that its programs should be less esoteric and should emphasize Pulitzer's favorite composers—Beethoven, Wagner, and Liszt. The struggle to establish aesthetic standards, to separate true art from the purely vulgar, was waged not only between such institutions as the New York Philharmonic and the larger society but within the institutions themselves. Men like Pulitzer did not mean their contributions to be solely financial; they had matters of taste and culture on their minds as well.* And they increasingly came to dominate the symphonic scene.[52]

---

*This pattern went beyond the orchestral scene. When John Crerar left a bequest to establish a library in Chicago, he established guidelines: "I desire that the books and periodicals be selected with a view to create and sustain a healthy moral and Christian sentiment in the community and that all nastiness and immorality be excluded. I do not mean by this that there shall be nothing but hymn books and sermons, but I mean that dirty French novels and all skeptical trash and works of questionable moral tone shall never be found in this library."

From its founding in 1842, the Philharmonic Society of New York had been a cooperative enterprise controlled by its musicians, who elected the conductor, chose the repertory, and shared the receipts. They also shared the insecurity and financial crises that led them to depend increasingly upon wealthy subscribers. As early as 1871 there were complaints that these affluent men and women were the recipients of favoritism and were exerting undue influence on the orchestra:

> The German Philharmonic
>   Rules the music of this town;
> It plays for pet subscribers—
>   The public is done brown.
> Its Music of the Future
>   On every pure ear palls;—
> Subscribers sit—the public stands,
>   As cattle stand in stalls.
> Then sing the Philharmonic,
>   Where Art-love reigns o'er all!
> When the Dollar looks almighty large
>   And Music very small!

In 1902 Andrew Carnegie and several associates offered to go beyond mere subscription to concerts and to establish a fund offsetting deficits if the musicians would share control of the orchestra with the contributors. The musicians' refusal kept them in authority—and adversity—for a few more years but by the 1908–9 season they accepted a guarantee of $90,000 for three years by a group including Carnegie, J. P. Morgan, and Joseph Pulitzer in return for the abandonment of the cooperative plan, the establishment of an outside board of control, the naming of a conductor who would have power over membership and musical affairs, and the expansion of the number of concerts.[53]

The pattern was repeated wherever symphonic music blossomed. The New York Symphony Orchestra, which had been established in 1878 by the conductor Leopold Damrosch and taken over by his son Walter in 1885, went through years of financial strain. Although it received help from such patrons as Andrew Carnegie—who was persuaded by Walter Damrosch to contribute funds for the symphony hall that opened in 1891 bearing its donor's name—J. P. Morgan, John D. Rockefeller, the Vanderbilts (Cornelius, George, and William), and Collis P. Huntington, it was forced to suspend operations between 1898 and 1903, when it was reorganized and gradually came under the financial aegis of Henry Harkness Flagler, who helped it steadily increase the number of its rehearsals and concerts and guarantee its members a fixed yearly salary. By 1914 Flagler was underwriting the orchestra's continuing deficits up to a guaranteed maximum of $100,000 a year, and in 1920 he treated it to a European tour, the first made by any American symphony orchestra. By 1925 the burden became too great for an individual, and Flagler had to turn to his fellow directors for help in covering the deficit. In 1928 the New York Symphony merged with the Philharmonic to form the New York Philharmonic-Symphony Orchestra under a new board composed of directors of both orchestras.[54]

Ultimately, then, it was not Higginson's mode of one-man rule but the corporate Chicago model that prevailed. The Philadelphia Orchestra, for example, was established in 1900 in a city that, according to Frances Anne Wister, a member of the orchestra's board from 1905 to 1956, "was still not ready to attend symphony concerts or support an orchestra at any general sacrifice to its own purse. The general attitude was that such a project must be supported by a few persons who had time and money to spend. Indifference was widespread." The stringent financial pressures forced the orchestra's first conductor, Fritz Scheel, to engage in what was becoming a familiar struggle for artistic purity. When some members of the board, appalled at the large losses averaging some $70,000 annually, insisted that Scheel reach out to the public by including waltzes in his programming, the conductor responded in a manner that in fact articulated the sentiments of the majority of the board: "You represent the business end of this association; I stand for art . . . As long as I am conductor of the Philadelphia Orchestra, waltzes will not be played on a symphony programme." The solution, in Philadelphia as in Boston and elsewhere, was to separate the wheat from the chaff; to mount a series of "popular concerts" for those who craved hearing Strauss's waltzes, Brahms's Hungarian Dances, Liszt's Hungarian Rhapsodies, and instrumental arrangements of Wagner's *Pilgrim's Chorus* and *Eve-*

ning Star or Verdi's arias, and to arrange the regular programming for those who preferred to have their culture unsullied by
compromise. When, in its third season, the orchestra mounted
Philadelphia's first Beethoven Cycle, presenting the nine symphonies in five concerts, the *Musical Courier* reported, "The cycle
was projected as an art undertaking pure and simple. Profit was
a secondary consideration. Flamboyant advertisement was es-
chewed. There were announcements dignified and to the point."
While the Philadelphia Orchestra was learning many new tunes,
Frances Wister reported, "the Board of Directors could remember but one . . . 'Where shall we get the money?' with variations."
Though general fund raising was tried continually, with mixed
results, the finger increasingly pointed in one direction. Of the
twenty-four founding board members of the Philadelphia Orchestra Association, nineteen were listed in the *Social Register of
Philadelphia*.* Representing the city's most affluent and socially
elite element, the Board of Directors came to exercise the responsibility for, and the authority over, the Philadelphia Orchestra. In 1899 a Philadelphia newspaper warned those planning to
establish a symphony orchestra that there was no evidence that
the general public hungered for so expensive a musical institution
sufficiently to justify relying on its financial support. Thus, the
paper concluded prophetically, "the promoters must expect to
pay the piper. And this being the case, we should say that those
who pay have an entire right to choose their piper—to organize
their orchestra in their own way and put it in charge of whom
they please."[55]

The Philadelphia story was the national story. In addition to
New York and Chicago, before World War I orchestras were
established in St. Louis, Cincinnati, Minneapolis, Pittsburgh, and
San Francisco based on a structure that lodged control in a board
of wealthy sponsors. In Boston itself, Higginson's dream of
leaving his orchestra a bequest sufficient to give it independence
was doomed by the economic reverses he suffered in his late

---

*This pattern continued: 84 of the 128 board members who served through
1969, and all but 1 of the Orchestra Association's presidents or chairmen of
the board from 1901 to 1969, were listed in the *Social Register*.

years. Though he had long resisted the suggestion that he place control of his orchestra under a board of trustees, Higginson's age and finances ultimately forced him to heed the counsel of Harvard President Eliot that the orchestra take on "a more institutional aspect." In the spring of 1918, little more than a year before his death, Higginson resigned from active control of the orchestra and transferred his authority to a board of nine trustees headed by Judge Frederick P. Cabot and including men who, like Higginson before them, were prominent in the nexus of cultural and financial institutions that ruled Boston.[56]

Since neither paternalistic royalty nor a paternalistic government was available for the support of symphonic music or any other aspect of expressive culture, it is hardly surprising, considering the prevailing paradigms and ethos of the turn of the century, that the alternative source of paternalistic capitalism was sought not only as a means of funds but as a model of organization as well. The new framework was used in the cultural arena—as it was being used increasingly in the economic arena—to win freedom from the pressures of the market place and to establish a new hierarchy whose effects upon culture, and especially upon the ways in which we think about culture, were to persist throughout this century. The new organizational structures lent themselves particularly well to the process of sacralization that was transforming the face of American culture.

IN 1848, in their sixth annual report, the directors of the Philharmonic Society of New York wrote, "It must be acknowledged that the science of Music as it exists in nature is not of human invention, but of divine appointment." The number of those who were willing to acknowledge this "divine appointment" was to grow with the coming years. The process of sacralization endowed the music it focused upon with unique aesthetic and spiritual properties that rendered it inviolate, exclusive, and eternal. This was not the mere ephemera of the world of entertainment but something lasting, something permanent. "The root of our success is *not* fashion," the Philharmonic directors announced in 1857, "it is art."[57]

George Templeton Strong wrote in his diary following a performance of Beethoven's Fifth Symphony in the spring of 1851, "It is music that I should think an orchestra of angels, such as one sees in old pictures before Raphael, might love to play. No mortal instruments can do justice to the andante and finale." This, he was convinced, was the only music a symphony orchestra should play. "Why should fifty violins, trombones, flutes, and so on, waste their time in laboriously rehearsing and studying out a production that is 'exceedingly clever,' . . . when they might be so much more profitably employed on truly great and transcendent works." Henry Theophilus Finck, the future music critic for Godkin's *Nation* and *New York Evening Post*, grew up on the outskirts of the village of Aurora Mills, Oregon, far removed from Strong's New York, but from an early age he shared Strong's orientation. Finck's father, who grew apples and gave music lessons, introduced him to the string quartets of Haydn, Mozart, and Beethoven, but since there was no local orchestra, he could only describe to his son the effects of their symphonic compositions. "When I think of such an orchestra an indescribable thrill runs through my heart," the teen-ager wrote in his diary in the 1860s. "I feel myself brought nearer to the immortal God . . . I feel inclined to fall on my knees and adore the Great Power, of whatever nature it may be, that could create music, the most divine of all gifts to man."[58]

Throughout his career there were those who saw in Theodore Thomas more than merely a musician. As early as 1856, when the young Thomas was first violinist in the Mason-Thomas Quartette, *Dwight's Journal of Music* wrote of his "reverence" for great music and commented, "Such men are, or ought to be, the true missionaries of art in this country." On January 8, 1905, just four days after Thomas's death, the Reverend Frank Wakely Gunsaulus told a memorial meeting, "We have said goodbye to a priest and prophet. It makes no difference that Theodore Thomas never acknowledged his divine call to a high and noble ministry. The art of interpreting great music comes as a duty, and Theodore Thomas, like a true minister, made it a privilege and joy." The Reverend Gunsaulus was not quite right; Thomas may not have acknowledged his "divine call" publicly but long before his death he had recognized it. His wife has testified that

Thomas refused to listen to vulgar talk, go to "questionable" plays, or read immoral books, for fear of poisoning his mind and rendering himself unfit to interpret the music of the classic masters. "I avoid trashy stuff," Thomas told his wife, "otherwise, when I come before the public to interpret master-works, and my soul should be inspired with noble and impressive emotions, these evil thoughts run around in my head like squirrels and spoil it all. A musician must keep his heart pure and his mind clean if he wishes to elevate, instead of debasing his art. And here we have the difference between the classic and the modern school of composers. Those old giants said their prayers when they wished to write an immortal work. The modern man takes a drink."*[59]

One important result of sacralization was to call into question the traditional practice of mixing musical genres and presenting audiences with an eclectic feast that John Sullivan Dwight now characterized in the *Atlantic Monthly* as "miscellaneous concerts, potpourris of the hackneyed sentimentalities or flash fancies of third and tenth rate composers." In the late 1870s *Dwight's Journal of Music* complained about the "musical babble," the "pandemonium of sounds," which pursued one everywhere: "Bands in the streets and gardens and on every steamboat, hand-organ grinders, whistlers of *Pinafore*, keep the air full of melodies that cross each other in all directions." *Dwight's Journal* called for an end to this "period of sentimental, superficial dilettantism" and for the adoption of "an authoritative standard," which would ensure that music would become "a more earnest matter among its votaries in our country than it ever was before."[60]

The artist's vocation, Edward Baxter Perry maintained in 1892, "is, or should be, a religion"; and when the musician

---

*A friend of Thomas's informed Charles Edward Russell that in the 1870s he had begun to tell Thomas an off-color story. "You must not tell me stories like that," Thomas admonished him. "Suppose you tell me this story and to-night when I am about to conduct some work of beauty and purity I catch sight of your face in the audience. Do you not see that involuntarily my mental state is distorted from the idea of purity I ought to have, and it will not be possible for me to give to that composition the interpretation of perfect purity that it demands?"

stepped upon the stage "in his capacity as high priest in the temple of the beautiful," his "devout fervor" should lift his audience above the "trivial, petty phases of mere sensuous pleasure or superficial enjoyment, to a higher . . . plane of spiritual aesthetic gratification." Unfortunately, too many artists failed to adhere to "strictly legitimate" compositions and sought favor with "a commonplace majority" by giving in to its "vulgar taste for the sensational and the frivolous." Henry T. Finck, now an influential critic, agreed, dismissing "Home Sweet Home," a favorite encore for opera singers, as "a cheap Sicilian ditty" unworthy of accompanying great music. When in 1882 the soprano Adelina Patti, who had made her debut in New York City in the 1850s, returned to the United States after an absence of many years during which she had become one of Europe's most famous prima donnas, and gave a recital of popular ballads, she offended many in her audience and was condemned by the critics. George William Curtis, the editor of *Harper's* attempted to help his readers comprehend her mistake. While Patti had been enchanting Europe, "she had not known the marvellous growth of the land that she had left." Indeed, even Jenny Lind, who had charmed "the rude and primitive" Americans of three decades earlier had by now "become a tuneful tradition heard by the newest America not without head-shakes and murmurs of incredulity." It was "another America" to which Patti returned:

> It was an America which had half outgrown the Italian opera, and which listened with delight to the music of the future. It was indeed the cultivated, intelligent musically developed America . . . accustomed to hear the greatest works of the greatest masters performed in a manner which would not discredit the Academie in Berlin, the Gewandhaus in Leipsic, the Conservatoire in Paris.

Patti had learned the hard way that New York City possessed "some taste, some sense of proportion, some knowledge of the fitness of things. It is not altogether a miner's camp upon the frontier." Patti's concert of petty popular airs, Curtis concluded, "was an error. It was presently repaired. It will not be repeated."[61]

During his visit to the United States in 1876, the German pianist Hans von Bülow acted out these convictions. The soprano Emma Thursby, who preceded von Bülow on the program, followed her rendition of songs by Schubert and Schumann by singing what the conductor Walter Damrosch called "a rather trivial song by Franz Abt." Von Bülow's "rage knew no bounds" at this "desecration" of a program composed of the works of great masters. When von Bülow came out on the stage, "he deliberately took out his handkerchief and carefully wiped the keys of the piano up and down in a noisy glissando scale and then began to improvise on the recitative from Beethoven's Ninth Symphony, 'Oh friends, not these tones . . .'" Von Bülow was not alone in believing that great music had a cleansing effect. When, in the fall of 1900, the Boston Symphony Orchestra moved into the newly completed Symphony Hall, the *New York Tribune* lamented that its former home, the old Music Hall,

> is now degraded to the level of a home for vaudeville shows. For a decade past it has harbored dog shows, cat shows, promenade concerts and meetings of all descriptions, yet has held its place in the love of Boston because of its gracious past and by reason of its weekly purification during the musical season.

The urge to deprecate popular musical genres was an important element in the process of sacralization. If symphonic music was, as Henry T. Finck believed, divine, then it followed that other genres must occupy a lesser region—which Finck also believed. One Thanksgiving, following a matinee of Wagner's *Parsifal*, he and his wife went to the home of the soprano Lillian Nordica. After dinner the Fincks and Enrico Caruso were invited to share Nordica's box at the Winter Garden. "So we went," Finck has recorded, "though I loathed vaudeville. After enduring the tortures of boredom for an hour we excused ourselves to our hostess, and on the way out I said to my wife emphatically: *'That's my idea of hell!'*" Toward the end of his life, Theodore Thomas would have agreed. "Light music, 'popular' so called," he wrote in his autobiography, "is the sensual side of the art and has more or less devil in it."[62]

That the symphonic conductors' function had become no less than the pursuance and preservation of what was often referred to as the "divine art," enhanced their position. European musicians like Gustav Mahler were stunned at the power and prestige conductors in America enjoyed. In urging a German colleague to take the post as conductor of the Boston Symphony Orchestra in 1908, Mahler argued that the position brought with it "an orchestra of the first rank. Unlimited sovereign power. A social standing such as the musician cannot obtain in Europe. A public of whose keenness to learn and whose gratitude the European can form no conception." A Cleveland reporter put it more simply: "In Boston the leader of the orchestra is a good deal bigger than the mayor." The process, of course, enhanced the prestige of the composer even more. Before the nineteenth century the names of composers were often omitted from concert programs. Though the Old City Concerts in late eighteenth-century New York centered on the music of Haydn, his name did not appear once on any of the programs. In the early 1850s the impresario Max Maretzek sent a pianist and basso on a concert tour. Maretzek's agent discovered that the musicians, who were well known in New York, Boston, and Philadelphia, were comparatively unknown in a New England town where they were to perform. Accordingly, he decided to make the names of the composers whose pieces they were playing a "larger feature" in the programs and posters than those of the performers themselves. The "trick," Maretzek wrote, succeeded and a good audience attended the concert. This practice of featuring the composers rather than the performers was evidently so novel that the confused hotel proprietors, according to Maretzek, billed not the performing artists but Mozart, Handel, Bellini, and Beethoven.[63]

The enhanced prestige of the composers and the sacralization of their work changed those long-standing attitudes toward them and their compositions that had prevailed throughout most of the nineteenth century. In 1855, Balbina Steffanone, scheduled to sing in Bellini's *I Puritani*, informed Max Maretzek on the day of the performance that she was unable to appear because of chills and fever. Maretzek recorded his response: "I rushed to her house, I begged, I implored, I promised to apologize to the public for any shortcomings; I advised to cut out the heaviest pieces of the opera, but to no avail. Steffanone would not sing." The ease with which Maretzek offered to "cut out the heaviest pieces of the opera" says much about attitudes of the period's promoters and performers toward the music: It was *theirs* to do with what they willed. That feeling faded rapidly with the coming of the new century. Just as actors were admonished not to take liberties with the text of a Shakespearean play, so singers and soloists were obliged increasingly to stick to the sacred text of the great masters. In 1867 George Templeton Strong heard a Mozart piano concerto in which the soloist introduced "two elaborate inane 'cadenzas' to shew off his fingering," and commented that it would have been as appropriate for him to have "exhibited a conjuring trick with cards or a bottle, or turned three back somersaults over his piano" as to introduce these "impertinent" phrases "into Mozart's pure crystalline music." In 1871 Strong called Leopold Damrosch's rendition of Beethoven's Violin Concerto in D brilliant but complained about his cadenza: "Who is worthy to append a bit of his own writing to a composition of Beethoven's?" Strong did not live to see his lonely grumblings echoed by an increasing number of influential critics and musicians. Conductors like Theodore Thomas, Wilhelm Gericke, and Karl Muck were suspicious of soloists altogether, constantly fearing that they would turn the music to their own purposes and encourage the audience to admire sensationalism rather than art. Musical lore was filled with stories of the tensions between conductors who insisted upon adherence to the score and soloists who wanted to take liberties with it in order to demonstrate their talents. During a rehearsal of a Handel oratorio, the soprano Adelina Patti, who was famous for altering the music she sang in order to display her impressive range, insisted on her right to sing the way she chose since she was the prima donna. "Excuse me, madam," Theodore Thomas rejoined, "but here *I* am prima donna." In a similar confrontation, Arturo Toscanini insisted repeatedly during rehearsals of Gluck's *Orfeo ed Euridice* that a contralto stop prolonging the high note in her major aria. When, during the performance, she persisted in having her way, Toscanini simply stayed with the score, brought the aria to a conclusion, and left the contralto alone with her high F.[64]

Conductors themselves often were judged by the same standards as soloists. In spite of his great prestige, when Gustav Mahler, who led the New York Philharmonic from 1909 to 1911, openly made changes in Beethoven's orchestration, proclaiming, "Of course the works of Beethoven need some editing," he was immediately and persistently attacked by the many guardians of the sanctity of the text, and most severely by the *New York Herald*'s influential critic Henry Edward Krehbiel, who was known as "the American high priest of Beethoven."* For much of the nineteenth century conductors had been free to present separate movements of concertos and symphonies. Even George Templeton Strong suggested, after attending a Philharmonic concert in 1871, "the Beethoven concerto, lovely as it is, might be advantageously abridged." As late as 1894 the Boston critic Philip Hale, complaining of the undue length of a Boston Symphony concert, suggested that the second and third movements of the Beethoven Violin Concerto "could well have been omitted." That same year the Boston Symphony Orchestra presented only movements three and two—in that order—of Beethoven's Ninth Symphony. This practice, which had not disturbed such composers as Mozart and Chopin, was not consistent with the growing aura of sanctity that surrounded symphonic compositions or the sense that a true work of art had an integrity which must not be interfered with by anyone, be it audience, soloist, or conductor, and was increasingly relegated to such manifestly less "serious" occasions as concerts of the Boston Pops Orchestra.[65]

Sacralization increased the distance between amateur and professional. The blurring of that distinction had been one of the characteristics of music in America for much of the nineteenth century. But by the end of the century the gap had widened. More and more it was asserted that it was only the highly trained professional who had the knowledge, the skill, and the will to understand and carry out the intentions of the creators of the divine art. The urge toward high art precipitated a marked decline of parlor music in the late nineteenth century. "I fear that the coming generation will lose one of the delights and comforts

---

*Mahler the composer embraced the same views as Mahler the conductor, at least rhetorically. According to the conductor Otto Klemperer, Mahler announced that if his Eighth Symphony did not sound good, anybody could "with an easy conscience" make changes in it.

of the last," a correspondent wrote to the *Atlantic Monthly* in 1891, "—the song which in the home circle moved to tears or smiles, and which thrilled with simple pathos or noble sentiment the hearts of those who were 'not too bright or good for human nature's daily food.'" There had been a time, an observer noted in 1894, when the title *amateur* "carried with it respect, dignity, and worth," but no longer.

> Amateur has collided with professional, and the former term has gradually but steadily declined in favor; in fact, it has become almost a term of opprobrium. The work of an amateur, the touch of the amateur, a mere amateur, amateurish, amateurishness—these are different current expressions which all mean the same thing, bad work.

In her 1939 autobiography, the American pianist, music critic, and teacher Olga Samaroff Stokowski demonstrated how radically attitudes had altered when she wrote with contempt of *Hausmusik*, which she contended had led generations of cultivated people to listen "to grotesque and inaccurate distortions of the music of Haydn and Mozart." Of all the creations "of human genius," only music, she insisted, had been treated so shabbily: "Bungling attempts at painting, sculpture or writing can do no harm. They do not ruin an art work created by somebody else. But the old idea of musical performance as an 'accomplishment' destined to be admired upon social occasions has been responsible for some pretty terrible vandalism."[66]

The process of sacralization reinforced the all too prevalent notion that for the source of divine inspiration and artistic creation one had to look not only upward but eastward toward Europe.* In 1889 Theodore Thomas described the study in his country home in New Hampshire. It included busts of Shakespeare and Bach, an engraving of Mozart at the court of Vienna,

---

*Indeed, Olga Samaroff Stokowski's very name was the result of this Eurocentrism. When, as the young American pianist Lucy Hickenlooper, she appeared in the office of the concert manager Henry Wolfsohn, she was told that her name was too "cold" for a musician and she was rechristened Olga Samaroff, to which was added still another Slavic surname after her marriage to the conductor Leopold Stokowski.

another of Beethoven "under whom I sit, before a writing table," a picture of Goethe as an old man, a picture of Schiller's house and garden in Weimar, a picture of Schubert and one of Schumann. "Here," Thomas wrote, "you have my *'Glaubens Bekenntnis'* [my creed]." Such icons formed the creed of most of Thomas's colleagues, as the young Charles Ives discovered when he attempted to inject American idioms into his Second Symphony, which he completed in 1901 or 1902. "Some of the themes in this symphony suggest Gospel Hymns and Steve Foster," Ives noted. "Some nice people, whenever they hear the words 'Gospel Hymns' or 'Stephen Foster,' say 'Mercy Me!', and a little high-brow smile creeps over their brow—'Can't you get something better than that in a symphony?'" "Imagine," one of his Yale professors told him, "in a symphony, hearing suggestions of street tunes like "Marching through Georgia" or a Moody and Sankey hymn!" Growing up in Danbury, Connecticut, Ives had learned from his father, George, a bandmaster and music teacher, that a sense of the divine did not rule out openness. In a note to the second movement of his Fourth Symphony, Charles Ives quoted an "unknown philosopher of a half century ago":

> How can there be any bad music? All music is from heaven. If there is anything bad in it, I put it there—by my implications and my limitations. Nature builds the mountains and the meadows and man puts in the fences and labels.

Whether these were actually the words of George Ives, they articulated the principles that guided him as a teacher and musician. No matter how strongly wedded the elder Ives was to the assumptions and structures of European art music, he never taught his son to ignore or disdain the vernacular tradition as a source of inspiration and ideas. "He started all the children of the family," Charles Ives recalled, "—and most of the children of the town for that matter—on Bach and Stephen Foster." The move from Danbury to New Haven and his education at Yale University taught Ives quickly enough that the catholicity that sprang from his father's vision of the divine was not in vogue. "I began to feel more and more," Ives wrote, "that, if I wanted to write music that, to me, seemed worth while, I must keep away from musicians."[67]

"Our National Music," 1888, makes clear the sacred, Eurocentric conceptions of "serious" music that were becoming prevalent toward the turn of the century and illustrates how little room there was for indigenous American composers or performers in the pantheon of culture.

Ives might have been better prepared for his experiences had he studied the career of the American pianist and composer Louis Moreau Gottschalk, who won more fame and recognition in Paris than in the United States. When he reviewed Gottschalk's Boston concert in 1853, John Sullivan Dwight complained that the pianist played only his own compositions which were based on such American songs as "Old Folks at Home" and "O Susanna." "Could a more trivial and insulting string of musical rigmarole have been offered to an audience of earnest music-lovers?" Though he did attain a degree of success in the United States as a performer, Gottschalk expressed the pain he felt on not being accepted as fully as he had hoped as a composer as well. In 1863 he complained of the type of critic he dubbed the "guardian of the flock" whose "immaculate, delicate taste" could feed "only on the divine ambrosia emanating from the masters (dead—this is important, and purified in the crucible consecrated by opinion and by time) . . . The great dead! How many little crimes are committed in their name!"* The "crimes" were to grow in frequency and influence with the coming years.[68]

After hearing the Jubilee Singers in 1897, Mark Twain wrote a friend, "I think that in the Jubilees and their songs America has produced the perfectest flower of the ages; and I wish it were a foreign product, so that she would worship it and lavish money on it and go properly crazy over it." So little did the arbiters of musical taste think of their own country's contributions that when in 1884 the critic Richard Grant White was invited to write a history of American music, he refused for lack of an American music to write about. American psalm-book makers and singing-school teachers were, White declared, "about as much in place in the history of musical art as a critical discussion of the whooping of Indians would be." White's attitude was common; Henry Finck also refused a commission to write a history of American music. "I declined," he tells us, "on the

---

*Gottschalk spoke for most of his American colleagues. In 1853 the composer William Henry Fry complained that "a composer in this country may as well burn his compositions for any opportunity he has for making himself heard. Our Opera Houses and Musical Societies are worse than useless so far [as] they foster American Art."

ground that there wasn't enough of it to go 'round." John
Sullivan Dwight called the seventeenth and eighteenth centuries
"Our Dark Age in Music," and complained that although he was
writing in 1882 there was still "nothing that properly can count
in the history of music here *as art*." Though there were some
who began to see in American and, especially, Afro-American
folk music evidence of an indigenous American musical tradition,
that notion flew too directly in the face of the comfortable
evolutionary predispositions of the day. In 1893 Frederick W.
Root explained to those attending the International Folk-Lore
Congress in Chicago that "the utterances of the savage people
were omitted, these being hardly developed to the point at which
they might be called music." In 1881 the critic Frederick Nast
dismissed "all plantation melodies and minstrel ballads" as products of "the lowest strata of society," and the Boston critic William Apthorp declared in the 1890s that such compositions as
Dvorak's *New World* Symphony and Edward MacDowell's *Indian*
Suite were futile attempts "to make civilized music by civilized
methods out of essentially barbaric material," resulting in "a mere
apotheosis of ugliness, distorted forms, and barbarous expression."[69]

Over the years, American writers felt the impact of this deference for things European, especially if they were hallowed by
age. In accepting the Nobel Prize for literature in 1930, Sinclair
Lewis condemned the false standards of those turn-of-the-cen-
tury critics who were "effusively seeking to guide America into
becoming a pale edition of an English cathedral town," and
remarked that to "true blue" professors of literature in American
universities, "literature is not something that a plain human
being, living today, painfully sits down to produce. No, it is
something dead; it is something magically produced by super-
human beings who must, if they are to be regarded as artists at
all, have died at least one hundred years before the diabolical
invention of the typewriter." Hamlin Garland complained that
so far as the late nineteenth-century literary magazines were
concerned, "Wisconsin, Minnesota and Iowa did not exist. Not
a picture, not a single poem or story, not even a reference to
those states could I discover in ten thousand pages of print." For
the genteel writers, Malcolm Cowley observed, England "was

'our old home,' to be regarded with a mixture of emulative jealousy and pride of kinship. Their literary models were English, with the result that much of their writing seemed less national than colonial." By the first world war Randolph Bourne was observing: "English snobberies, English religion, English literary styles, English literary reverences and canons, English ethics, English superiorities, have been the cultural food that we have drunk in from our mothers' breasts."[70]

In 1927, contemplating the reasons for the demise of Theodore Thomas' American Opera Company forty years earlier, Charles Edward Russell speculated that the name of the company was unfortunate. "'American Opera' connoted bad opera. To this day 'American artist' means to the average American soul inferior artist; 'American composer' means inferior composer." The distaste for things American could even extend to the natural world. "Nature," Charles Eliot Norton declared in 1873, "certainly did not show half so much poetic imagination in the construction of America as she did in Europe." In 1887 he wrote George Edward Woodberry, "Nature to be really beautiful to us must be associated with the thoughts and feelings of men. An Italian sunset is better than a Californian for this reason; a daisy of more worth than a mayflower." Similarly, Henry James commented that "even nature, in the western world, has the peculiarity of seeming rather crude and immature." The painter Thomas Cole compared America and Italy: "He who stands on Mont Albano and looks down on ancient Rome, has his mind peopled with the gigantic associations of the storied past; but he who stands on the mounds of the West, the most venerable remains of American antiquity, *may* experience the emotion of the sublime, but it is the sublimity of a shoreless ocean unislanded by the recorded deeds of man." Indeed, American nature became worthy of consideration only after it was filtered through European sensibilities. George E. Adams, a trustee of Chicago's Newberry Library and Field Columbian Museum and a former president of its Orchestral Association, informed the members of the Chicago Literary Club in 1905 that before the European explorers and colonists had come to the New World, the beauty of the New Hampshire mountains was nonexistent, "because there was no eye to see, no soul to feel it. True, the Indians were there . . . But the red Indian, being a primitive man, did not have that delicate sense of beauty, of form and color, which has been developed in the modern man, the heir of centuries of civilization."[71]

These attitudes were part of a development that saw the very word "culture" becoming synonymous with the Eurocentric products of the symphonic hall, the opera house, the museum, and the library, all of which, the American people were taught, must be approached with a disciplined, knowledgeable serious-ness of purpose, and—most important of all—with a feeling of reverence. "Certain things are not disputable," *Harper's* pro-claimed:

> Homer, Shakespeare, Dante, Raphael, Michael Angelo, Handel, Beethoven, Mozart, they are towering facts like the Alps or the Himalayas. They are the heaven-kissing peaks, and are universally acknowledged. It is not conceivable that the judgment of mankind upon those names will ever be reversed.[72]

Thus by the early decades of this century the changes that had either begun or gained velocity in the last third of the nineteenth century were in place: the masterworks of the classic composers were to be performed in their entirety by highly trained musicians on programs free from the contamination of lesser works or lesser genres, free from the interference of audi-ence or performer, free from the distractions of the mundane; audiences were to approach the masters and their works with proper respect and proper seriousness, for aesthetic and spiritual elevation rather than mere entertainment was the goal. This transition was not confined to the worlds of symphonic and operatic music or of Shakespearean drama; it was manifest in other important areas of expressive culture as well.

American museums went through a familiar pattern of devel-opment from the general and eclectic to the exclusive and specific. Neil Harris has summed up the state of museums in the first half of the nineteenth century: "Paintings and sculpture stood along-side mummies, mastodon bones and stuffed animals. American museums were not, in the antebellum period, segregated temples of the fine arts, but repositories of information, collections of strange or doubtful data." "A Repository of learned Curiosities," was in fact precisely how Dr. Samuel Johnson defined museums in his 1755 *Dictionary*. These repositories competed freely for the public's attention. Even so serious a museum head as the artist Charles Willson Peale, who opened his museum of paintings and natural curiosities in Philadelphia in 1786, was not above publicizing his new Mammoth Room by dressing his handyman in American Indian garb and parading him through the streets on a white horse preceded by a trumpeter. The eclectic nature of Peale's museum is revealed in his famous painting *The Artist in His Museum* (1822), in which Peale portrayed himself lifting a curtain beyond which lies the Long Room of his museum. The walls are covered with cases containing stuffed birds, in reconstructed natural habitats—an exhibition technique pioneered by Peale. Portraits of the heroes of the American Revolution decorate the spaces above the cases. In the foreground are several mastodon bones, the fully reconstructed skeleton of a mastodon, a stuffed wild turkey, the tools of a taxidermist, and the palette and brushes of an artist. The people in the room are equally varied: a man with folded arms seriously studying the birds, a father instructing his young son, and a woman standing in astonishment before the mastodon testified to Peale's desire to make his museum a source of enlightenment *and* "rational amusement." In addition to what he depicted in his painting, Peale's museum featured a large variety of mounted animals, fishes, snakes, and insects, a collection of minerals, fossils, and shells, ethnographic exhibits focusing especially on the clothing and utensils of North American Indians, a picture gallery containing many portraits of patriots and scientists, ultimately including every president through Andrew Jackson, a menagerie of live animals, a botanical exhibit featuring rare trees and plants, electrical and technological equipment including a model of a perpetual-motion machine, and such curiosities as a mounted five-legged, double-tailed cow giving milk to a two-headed calf.[73]

This variety was typical. Boston's first museum, which opened in 1791 and became known as the Columbian Museum in 1795, exhibited a series of wax figures of such notables as John Adams,

Charles Willson Peale, *The Artist in His Museum*, 1822, oil on canvas.

George Washington, and Benjamin Franklin, and 123 paintings with such titles as *Mr. Garrick Speaking the Ode to Shakespeare, Scene in the Third Act of King Lear, Mr. Lowndes and Family of Maryland, A Beautiful Grecian Lady*, along with a live rattlesnake, alligator, and eagle. During the early years of the nineteenth century the Columbian Museum added to these exhibitions and featured statuary and a fine collection of miniature paintings. In New York City a series of museums, from the Tammany American Museum in 1791 to the New American Museum in 1816, featured natural history, waxworks, African, Indian, and Chinese ornaments, weapons, and relics, such technological exhibits as an air gun and a guillotine complete with a recently beheaded wax figure, a panorama of Charleston, a full-length portrait of George Washington by Gilbert Stuart, and 200 paintings and prints. Museums of this nature adorned American cities from Utica, Syracuse, and Niagara Falls in New York State, to Pittsburgh, Charleston, Cincinnati, Lexington, and St. Louis. Audiences were attracted to these museums not only by the regular exhibits but by learned lectures, sensational scientific demonstrations, and enticing performances of music and drama such as Signor Hellene, the one-man band, who appeared in Peale's museum simultaneously playing the viola, Turkish cymbals, tenor drum, Pandean pipes, and Chinese bells. In 1819, just one year after Boston's Gallery of Fine Arts advertised an exhibition of 111 of Hogarth's engravings, it featured two dwarfs called "The Lilliputian Songsters," who sang tunes "modern, fashionable, and patriotic" and were worth seeing because of "their intelligence and genteel deportment." It is clear what models P. T. Barnum drew upon when he founded his series of "American Museums" beginning in the 1840s.[74]

No more than drama, opera, or instrumental music, then, were painting and sculpture elevated above other forms of expressive culture in the first half of the nineteenth century; they were part of the general culture and were experienced in the midst of a broad range of other cultural genres by a catholic audience that cut through class and social lines. This situation began to change after mid-century and, characteristically, the change was accompanied by sacred language and religious analogies. "If we want to drive far from us, vice and crime—if we want to outbid the wine-cup and the gaming-table, we must adorn," the Reverend Frederick W. Sawyer wrote in 1860. "We must adorn our parks and gardens; adorn our churches and public edifices. We must have something to claim the attention, to mould the taste, to cultivate." A number of ministers, ranging from Episcopalian to Methodist, began to assert that religion needed art if it was to continue to attract followers in the future. "A religion that renounces the beautiful, and true and tasteful in Nature and Art," the Methodist *National Magazine* warned, "is either mere affectation, or will one day drive its votaries to the hermit's cell or the monastery." This thrust helped men of God discover the divine element in the fine arts. "Is there not something quite kindred between your profession and ours?" the Reverend Samuel Osgood asked artists in the summer of 1855. Several months later he discovered that "God himself is the Master Artist." In his novel *Norwood* (1867), the nation's best known minister, Henry Ward Beecher, had his protagonist tell a young man who is thinking of abandoning art for the ministry to stick to his last: "You can seek the moral benefit of society by your art, as really as by sermons, and probably with far greater success . . . Your profession is . . . the education of the community by the ministration of Beauty." James Jackson Jarves, the influential American art critic and follower of John Ruskin, referred to the European art in churches and galleries as "these sacred writings on the wall," which he asserted "every American who goes abroad . . . if he would do his duty to his own country," had the obligation "of reading and interpreting to his countrymen, so far as in him lies." In his novel *Roderick Hudson* (1875), Henry James portrayed this increasingly common attitude by having a midwestern patron of the arts reflect that "the office of art is second only to that of religion." A number of artists agreed with this elevated definition of their calling. George Inness insisted that "*the true artistic impulse is divine*," and Asher Durand argued that the purpose of art was neither riches nor decoration: "It is only through the religious integrity of motive by which all real Artists have ever been activated." The development of artistic taste, *Scribner's Monthly* announced in 1877, "may be compared with what the religious call a 'growth in grace.' There is such a thing as 'the witness of the spirit,' in art as in religion."[75]

These attitudinal changes were to become embodied gradually in institutions. The Boston Museum of Fine Arts, as Paul DiMaggio has argued so persuasively, provides a fine example of the process by which art museums in America became sacralized. Incorporated by an act of the Massachusetts legislature in 1870, and fully opened to the public in 1876, the museum's first purpose was educational; the act of incorporation stipulating that the museum "ought to be a popular institution, in the widest sense of the term," and be open free to the public as many days a week as feasible. The immediate stimulus for its creation was the desire of the Boston Athenaeum to house a valuable armor collection bequeathed to it in 1869, the desire of the Massachusetts Institute of Technology to find a home for its large collection of architectural casts, and the quest of the Harvard Board of Overseers for a fireproof home for its collection of engravings. Thus from the outset the new museum's collection was a combination of art and artifact, originals and reproductions. This blend suited its didactic purposes. At its first meeting the Board of Trustees agreed that the museum should be "a comprehensive gallery of reproductions, through plaster casts of the many treasures of Antique and Medieval Art, or photographs of original drawings by the most renowned artists of all periods." One of the trustees voiced the hope that the very nature of the board, which included not only a fair number of Boston Brahmins but also the mayor, the chairman of the board of the Boston Public Library, the secretary of the State Board of Education and the superintendent of Boston's schools, would prevent the museum's managers "from squandering their funds upon the private fancies of would-be connoisseurs." During its first two decades the museum owned relatively few paintings and filled its galleries with photographs of European masterpieces and casts of classical sculpture and architecture. The museum's primary purpose, one of its founders, Charles C. Perkins, declared in 1870, was "collecting material for the education of a nation in art," rather than "making collections of objects of art." In 1879 the *Boston Advertiser* applauded this course: "Our aim must be to bring these [masterworks] within the reach of our people by means of the best available copies and this is exactly what the directors of the museum . . . have done." At the dedication of the museum's

Victorian Gothic building on July 3, 1876, Boston's mayor declared that "all classes of our people will derive benefit and
pleasure" from the museum, which he hailed as the "crown of
our educational system."[76]

It was not a crown destined to remain in place for very long.
Just as Theodore Thomas underwent a transition from an educator who spread the joys of symphonic music across the nation
to a conserver of the purity of classic compositions, so too the
museum, armed with an increasing number of bequests of money
and original works of art, gradually began to relegate the photographs, casts, and a variety of "curiosities" to storage and
dedicate its galleries to what its director in 1912 called "higher
things." When the original Greek sculpture began to take its
place in the museum, he wrote, "What a revelation it was . . .
The casts became mere plaster without a soul and we recognized
the magic of the craftsmen's hands, the beauty of texture and the
nobility of form." As the museum increased its store of original
paintings,* a jockeying for precedence took place and exploded
into a struggle over the very nature and purpose of the institution. For those—including the curator of classical antiquities,
Edward Robinson, who became director in 1902—who held to
the museum's original didactic thrust, the casts remained a central
vehicle for reaching the public. In 1904 Robinson proposed
expanding the cast collection, arguing that the museum could
become "a national factor in artistic education, if it were to offer
the country a standard collection that could be followed more
or less completely in other places." For the increasing number
of those who disagreed, led by Matthew Stewart Prichard, who
became assistant director in 1903, and backed by Board President
Samuel D. Warren, the casts were a profanation. The "first and
great commandment" of an art museum, Prichard insisted, "is
to establish and maintain in the community a high standard of
aesthetic taste," to which all other aims, such as supplying information to the public, were secondary. The purpose of art, ac-

---

*The museum spent $7,500 for the acquisition of original art in its first seven
years of operation. In the ten years following 1894 it spent $1,324,000.

Part of the much disputed cast collection of the Boston Museum of Fine Arts. Collections similar to this became the center of controversies over the nature and purposes of art museums in New York City and Chicago as well.

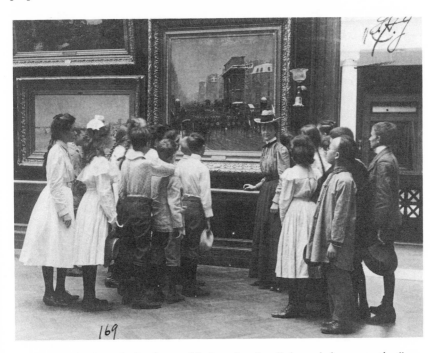

A schoolteacher introducing her well-behaved and well-dressed charges to the "contemplation of the perfect" at the Corcoran Gallery of Art, Washington, D.C., around 1900.

cording to Prichard "is the pleasure derived from a contemplation of the perfect." Casts were worse than merely imperfect, they were subversive; as "data mechanically produced," casts were "the Pianola of the Arts" and no more belonged in an art museum than mechanical music belonged in a symphony hall. Casts were "engines of education and should not be shown near objects of inspiration." The opponents of casts, paying heed to the caveat of the museum's first president, Walter Brimmer, that care must be taken to "carefully guard against the inroad of pictorial rubbish," also attempted to deaccession unworthy originals and to confine some of the best works to study collections intended not for the casual viewer but for connoisseurs. "Naturally the higher the standard of excellence it is wished to maintain, the larger will be the size of the study series, and the fewer the objects it is possible to show to the public," Prichard observed. "The air grows rarer the nearer you reach the summit of the mountain."[77]

Though both Robinson and Prichard resigned—the former in 1905, the latter in 1906—Prichard's philosophy was triumphant. In 1909 the casts—and many of the museum's original goals— were relegated to the basement of the museum's new building in a more exclusive neighborhood. The casts were scheduled to be housed in a separate structure, well removed from true works of art, but that building was never constructed and the casts were never exhibited again. In its original location and with its original philosophy, the museum had frequently drawn large and diverse crowds, including, according to Prichard, "loquacious Italians" on Sundays when admission was free. It was doubtless these crowds that the trustees had in mind when they warned that "convenient study of the many valuable objects" was rendered "impossible on free days," and concluded that "nothing contributes so much to the real enjoyment of, and the good to be derived from a work of art as freedom from oppressive interruption in the process of examining it." Benjamin Ives Gilman, the museum's secretary, set the tone for the new century when, in his comparison of a museum of natural history or science and a museum of art, he declared that "a collection of science is gathered primarily in the interest of the real; a collection of art primarily in the interest of the ideal. . . . A museum of science is in essence a school; a museum of art is in essence a temple."*[78]

The debate over the place of art occurred not only in the world of museums but also in the realm of art education. Peter Marzio has shown that during the first half of the nineteenth century there was a "crusade" to spread art among the masses. Professional artists like John Rubens Smith, Rembrandt Peale, and John Gadsby Chapman created drawing manuals designed to educate the untrained populace and to spread democracy from the political realm to the world of art, to take the mystery out of art and create a democracy of citizen artists, "a nation of draftsmen." The motto of Chapman's *American Drawing Book* was "Anyone who can learn to write, can learn to draw." The history of art, the *United States Democratic Review* observed in 1858, "is a prolonged record of the patronage of princes and nobles, blossoming only in royal gardens and beneath the sunshine of opulence and wealth. *Democratic art, until within a few years, was a thing unknown.*" Happily, the *Review* announced, a democracy possessed the power and the will "to republicanize art—to impart to its exquisite language an intonation whose lulling melodies are heard in the cottage as well as in the palace." By the closing decades of the century the crusade was over. The artist William Morris Hunt, who won great fame as a teacher in the 1870s, insisted that the "way to educate artists," was to place them in studios "divorced from everyday affairs." Hunt, and most of his peers, did not conceive of art as a democratic enterprise but as a special skill exercised by creative individuals. "To draw!" Hunt exclaimed, dismissing the epigram of Chapman and his associates. "What is it to draw? Any idiot who could learn to write could learn to draw! Not to draw well; for that seems to me to require more skill than anything else in the world."[79]

The drama that took place within the precincts of the Boston

---

*This sentiment was to be repeated many times in similar settings. "A large number of our visitors are foreign born or of foreign parents," a trustee of the Philadelphia Art Museum explained in 1922. "To them the museum must take the place of the cathedral."

Museum of Fine Arts at the turn of the century—and which was paralleled to a large extent by events at New York's Metropolitan Museum of Art and Chicago's Art Institute—had already been rehearsed earlier in the nation's capital in the struggle over the nature of the Smithsonian Institution. In 1846 Congress utilized the more than half a million dollars left to the United States by the Englishman James Smithson to found the Smithsonian Institution for—and here Congress used the exact wording of Smithson's will—"the increase and diffusion of knowledge among men." This language became the catalyst for fierce disagreement over the purposes of the new institution. To the Smithsonian's first secretary, Joseph Henry, the terms "increase" and "diffusion" were not comparable. Without increased knowledge there could be no diffusion, therefore the primacy of the former function was unmistakable; the essential purpose of the Smithsonian was not to be education but creation, its goal was not merely to spread knowledge but to add to it. Thus throughout his long tenure from 1846 to 1878, Henry resisted with his full force the many attempts to make the Smithsonian primarily the keeper of a national museum, library, or art gallery. He was forced to compromise again and again but never abandoned his vision of what the Smithsonian was meant to be. Henry was not opposed to museums, libraries, or galleries per se, but was convinced that if the Smithsonian was ever forced to administer one or more of these, its main vitality would be channeled into the direction of diffusion rather than the higher purpose of creating and enlarging the boundaries of human thought. He was successful in transferring his books to the national library being shaped on Capitol Hill, and in sending the art foisted on him to both the library and the newly formed Corcoran Gallery, but he was not able to completely stave off the creation of a national museum inside his institution. Still, he fought successfully to keep the museum within bounds, always warning that without vigilance the tail might begin to wag the dog; always reminding anyone who would listen that "the objects of the Smithsonian Institution are not educational," that "if we would advance to a higher civilization" it was crucial not only to diffuse or apply science, "but, primarily to increase it," and that the collections of the Smithsonian were intended essentially for study and not "to gratify an unenlightened curiosity." When a member of Congress advised Henry that by a few changes in his policies he could make the Smithsonian a popular institution, Henry was quick to reply that his "self-imposed mission and deliberate purpose was to prevent, as far as in him lay, precisely that consummation." Henry was never shy about his rejection of the notion that it was his function to win the favor of the public. In his *Annual Report for 1876* he maintained:

> It has been supposed that the Institution has derived much benefit from its connection with the Museum in the way of adding to its popularity, but it should be recollected that the Institution is not a popular establishment and that it does not depend for its support upon public patronage . . . and that the very nature of its operations, involving study and investigation, is in a considerable degree incompatible with continued interruption from large numbers of visitors.[80]

In spite of all the compromises he had to make, Henry never gave up. In the last year of his life he was still insisting that "for the safe administration of the Smithson fund in the future, it ought to be entirely separated from what we have denominated a 'National Museum.'" That separation, of course, was never to take place. For Henry, final defeat came only with his death in 1878. His successors were neither as able to withstand the pressures of Congress nor as convinced of the perils of tying the Smithsonian's destiny to a public museum, and precisely what Henry feared would happen did happen: the Smithsonian became engaged in what Henry considered the lesser task of disseminating knowledge to the nation and, to a much larger extent than Henry would ever have reconciled himself to, relinquished to the new universities the higher cultural task Henry had conceived for it.* It is possible that in Henry's fate more than a few

---

*Three years after Henry's death, the Smithsonian opened a new museum building and just two years later it was petitioning Congress for still more museum space. Henry's successors also took steps to recover some of the art Henry had sent to the Library of Congress and the Corcoran Gallery. To symbolize how far they had moved from his conception of the Smithsonian, in 1890 they opened a zoo and in 1894 they reclaimed the National Herbarium, which Henry had relinquished to the Department of Agriculture in 1869.

cultural leaders saw both the perils of too close an involvement with government and the wisdom of the form of autonomous corporate organization they were adopting for the governance of museums, opera companies, symphonic associations, and other cultural institutions. Indeed, as early as 1869, those who gathered in New York City to create the Metropolitan Museum of Art declared that "it would be folly to depend upon our governments, either municipal or national, for judicious support or control in such an institution."[81]

The tensions between the didactic and the ideal were manifest in a wide range of institutions in the late nineteenth century. Whether a library existed to disseminate or conserve knowledge was a common matter of debate throughout these years. An anecdote that made the rounds had Harvard President Charles W. Eliot meet his librarian, Justin Winsor, in Harvard Yard around 1880 and inquire how the library was progressing. "Excellently, excellently," Winsor is supposed to have replied. "All the books are on the shelf except one that Agassiz has, and I'm going after it now." In 1884 *Life* magazine published a lengthy imaginary dialogue concerning New York's Lenox Library:

> *What is this?*
> This, dear, is the great Lenox Library
>
> *But why are the doors locked?*
> To keep people out
>
> *But why?*
> To keep the pretty books from being spoiled.
>
> *Why! who would spoil the pretty books?*
> The public.
>
> *How?*
> By reading them.[82]

The question, of course, was not merely quantitative; the debate over the nature of libraries went beyond the matter of accessibility to embrace the question of the quality of the books to be made available. The Chicago Public Library was established as a repository for books donated to replace those destroyed in the Great Fire of 1871. At the outset its mandate was broad, as its first annual report in 1873 made clear:

> Every person in the community, however humble, or lacking in literary culture, has a right to be supplied with books adapted to his taste and mental capacity. The masses of readers are not scholars, and have little of what passes in the world as literary culture; hence they read largely works of the imagination and the lighter class of literature, and are benefited thereby. To deprive them of such books is to exclude them from the use of the library.

Accordingly, the library carefully distinguished itself from the Newberry Library, the city's new reference and research center; it kept generous hours, established outlets throughout the city where books could be called for and returned, cooperated with the public schools, and was responsive to the request of ethnic groups that books in their native languages be made available. Ultimately, the determination to fulfill the public's felt needs was weakened by the desire to cultivate their tastes. There were few librarians in Chicago, or elsewhere, who added their voices to that of the Newark Public Library's John Cotton Dana in insisting: "Better a shallow mind than an empty one. It is a proper function of a library to amuse." Almost as if its magnificent new classical building—replete with mosaics, marble, and the names of great authors on the walls—symbolized new priorities, the Chicago Public Library curtailed hours, closed decentralized delivery stations, placed new emphasis on reference collections, and no longer so avidly consulted the desires of disparate groups. "Like the Art Institute," Helen Lefkowitz Horowitz has concluded, "the Chicago Public Library building was to act on its visitors as a stimulus to the higher life. The supply of desired books took second place to the splendor of a house of culture." None of this would have surprised Finley Peter Dunne's bartender, Mr. Dooley. When his friend Hennessy inquired whether Andrew Carnegie supplied the books for the libraries he was donating, Dooley exclaimed:

> Books? What ar-re ye talkin' about? . . . A Carnaygie libry is archytechoor, not lithrachoor. Lithrachoor will be riprisinted. Th' most cillybrated dead authors will be honored be havin' their

names painted on th' wall in distinguished comp'ny . . . so that
whin a man comes along that niver heerd iv Shakespeare he'll
know he was somebody, because there he is on th' wall.[83]

THE PROCESS of sacralization could operate to dethrone culture as well as to elevate it. From 1840 to 1900, chromolithography—the process by which original paintings were reproduced lithographically in color and sold in the millions to all
segments of the population—was one of the most familiar art
forms in the nation. It was hailed as a vehicle for bringing art
"within the reach of all classes of society" and praised as "art
republicanized and naturalized in America." These very characteristics made chromolithography anathema to E. L. Godkin of
the *Nation* and the genteel group for whom he spoke. Once
again, as with theater, opera, and symphonic music, a medium
that had the effect of widely disseminating a form of artistic
expression was perceived as a force for cultural dilution. To
Godkin, chromolithography symbolized the packaged "pseudoculture" that "diffused through the community a kind of smat-
tering of all sorts of knowledge" and gave people the false confidence of being "cultured." "A society of ignoramuses who know
they are ignoramuses, might lead to a tolerably happy and useful
existence," he wrote, "but a society of ignoramuses each of whom
thinks he is a Solon, would be an approach to Bedlam let loose
. . . The result is a kind of mental and moral chaos." Godkin's
view prevailed. By the 1890s the term "chromo" had come to
mean "ugly" or "offensive." Thus while at the Philadelphia Centennial Exposition in 1876 chromolithographs were exhibited as
"fine" arts along with sculpture, painting, and engravings, seventeen years later at Chicago's Columbian Exposition of 1893
they were classified as, and exhibited with, "industrial" or "commercial" arts.[84]

Closely related to the cultural demotion of lithography was
the cultural exclusion of photography. Since one of the early
functions of photography was to reproduce works of art, it is
understandable that the camera should have been considered by
many a vehicle for mimicking rather than creating art. But the

feeling against photography ran much deeper than this. A process that rendered an expressive form relatively simple, definitely accessible to large numbers of untrained amateurs, and almost infinitely reproducible, was a radical departure from an ethos that judged art and culture to be the sacred, unique products of the rare individual spirit. Photography was a far more serious threat to those who were sacralizing art than chromolithography for while both the chromolithograph and the camera could disseminate art among the masses, the camera could do far more: it could give a wide spectrum of people the very means of *creating* art. It was the perfect instrument for a society with a burgeoning middle class, which could now satisfy itself with processes and images that had previously been confined to elite circles. It was this that led to Charles Baudelaire's angry outburst in France in 1859 denouncing "our squalid society" for rushing "Narcissus to a man, to gaze at its trivial image on a scrap of metal," and warning that photography was "a cheap method of disseminating a loathing for history and for painting among the people." In the United States the photographer Alfred Stieglitz, who labored to have the camera recognized as a legitimate alternative for "those who loved art and sought some medium other than brush or pencil through which to give expression to their ideas," put his finger on the primary obstacle: "The placing in the hands of the general public a means of making pictures with but little labor and requiring less knowledge has of necessity been followed by the production of millions of photographs. It is due to this fatal facility that photography as a picture-making medium has fallen into disrepute."[85]

Some arts are immortal, *Appleton's Journal* announced in 1875, pointedly excluding photography or mass-produced sculpture and painting, which could never give "the tone, the feeling, the quality that come from the finger ends of a man charged with art-feeling." Photography, W. J. Stillman announced in the *Atlantic Monthly* in 1892, "is the absolute negation of art," since the photographer was a realist depicting what existed whereas the artist was an idealist expressing reality through his own vision. In the Boston journal *Living Age*, the English critic Joseph Pennell likened the urge of photographers to be considered artists to the desire of "the Italian, with his hurdy-gurdy" to "win for himself the reputation and fortune of Paderewski." There was no more art in producing "machine-made pictures" than there was in producing "machine-made shirts and carpets." Photography had cheapened art: "It has lowered the standard with a public that instinctively prefers the sham and the machine-made and the microscopic; it has reduced the artist to a demoralizing struggle with the amateur simply to get his bread." Photography, Pennell was saying in effect, had to be excluded from the canon because it desacralized art. The English photographer Peter Henry Emerson, whose *Naturalistic Photography* went through three editions in the United States, charged that the photographer, "does not make his picture—A MACHINE DOES IT ALL FOR HIM." Ultimately, Emerson advised his readers, one had to heed the judgment of experts and in this case the experts, "the best artists," "are unanimous that photography is not art, and never can be . . . Art is personal; photographs are machine-made goods, useful, as is machine-made furniture, machine-made fabrics, and perhaps—for the slums—machine-made music." Those who maintained, as did Charles Caffin in 1901, that photography was becoming a fine art were quickly answered by such journals as the *Nation*, which asserted that photography could never be an art simply because the true artist was a creative spirit who worked from *within*, "from a preconceived notion of what he wishes to do, often without any reference at all to nature," whereas the photographer, tied to an external machine, "may record accidental composition when he finds it, but he can never compose . . . Photography is not a fine art because it can invent nothing."[86]

In the end, the debate centered on the nature of photography rather than the nature of art, about which there was apparently widespread agreement. In its infancy, Stieglitz admitted in 1899, photography had been dominated by "mechanism," and photographs bore "the crude stiffness and vulgarity of chromos and other like productions." In recent years, however, the "proper hands" of "the more serious of the photographic workers" had transformed the camera, lens, plate, developing-baths, printing process and the like into "pliant tools and not mechanical tyrants." The result was that "the photographer has moved onward first by steps, and finally by strides and leaps and . . . has brought his art to its present state of perfection. This is the real photography, the photography of today, and that which the world is accustomed to regard as pictorial photography is not the real photography but an ignorant imposition." The eventual victory that Stieglitz and his successors experienced in establishing photography as a legitimate art form was not, in the short run at least, a defeat for the sacred conceptions of art formulated at the turn of the century, since the terms of victory—which Allan Sekula has correctly dubbed "the invention of photography as high art"—mandated that photographic art imitate the canons of painterly art with emphasis upon the individual unique creator and the single image. "For decades," the photographer Arthur Rothstein wrote in 1986, "the photographers continued to imitate painters, and some photographers do this even today . . . It seemed as though the users of the camera suffered from an inferiority complex and could not recognize nor admit to the unique virtues of photography, such as the ability to show detail and stop action."[87]

When Matthew Prichard denounced plaster casts as "the Pianola of the Arts," he was expressing a widely shared feeling. Throughout these years anything mechanically reproduced—any expressive form in which a mechanical process stood between the creator and the product—struck many of the arbiters of culture as inauthentic and therefore not to be accorded artistic status. The Industrial Revolution had produced sufficiently unwelcome changes from within its factory citadels, it could not be allowed to invade the precincts of Art. "There is no use in talking aesthetics if you are satisfied with machine-made furniture," Norman Hapgood declared in 1903. If the ethos of the artisan was doomed in the industrial marketplace, it could at least be kept alive in the realm of expressive culture. In 1906 John Philip Sousa, who was himself so often attacked for diluting culture, warned the nation of a new menace: the proliferation of phonographs and player pianos, which were transforming musical expression into "a mathematical system of megaphones, wheels, cogs, disks, cylinders, and all manner of revolving things" that had nothing to do with "real art." If children were crooned to sleep not by their mothers' sweet lullabies but by the "canned music" of the phonograph, would they not grow up to sing "if they sing at all, in imitation and finally become simply human phonographs—without soul or expression?" Music, he pleaded, "teaches all that is beautiful in this world. Let us not hamper it with a machine that tells the story day by day, without variation, without soul, barren of the joy, the passion, the ardor that is the inheritance of man alone."*[88]

As Susan Sontag has argued, the emerging distinction between high and low culture was based in part on an evaluation of the difference between unique and mass-produced objects. No one expressed this more forcefully than Walter Benjamin, who maintained in 1936 that in "the age of mechanical reproduction" the "aura" of a work of art, its unique existence, withered and its traditional value was liquidated: "The technique of reproduction detaches the reproduced object from the domain of tradition. By making many reproductions it substitutes a plurality of copies for a unique existence." Indeed, Benjamin went so far as to argue that "the poorest provincial staging of *Faust* is superior to a Faust film in that, ideally, it competes with the first performance at Weimar." In the final chapter I will examine this same insistence on unencumbered individual uniqueness as it surfaced with regard to the consumption of art. Matthew Arnold, to whom the arbiters of culture paid close attention, insisted that culture was "above all, an inward operation . . . Culture . . . places human perfection in an *internal* condition." Thus though theaters, museums, symphonic halls, and parks were public places, they were meant to create an environment in which a person could contemplate and appreciate the society's store of great culture *individually*. Anything that produced a group atmosphere, a mass ethos, was culturally suspect.[89]

---

*In spite of these attitudes, Sousa himself could not withstand the new technology. By 1912 Sousa had recorded fifteen to twenty sides for Victor Records including music by Verdi, Berlioz, and Wagner, as well as a number of his own marches. In the 1920s, Sousa's attitude toward the radio was a bit more benign. He admitted that "through this medium the masses are becoming acquainted as never before with the best of the world's music," but insisted that radio could never replace the personal performance. "The rapport between performer and audience is invaluable . . . I have refrained from broadcasting for this very reason; I am reluctant to lose the warm personal touch with my audience." After writing this in 1928, Sousa did broadcast a series of concerts in 1929 and again in 1931.

The assault on "inauthentic" cultural forms was not limited to the mechanical. Band music, which from the 1830s through the Civil War was one of the most widely shared and popular forms of music in America, and which as we saw earlier in this chapter encompassed a wide spectrum of the musical repertory, came under attack in the closing decades of the nineteenth century for much the same reasons as chromolithography had—because it represented impure art, pseudoculture, and disorder. In this as in so much else, John Sullivan Dwight was a pioneer. "Last week we had commencement—commencement at old Harvard," Dwight informed his readers in 1856, "and as usual, a Boston band assisted at the exercises. But—Ichabod!—the glory has departed. Brass, brass, brass,—nothing but brass." Dwight was to have a good deal of company in the coming decades. "Brass band music," the young Henry Finck wrote, "always reminds me of a threshing machine through which live cats are being chased." In the summer of 1880 the *New York Times* printed three remarkable editorials calling the growth of "the horrible thirst for brass" a "devastating vice," a "giant evil," compared with which "the prevalence of drunkenness becomes insignificant and opium eating hardly deserves notice." Brass bands were contaminating the taste of "the young and thoughtless" whose desire to play brass instruments was making thousands of homes and neighborhoods "wretched." Brass bands had "the musical character of a machine shop in busy operation," and their bedlam could be tolerated only if bandstands were placed on a pivot at seaside hotels "so that when the terrible creature within begins to lash itself into fury" the stage could be turned facing the water, "and the horrid voice of the monster poured out upon the illimitable ocean." Shortly after his death in 1892, several newspapers branded Patrick Gilmore a panderer to mass tastes. The *New York World* argued that Gilmore's fame "was not based upon the satisfaction he gave our intellect; it rested upon the gratification he furnished to our senses," while the *Kansas City Journal* dismissed him as "more a caterer than a teacher."[90]

Insofar as John Philip Sousa, who replaced Gilmore as the towering bandmaster of his age, escaped this kind of criticism, it was because he came to symbolize good taste and order and was perceived as muting some of the most grating features of bands. Many reviewers praised Sousa's ability to emulate the sounds of a concert orchestra by increasing the proportion of reed instruments.* "The reeds temper the blare of the brass," the *Wilkes-Barre Truth* noted approvingly. The *Philadelphia Enquirer* called the new band Sousa formed in 1892 "a compromise between an orchestra and a field band. There is not the loud twanging that has made the indoor playing of the old organization objectionable." The *Boston Herald* praised Sousa for taking a military band and making it "capable of producing the effects commonly confined to the players of a concert orchestra." Words like "dignity," "refinement," "quality," were often used to describe the tone he and his musicians set. Nevertheless, Sousa too was often attacked for squandering his great talents on "empty and meaningless music," and profaning the great compositions of Wagner and Grieg by combining them with such popular songs as "Molly and I and the Baby" or "Has Anybody Here Seen Kelly?" Though Sousa could react aggressively to these charges, he frequently espoused the values of his critics and merely advocated different tactics. Sounding like Theodore Thomas in the early years of his career, Sousa insisted that public appreciation of "high class" music would increase if it was "mixed judiciously with favorite tunes and dealt out in small doses." "I have made 'Tannhaeuser Overture' as popular as 'The Stars and Stripes,'" Sousa insisted in 1899. "I think I have done more missionary work for the better class of music than all the rest of them together." The *Chicago Herald* agreed and asked its readers to bear in mind "that upon him, in a measure, devolves the responsibility of educating the taste of the people so that they may eventually learn to appreciate the higher forms of orchestral music. For band music always appeals to the masses and can thus be made a stepping stone to something higher."[91]

---

*In fact, Sousa was carrying forward a change that Gilmore had done much to inaugurate. Three years after Gilmore's death, Victor Herbert wrote: "From the old band which depended on the loud brasses and drums, all forced to their utmost to make the most noise possible, to the bands of the present day which interpret the works of the greatest so as to satisfy even the most exacting musician, has been a hard but glorious struggle up the steeps of Parnassus, and to Patrick Sarsfield Gilmore belongs most of the glory."

THE CHANGES DISCUSSED in this chapter were not etched in stone. The museums that reached out to the general public in the last decades of the nineteenth century only to retrench with the coming of the new century, would reach out again at various times in the twentieth century, and this was true of other cultural institutions as well. What was transpiring in the years dealt with here was something more fundamental than mere outreach programs. The meaning of culture itself was being defined and its parameters laid out in ways that would affect culture profoundly throughout this century. The primary debate was less over who should enter the precincts of the art museum, the symphony hall, the opera house as over what they should experience once they did enter, what the essential purpose of these temples of culture was in the first place. The "fences and labels" that Charles Ives's "unknown philosopher" spoke of in the nineteenth century, were firmly in place by the early decades of the twentieth century. Specific policies would come and go; arguments about this and that would wax hot, simmer for a time, and grow cold. But the essential debate, the central policy, was settled: the meaning and purpose of the halls of culture—and of culture itself—was established; all else was commentary.

It is important to understand that although sacralization became a cultural fact and shaped twentieth-century cultural attitudes and practices, it never became a cultural reality. By its very nature it remained an ideal. The Toscanini who struggled so successfully to compel his audiences and musicians to respect the purity of the compositions they were hearing and performing, the Toscanini who affirmed his allegiance to the composers' intentions by asserting that while to some the first movement of Beethoven's *Eroica* "is philosophical struggle; to me it is Allegro con brio," the Toscanini who was hailed by music critics for his absolute "fidelity to the score," the Toscanini who became the very symbol of a perfectly sacralized culture, was himself interpreting, rescoring, and adjusting the musical texts he presented. It was one thing for a non-musician like George Templeton Strong to insist on musical purity and the total integrity of the sacred text, it was another thing for a musician to implement such ideals. The truth Charles Lamb perceived—that the moment

Shakespeare was performed he was altered—applied to music as well as drama, though it is difficult to find a musician who adopted Lamb's solution: that the integrity of the creator's work be preserved by no longer performing it. And even here the fact is that the Lamb who concluded that Shakespearean plays were *intended* not to be performed but only to be read, is the same man who won fame by abridging and retelling those plays in his own versions and his own language.[92]

To say that sacralization remained an ideal only imperfectly realized is not to deny that it became a cultural force. As with many ideals, the contradictions were resolved not primarily by denying them but more powerfully by failing to recognize them. Thus the great Hollywood director Frank Capra, who was, as all directors are, dependent upon writers, cameramen, editors, and actors, could assert as his credo and the reality of his career: "One man, one film." Film directors who ignored, or down-played, the collective nature of their art and conceived of themselves as *auteurs*, with the model of the novelist so clearly in mind, were not aberrations. They were closely related to other artists and performers—such as photographers who neglected the full potentialities of their cameras to emulate painters—who struggled diligently to win cultural legitimization under the new standards that prevailed from the turn of the century on. This entire panoply of cultural confusion was the inevitable product of sacralization; of the adoption of a single version of cultural truth, of a single model of cultural creation.[93]

When Hegel wrote in the early nineteenth century, "We are beyond the stage of reverence for works of art as divine and objects deserving our worship," he was being a touch optimistic.[94] In late nineteenth-century America the momentum was in the other direction.

Three

Order, Hierarchy,
and Culture

THE CHILD BORN in 1900 would, then, be born into a new world which would not be a unity but a multiple." This terse comment, appearing only toward the end of Henry Adams's *Education*, was in fact a central thread that Adams embroidered throughout the third-person narrative of his life and times. "He had become an estray; a flotsam or jetsam of wreckage," Adams wrote of himself. "His world was dead. Not a Polish Jew fresh from Warsaw or Cracow . . . still reeking of the Ghetto, snarling a weird Yiddish to the officers of the customs—but had a keener instinct, an intenser energy, and a freer hand than he—American of Americans, with Heaven knew how many Puritans and Patriots behind him . . . he was no worse off than the Indians or the buffalo who had been ejected from their heritage by his own people." Shortly before Adams had his autobiography privately printed and circulated among a small group of friends in 1907, the period's other famous Henry—Henry James—visited his native land after almost a quarter of a century of self-exile. Like Adams, James was seeking to recover "some echo of the dreams of youth, the titles of tales, the communities of friendship, the sympathies and patiences . . ." Like Adams, he was to find "among the ruins" of his country, not the "New England homogeneous" he remembered, not the unity he sought, but rather "multiplication, multiplication of everything . . . multiplication with a vengeance."[1]

For James, as for Adams, the word "multiple" came to symbolize the new world. For James, as for Adams, the immigrant was a convenient and tangible sign of a transition that left him with "a horrible, hateful sense of personal antiquity," with a numbing sense of being an alien in his own land. He visited Ellis Island and came away like a person "who has had an apparition, seen a ghost in his supposedly safe old house." He toured New

York's Lower East Side and felt "the 'ethnic' apparition again sit like a skeleton at the feast. It was fairly as if I could see the spectre grin." He rode on the electric cars and gazed upon "a row of faces, up and down, testifying, without exception, to alienism unmistakable, alienism undisguised and unashamed," which made him "gasp with the sense of isolation." He walked the streets and found that "face after face, unmistakably, was 'low'—particularly in the men." Even in Boston, where he stood on Beacon Hill one late winter Sunday afternoon, close to the State House and the statues, observing the strolling crowds of workers "of the simpler sort" dressed in their Sunday best, he discovered that "no sound of English, in a single instance, escaped their lips; the greater number spoke a rude form of Italian, the others some outland dialect unknown to me . . . No note of any shade of American speech struck my ear, . . . the people before me were gross aliens to a man, and they were in serene and triumphant possession." The general movement, he lamented "was *away*—away always and everywhere, from the old presumptions and conceivabilities."[2]

It was not only the immigrants, their numbers and manners, that filled James with "the dreadful chill of change," but the general tone and tenor of his native land, where "*the will to grow* was everywhere written large, and to grow at no matter what or whose expense." He was shocked by the "vision of waste" that left rows of houses "marked for removal, for extinction, in their prime." There was no better symbol of the "profane overhauling" that had left America a "hustling, bustling desert" than the "insolent" skyscrapers, those "vast money-making" structures, those "impudently new . . . payers of dividends," those "monsters of the mere market," which now overwhelmed such aesthetically and spiritually satisfying landmarks as New York's Trinity Church or Castle Garden, from whose stage the young Henry James had heard the young soprano Adelina Patti "warbling like a tiny thrush even in the nest." Today this "ancient rotunda" was "shabby, shrunken, barely discernible." Worse still, Boston's Athenaeum, "this honored haunt of all the most civilized—library, gallery, temple of culture," was now "put completely out of countenance by the mere masses of brute ugliness . . . above the comparatively small refined facade . . . It was heart-breaking." It was not merely tradition that was in danger but taste itself. James complained that "the huge democratic broom" had swept away the old and ushered in an age of "the new, the simple, the cheap, the common, the commercial, the immediate, and, all too often, the ugly." Everywhere in this "vast crude democracy of trade" James was assaulted by the "overwhelming preponderance" of the businessman. In this "heaped industrial battle-field" James was "haunted" by a "sense of dispossession." Constantly he was forced to tighten his "aesthetic waistband," to protect himself against "the consummate monotonous commonness, . . . in which relief, detachment, dignity, meaning, perished utterly and lost all rights."[3]

The lament that the two Henrys sang, almost in chorus, though it had grown in intensity and significance by the turn of the century, was not unique. Men of their class had been fashioning this particular jeremiad for decades. Philip Hone and George Templeton Strong, two of the century's great chroniclers, filled pages of their fascinating diaries with a sense of loss, looming disorder and chaos. Sitting alone at night recalling the day's events, Hone made note again and again of riots, civil disturbance, political fanaticism, public corruption, horrible disasters, frightening excesses of "the vulgar and uneducated masses," all of them constituting what he termed in 1839 "the vile disorganizing spirit which overspreads the land like a cloud and daily increases in darkness." He greeted the year 1840 by observing that "riot, disorder, and violence increase in our city; every night is marked by some outrage committed by the gangs of young ruffians who prowl the streets insulting females, breaking into the houses of unoffending publicans, making night hideous by yells of disgusting inebriety, and—unchecked by the city authorities—committing every sort of enormity with apparent impunity." In May of that year he complained of "the overwhelming flood of vulgarity which is sweeping over our land." Election day found him witnessing "scenes of violence, disorder, and riot" and concluding that "the heterogenous mass of vile humanity in our population" had put "unrestrained power in the hands of a mob of political desperadoes." Disorder followed Hone wherever he roamed. In the spring of 1842 he traveled to Long Island to witness a horse race. The day was lovely, the race exciting. Unfortunately for Hone and his companions, "tens of thousands of the sovereign people" wanted to see the race as well. When they found that the trains were not sufficient to carry them they "became riotous, upset the cars, placed obstructions on the rails, and indulged in all sorts of violence." The "crowd and the dust and the danger and difficulty of getting on and off the course with a carriage," Hone concluded, "are scarcely compensated by any pleasure to be derived from the amusement." There seemed to be no escape from the chaos that surrounded him. Even in the privacy of his own home the daily papers brought him a steady diet of railroad and steamboat accidents. "I never take up a paper that does not contain accounts of loss of life, dreadful mutilation of limbs, and destruction of property, with which these reckless, dangerous, murderous modes of locomotion are attended," he wrote in 1847. Hone refused to believe that these disasters were really accidents; they stemmed from the anarchic streak increasingly evident in his countrymen: "We have become the most careless, reckless, headlong people on the face of the earth. 'Go ahead' is our maxim and password; and we do go ahead with a vengeance, regardless of consequences and indifferent about the value of human life." "I think the world is worse than it used to be," Hone moaned in 1840. Nothing occurred before his death a decade later to change his mind.[4]

Hone's fellow New Yorker George Templeton Strong possessed a similarly restless curiosity which propelled him out into streets "absolutely swarming, alive and crawling with the unwashed Democracy," to record the unhappy developments of his age. He filled pages of his diary with accounts of the disorder that accompanied the financial distress of 1857. In February he noted: "An epidemic of crime this winter. 'Garotting' stories abound . . . Most of my friends are investing in revolvers and carry them about at night." In July New York erupted into bloody gang warfare. "We're in a 'state of siege,'" Strong commented on July 5, "and if half the stories one hears be true, in something like a state of anarchy." In the summer of 1863 he witnessed the New York Draft Riots, in which what Strong called a mob of "pure Celtic" "rabble" attacked "unoffending niggers" on the streets and then besieged the Colored Orphan Asylum. "The beastly ruffians were masters of the situation and of the city," Strong wrote. "I could endure the disgraceful, sickening sight no longer, and what could I *do*?" Disorder came in less dramatic forms as well. On a bright March afternoon in 1865, Strong stood on Fifth Avenue and Forty-ninth Street watching a throng of fancy carriages make their way to Central Park. This "vehicular gentility," Strong noted caustically, had been enriched during the Civil War by "profits of shoddy and of petroleum . . . Not a few of the ladies who were driving in the most sumptuous turn-outs, with liveried servants, looked as if they might have been cooks or chambermaids a very few years ago." Like Adams, James, and Hone, Strong was bewildered by the cultural behavior of the immigrants with whom he was forced to share his city. In 1857 he stumbled across an accident in which two Irish laborers had been killed and observed a group of Irish women

> raising a wild, unearthly cry, half shriek and half song, wailing as a score of daylight banshees, clapping their hands and gesticulating passionately. Now and then one of them would throw herself down on one of the corpses, or wipe some trace of defilement from the face of the dead man with her apron, slowly and carefully, and then resume her lament. It was an uncanny sound to hear, quite new to me . . . Our Celtic fellow citizens are almost as remote from us in temperament and constitution as the Chinese.

Strong's greatest ire was vented on his temporal rulers. "The New Yorker belongs to a community worse governed by lower and baser blackguard scum than any city in Western Christendom, or in the world . . . we submit to the rod and the sceptre of Maguires and O'Tooles and O'Shanes." In the last years of his life he warned that corruption was so pervasive, the rule of such "*canaille*" as the railroad kings Fisk and Vanderbilt and the political leader Boss Tweed so flagrant, that revolutionary action was "in the air." "If misrule could ever justify assassination of the ruler, ours would justify it."[5]

The unity that Adams and his peers envisioned as a historical reality was largely an ideal. From early in American history multiplicity had been the reality, but the multiplicity that Adams and James and others of their class experienced at the turn of the century, if not a new phenomenon, was more complex, more intricate, more varied, more immediate and undeniable. Charles Francis Adams, Jr., recalled the Quincy, Massachusetts, he grew up in before foreigners "and more particularly the Irish element had . . . reached the self-asserting point," and concluded, "the place I as a child loved so well no longer exists . . . As I pass to-and-fro in Quincy I now seem to wander with ghosts." Even in as large a city as New York, Frederic J. DePeyster remembered a time when he and his friends had not been "strangers in our own city," and complained that "the mighty city of today knows little or nothing of our traditions." In his reminiscence of the poet James Russell Lowell, Charles Eliot Norton, whom Henry May has called "perhaps the most important late nineteenth-century arbiter of elegant American taste," demonstrated just how rooted in the past he could be as he described "the age of greater simplicity and tranquility of life" in which Lowell had grown to manhood and pronounced it "a time for poets."

> There were no railroads with their tremendous revolutionary forces; no great manufacturing cities; no flood of immigrants; no modern democracy. Old forms of life and old traditions prevailed . . . The days before the advent of General Jackson are pleasant to look back upon.[6]

In an industrializing, urbanizing nation absorbing millions of immigrants from alien cultures and experiencing an almost incomprehensible degree of structural change and spatial mobility, with anonymous institutions becoming ever larger and more central and with populations shifting from the countryside and small town to the city, from city to city, and from one urban neighborhood to another, the sense of anarchic change, of looming chaos, of fragmentation, which seemed to imperil the very basis of the traditional order, was not confined to a handful of aristocrats. Indeed, the elites had more allies than they were ever comfortable with, for to many of the new industrialists as well as many members of the new middle classes, following the lead of the arbiters of culture promised both relief from impending disorder and an avenue to cultural legitimacy.

As he surveyed the changes in his country in the early years of this century, Henry James lamented that there was no escape "into the future, or even into the present; there was an escape but into the past." James was not quite accurate. For him and for many others there was also an escape into Culture, which became one of the mechanisms that made it possible to identify, distinguish, and order this new universe of strangers. As long as these strangers had stayed within their own precincts and retained their own peculiar ways, they remained containable and could be dealt with: Afro-Americans dancing their strange ritual dances to exotic rhythms within their own churches; Irish women "keening" [wailing] weird melodies over their dead at their own wakes; Germans entertaining family and friends in their own beer gardens. But these worlds of strangers did not remain contained; they spilled over into the public spaces that characterized nineteenth-century America and that included theaters, music halls, opera houses, museums, parks, fairs, and the rich public cultural life that took place daily on the streets of American cities. This is precisely where the threat lay and the response of the elites was a tripartite one: to retreat into their own private spaces whenever possible; to transform public spaces by rules, systems of taste, and canons of behavior of their own choosing; and, finally, to convert the strangers so that their modes of behavior and cultural predilections emulated those of the elites—an urge that I will try to show always remained shrouded in ambivalence. Martin Green has said of Charles Eliot Norton that "he and his colleagues brushed back an ocean in which they fully expected to drown." Norton himself, governed by his characteristic pessimism about the future, probably would not have agreed, but in retrospect it is fair to say that he and his peers were more successful than they could have expected. They left behind them—firmly planted on high ground—enclaves of culture that functioned as alternatives to the disorderly outside world and represented the standards, if not the total way of life, they believed in.[7]

O NE OF THE SEVERAL factors underlying John Philip Sousa's importance as a cultural figure at the turn of the century was his image as an apostle of order in an unstable universe. The *Worcester Telegram* described how Sousa got what he wanted from his men with the "simple lash of his eye, the motion of his little finger." In 1892 a newspaper in Rockford, Illinois, commented that Sousa "woos the harmony out of the men with the air of a master." Sousa was hailed as a leader and commonly compared to a general, a figure he certainly resembled in his smart military uniform. "Not the least enjoyable thing about a Sousa band concert," the *Detroit Tribune* observed in 1899, "is the masterly control of the leader over the human instrumentality before him." Sousa himself encouraged these views. "I have to work so that I feel every one of my fifty-eight musicians is linked up with me by a cable of magnetism," he told a reporter. "I know precisely what every one of my musicians is doing every second or fraction of a second that I am conducting. I know this because every single member of my band is doing exactly what I make him do."[8]

In depicting himself as a force for disciplined order, Sousa touched a chord that ran deep at the turn of the century. "America! America!" school children were taught to sing in the 1890s,

> God mend thine ev'ry flaw,
> Confirm thy soul in self-control
> Thy liberty in law.

In 1914, shortly after the outbreak of war in Europe, Henry Lee Higginson, now almost eighty years old, stood before his orchestra and pleaded with his musicians for order:

> We meet again under difficult circumstances; we are of many nationalities . . . and we are all on American soil, which is neutral. Therefore, we must use every effort to avoid all unpleasant words or looks, for our task is to make harmony above all things— harmony even in the most modern music. I expect only harmony.

If Higginson was particularly insistent that his musicians treat one another harmoniously it was because he had long understood that before culture could spread order and harmony throughout the land it had to clean its own house, discipline its audiences and performers, and stand as an exemplar for the nation.[9]

"Harmony" and "order" are hardly the words one would choose to describe American audiences from the eighteenth to the late nineteenth centuries. In 1766 Edward Bardin announced a series of outdoor concerts in New York City and felt it necessary to declare that "every possible precaution will be used to prevent disorder and irregularity." The playbill advertising a Baltimore concert in the late summer of 1796 featuring the music of Haydn, Playel, and Bach, concluded by noting, "A number of constables will attend to preserve order." That such precautions were needed is attested to by an indignant letter in the *New York Post Boy* in the waning days of 1764 from "a dear lover of music" who complained that "instead of a modest and becoming silence nothing is heard during the whole performance, but laughing and talking very loud, squalling, overturning the benches, etc.—behaviour more suited to a *broglio* than a musical entertainment." Such scenes were evidently common enough that newspapers often reviewed the audience as well as the performers. In 1786 the *Pennsylvania Packet* concluded a review of Handel's *Messiah* by noting, with what seemed relief, "No interruption from within, no disturbance from without, prevented the full enjoyment of this *Grand Concert.*"[10]

The tendency for undisciplined audiences to treat theaters, concert halls, opera houses, even lecture halls, not as sacred precincts but as places of entertainment where they could act naturally, continued well into the nineteenth century as we have seen in the last two chapters. The very ethos of the times encouraged active audience participation. "It is the *American people* who support the theatre," the *Boston Weekly Magazine* asserted in 1824, "and this being the case, the people have an *undoubted right* to see and applaud who they please, and we trust this right will never be relinquished. No, never!" The *New York Mirror* urged its readers in 1836 to make themselves heard: "*Applaud* whenever there is the least thing meriting admiration. It sustains, cheers and inspires the actor, warms him into full exertion, and often, in laborious scenes, affords him a moment of sweet and necessary repose. It also cheers the audience themselves, breaks the monotony of a continued and perhaps crowded confinement in one position, and renders them as much more able to appreciate excellence as it does the performer to exhibit it . . . *Applaud the performers!!*" Ticket holders, a New Orleans judge ruled in 1853, had the legal right to hiss and stamp in the theater. Audiences of the period seemed fully prepared to heed this advice and exercise their rights.[11]

The gap between the stage and the pit or orchestra, which we have learned to treat as a boundary separating two worlds, was perceived by audiences for much of the nineteenth century as an archway inviting participation. In his memoirs, Max Maretzek described a complicated feud that Edward P. Fry, the manager of the Astor Place Opera House, had with three of his singers and their ally, the publisher James Gordon Bennett of the *New York Herald*. As with the Forrest-Macready feud, it did not take long for the audience to get into the fray. During a performance of *Norma* in December 1848, the tenor Sesto Benedetti walked onto the stage and according to Maretzek, "He was immediately greeted by a storm of hisses, which were as quickly broken in upon by thunderous acclamation. This at length stilled and he began to sing." His singing was accompanied by "screams, whistles, clapping of hands, hisses, trampling of feet, roaring, menacing outcries and gesticulations of every kind." Maretzek imagined that "the inmates of some half a hundred mad-houses had broken loose." After numerous attempts, Fry was able to address the audience and convince it to allow the opera to continue, but the audience remained rambunctious and difficult, laughing hilariously even at lines in Italian they could not have known the meaning of. Some yelled for Benedetti to sing "Yankee Doodle," others shouted "We don't want 'Yankee Doodle' 'Carry him back to Old Virginey.'"[12]

Audiences remained proudly independent and insisted upon receiving what they had been promised and judging openly what they received. When he was touring the United States, the British actor Henry Irving was told of a city in Colorado where the manager of a traveling company, in order to catch a train taking his troupe to their next engagement, condensed the performance of his play into an hour and a half. The next time the company visited that city "they were met *en route*, some fifty miles out, by the sheriff, who warned them to pass on by some other way, as their coming was awaited by a large section of the able-bodied male population armed with shot guns." As late as 1907, the audience at a performance of *The Barber of Seville* in El Paso, Texas, erupted into riotous behavior when the advertised tenor, Leandro Campanari, failed to appear and a scene in Act I, and several scenes in Act II were omitted. In spite of the insistence of the company's manager, Henry Russell, that the performance was precisely the one given in every other city and the efforts of the soprano Alice Nielsen to appease the crowd by singing "Swanee River," "Coming through the Rye," and "Annie Laurie," for which effort she was roundly hissed, the knowledgeable audience demanded a complete rendition of the opera they had paid to hear. Even the arrival of police failed to quell the audience, which stormed the box office in an ultimately successful effort to have their money refunded.[13]

Although audiences did not generally express themselves quite so dramatically, their independence was commonly manifest. After a concert in Stamford, Connecticut, in 1863, Louis Moreau Gottschalk noted in his journal, "The concert was deplorable this evening. Complete silence. I correct myself. Silence when I entered and when I went out, but animated conversation all the time I was playing." So unruly were his audiences that when a young man tiptoed quietly and unobtrusively across the hall during his concert in Williamsport, Pennsylvania, Gottschalk wrote, "Incomparable young man! How I regret not being able to inscribe thy name on my tablets or have it engraved in letters of gold, in order that it may be handed down to the admiration of posterity!" The young Henry Finck complained of the lack of musical culture and manners in the Oregon town where he grew up. On one occasion a "young rowdy began, while we played, to whistle a comic song—yes, *while we played!*" He wrote bitterly of those who "when you play a sonata of Beethoven or an overture by Mozart for them . . . listen a few moments then start up from their chairs, whistle 'Marching Through Georgia' and show their ill breeding in all other possible ways." Though he lived far from Oregon, George Templeton Strong often felt as if he too was a denizen of the frontier. After attending a New York Philharmonic concert in 1858 he commented in his diary, "crowded and garrulous, like a square mile of tropical forest with its flocks of squalling paroquets and troops of chattering monkeys." There were exceptions to this disorder, of course, and Strong wrote happily of the "great, silent, appreciative crowd of Teutons" among whom he sat at an 1859 concert commemorating the centennial of Schiller's birth, but such homogeneity of people and purpose was hard to come by.[14]

That Strong's complaints were not the product of a crotchety imagination is made clear by the actions of the Philharmonic's board. In their thirteenth annual report (1855), the directors complained of "the disgraceful habit of talking aloud at the rehearsals while the performance is going on," and rebuked those who "would seem to be more attracted and charmed by the sounds of their own voices, than by the inspiring, solemn, majestic tones of BEETHOVEN or MENDELSSOHN." In 1875 John Sullivan Dwight wrote of "those illbred and ignorant people" at Theodore Thomas's New York concerts "who keep up a continued buzzing during the performance of the music to the annoyance of all decent folk." At the American premiere of *Lohengrin* in 1871 at the Stadt Theatre in New York City, a reviewer was shocked by those in the audience who waited for the program to begin by chewing on oranges and spitting out the rinds. Others were no less surprised at the decision of the society leader Mrs. W. Bayard Cutting to break the monotony of a lengthy program at the Metropolitan Opera by having the contents of a sandwich hamper distributed among her guests, who nibbled bonbons and other delicacies during the singing. In 1891 the Board of Directors of the Metropolitan Opera House felt compelled to post the following notice in every box:

> Many complaints having been made to the directors of the Opera House of the annoyance produced by the talking in the boxes during the performance, the Board requests that it be discontinued.

Whispering, talking, laughing, coughing, shouting, shuffling, arriving late, leaving early, prematurely donning outer garments during the final number, noisily turning the pages of programs, stamping of the feet, applauding promiscuously, insistently demanding encores, sneaking snacks, spitting tobacco—the list of audience sins was long and troublesome.[15]

Some of these sins were manifest in the nation's art museums as well. When in 1891 New York's Metropolitan Museum of Art, after prolonged prodding by political leaders, decided to open its doors to the public on Sunday afternoons, the staff braced itself to greet a crowd of twelve thousand that was younger, more working class in its composition, and less used to the decorum of art museums than the Metropolitan's usual run of visitors. The *New York Times* announced that "Kodak camera fiends" would be barred and that visitors would have to check canes and umbrellas at the door "so that no chance should be given for anyone to prod a hole through a valuable painting, or to knock off any portion of a cast." A *Boston Herald* reporter testified that many came armed with large baskets of lunch and restless babies. Some, according to Louis P. di Cesnola, the Metropolitan's director, "brought with them peculiar habits which were repulsive and unclean." Cesnola noted that the visitors were accustomed to the Dime Museums on the Bowery "and had come here fully expecting to see freaks and monstrosities similar to those found there. Many visitors took the liberty of handling every object within reach; some went to the length of marring, scratching, and breaking articles unprotected by glass; a few proved to be pick-pockets." The *New York Times*, which had been a strong advocate of Sunday opening, had a more benign view of the results than Cesnola, though even its account transmits a sense of the disorder that so troubled the Metropolitan's patrons: "Not an arrest was made and not a person was violently ejected," it reported. "Gleeful voices were heard through the corridors . . . Boys tagged at their mothers' heels and laughed at the queer-shaped pottery of the Egyptians. But they did no harm. A few could not help putting a hand on the piece of statuary now and then, but this is done just as much on a week day, and cannot be spoken of as an evil exclusively attending Sunday opening."[16]

Almost as soon as he became superintendent of New York's Central Park in 1857, Frederick Law Olmsted complained of a "certain class" of visitors which believed "that all trees, shrubs, fruit and flowers are common property," and would not hesitate to graze their animals and gather firewood and any available flowers and fruits. "A large part of the people of New York," he observed, "are ignorant of a park . . . They will need to be trained to the proper use of it, to be restrained in the abuse of it." Three years later he complained to the park's Board of Commissioners that inadequate policing had led to robbery, "wanton defacement" of park property, tobacco spitting, garbage dumping, "and other filthy practices." The problem of unruly audiences invaded even the staid precincts of the Smithsonian Institution. In his report of 1859, Joseph Henry commented that while many of those attending the institution's lecture series did so "for the sake of the advantage to be derived from them," many others "attend as a mere pastime, or assemble in the lecture room as a convenient place of resort, and by their whispering annoy those who sit near them." Since Henry was never convinced that such public lectures ought to be part of the Smithsonian's mission, he simply took advantage of the fire of 1865 and had his building reconstructed without a lecture hall.[17]

Other cultural leaders lacked this easy resolution and were compelled to confront the disorder directly. Even as they were successfully establishing canons that identified the legitimate forms of drama, music, and art and the valid modes of performing and displaying them, the arbiters of culture turned their attention to establishing appropriate means of receiving culture. The authority that they first established over theaters, actors, orchestras, musicians, and art museums, they now extended to the audience. Their general success in disciplining and training audiences constitutes one of those cultural transformations that have been almost totally ignored by historians.

A<small>T THE TURN</small> of the century, European playwrights, frustrated at having to see and hear their creations filtered through the overbearing egoism of actors, began to express their attraction for impersonal, obedient marionettes. "I love a marionette-show," Joseph Conrad declared. "I love the marionettes that are without life, that come so near to being immortal!" Without necessarily articulating or even realizing it, this was precisely what American reformers of the stage, the concert hall, the opera house were attempting to do to performers at the turn of the century: transform them into a species of marionettes who would obey the dictates of the artist; who would speak the words, act the part, play the notes, sing the songs of the masters without imposing their own wills, without interjecting their own art, without expressing their inner selves. What was true of performers was true of audiences as well. To make art possible, performers and audiences had to submit to creators and become mere instruments of the will, mere auditors of the productions of the artist. It may well have been an unrealizable urge, but it was one that transformed not only a good part of the culture of the period but the very conception of culture.[18]

By the close of its first year of Sunday attendance, the Metropolitan Museum of Art reported that Sunday visitors, who numbered some 30 percent of all visitors, had, through a rigorous policy of protection and education, become "respectable, law-abiding, and intelligent." The entire staff, including the curators and the director, were in the galleries every Sunday to answer questions and keep order. Mark Twain ridiculed these precautions. The story circulated that during a visit to the museum he was requested to leave his cane in the cloakroom, to which he responded: "Leave my cane! Leave my cane! Then how do you expect me to poke holes through the oil paintings?" Director Louis di Cesnola insisted that this vigilance was necessary to the museum's survival. When his staff's refusal to allow a plumber in overalls to enter the museum on a weekday afternoon in 1897 generated such unfriendly headlines as

SOBER WORKMAN HAS TO LEAVE ART GALLERIES

ART FOR THE WELL DRESSED

SENSITIVE AND REFINED PLUMBER AFFRONTED

Cesnola reminded the city that the museum was "a closed corporation" that had the right and obligation to monitor behavior: "We do not want, nor will we permit a person who has been digging in a filthy sewer or working among grease and oil to come in here, and, by offensive odors emitted from the dirt on their apparel, make the surroundings uncomfortable for others." He reiterated the great progress the museum had made in training its visitors:

> You do not see any more persons in the picture galleries blowing their nose with their fingers; no more dogs brought into the Museum openly or concealed in baskets. There is no more spitting tobacco juice on the gallery floors, to the disgust of all other visitors. There are no more nurses taking children to some corner to defile the floors of the Museum. No persons come now with "Kodaks" to take "snap views" of things and visitors. No more

whistling, singing, or calling aloud to people from one gallery to another.[19]

Referring to his ambitious project in Central Park, Frederick Law Olmsted testified that "the difficulty of preventing ruffianism and disorder in a park to be frequented indiscriminately by such a population as that of New York, was from the first regarded as the greatest of all those which the [Park] Commission had to meet and the means of overcoming it cost more study than all other things." Olmsted and his associates relied upon a host of regulations and policemen called Park-Keepers to enforce them. In addition to proscribing climbing trees, molesting birds, racing carriages, grazing animals, destroying plants, and shooting firearms, the regulations, as reported by an observer in 1868, isolated the park from the disorderly world surrounding it:

> No shows of any kind are allowed on the Park's grounds; no jugglers, gamblers—except those disguised as gentlemen—puppet shows, peddlers of flowers, players upon so-called musical instruments, ballad singers, nor hand-organ men; in fact none of the great army of small persecutors who torment the outside world, can enter into this pleasant place to make us miserable in it.

Olmsted's Central Park, and many of the other urban parks of the period, afforded what Robert Weyeneth has aptly called a "didactic landscape," a "moral space," which could only function as intended if the proper order was maintained.[20]

The nation's music lovers experienced the same disciplinary process as those who visited museums and parks. When he became president of the New York Philharmonic in 1870, George Templeton Strong began an active campaign against audience unruliness. In the fall he commented gratefully on the "blessed novelties" of a closely attentive audience and "the absence of clack," though he noted that people still came in late and took their seats during the first movement of the symphony, and vowed, "We must enforce our regulation against that abuse more strictly." After a concert in the opening days of 1871, he noted in his diary, "Some good done by my rather strong printed notice as to the ill-breeding of entering the house while music is in progress and thereby disturbing those who have taken their seats in good season. Several snobs marched in during the first movement of the symphony; but quite a throng steamed in at its conclusion, having courteously waited in the lobby for a pause." "I often hear it said that the vile habit of talking and giggling is much less general than heretofore," he noted in the spring of 1871 and attributed the change "to our daring handbills requesting silence and to the printed notices that have been delivered with our programmes." That as late as 1871 Strong characterized handbills requesting silence as "daring," is a sign of how significant the departure from past practice was.[21]

Theodore Thomas was equally active in the struggle for decorum and order. When, during a performance of the second movement of Beethoven's Eighth Symphony at a Central Park Garden concert, a young man in the front row, who had been talking incessantly to the lady with him, began to snap one "explosive" match after another in a futile attempt to ignite his cigar, Thomas, according to an observer, "gave the signal to his orchestra to stop, laid down his baton, turned to the young man, and said with one of his sweetest and most cynical smiles, in a voice audible to all around him, 'Go on, sir! Don't mind us! We can all wait until you light your cigar.' The cigar was not lit, and the couple were quiet through the rest of the concert." During a performance of Mendelssohn's *Midsummer Night's Dream*, Thomas suddenly gave the signal for a long drum roll during which he stared at a couple who had been chatting and then resumed the Mendelssohn. Thomas often reacted to the incessant noise by standing with his hands in the air until silence prevailed or by stopping his orchestra and apologizing to the audience for interrupting their conversation. When he conducted Handel at the Cincinnati Festival of 1873 he gave instructions that the doors be closed when he began and no one be admitted until the first part was finished. The sponsoring committee was reluctant to implement this lest the public be offended but Thomas was adamant: "It must be done. When you play Offenbach or Yankee Doodle, you can keep your doors open. When I play Handel's 'Te Deum,' they must be shut. Those who appreciate music will be here on time." The opera star Lilli Lehmann has written with admiration of Thomas's reaction to a rebellious New York audience that interrupted his premiere of Liszt's *Mephisto Waltz* with a barrage of whistles and hissing. After several futile attempts to resume, Thomas took out a watch and told the audience: "I give you five minutes to leave the hall; then we shall play the waltz from the beginning to the end. Who wishes to listen without making a demonstration may do so; I request all others to go. I will carry out my purpose if I have to remain standing here until two o'clock in the morning—I have plenty of time." "He often gained such victories," Lehmann observed, "and showed himself master."[22]

Harper's Magazine watched Thomas's campaign with interest and suggested that his approach form the basis of enforcing order in the opera house. *Harper's* suggestion was either to "let the performance be arrested in mid-career, and an appeal be made to the audience whether the singers or the talkers shall stop," or to have all those in the audience who were annoyed "turn *en masse* and silently fix their gaze upon the vulgar disturbers! That still concentrated look would quell the rioters." Disrupters at the Metropolitan, and other opera houses and concert halls, were subdued finally not by the audience but by conductors and the management. When Arturo Toscanini conducted at the Metropolitan Opera, he insisted that latecomers to *Tristan* be made to wait until the Prelude was completed, and interrupted a performance of Weber's *Euryanthe* to rap with his baton until the whispering stopped. Such tactics became commonplace. Frederick Stock, Thomas's successor in Chicago, would wave his handkerchief when the audience's coughing interfered with his music and once interrupted a performance of Smetana's *Moldau* to rebuke those who were putting on their wraps. At a concert in Nashville, Victor Herbert turned to those—including the governor of Tennessee—who were stirring to leave prematurely and announced, "It will take ten minutes to play this piece. You who are in a hurry perhaps had better leave now." According to a reporter, there was immediate order, the governor and all the other guilty parties took their seats obediently and remained for the rest of the concert. Pierre Monteux, who took over the Boston Symphony Orchestra in 1919, would sharply rap on his podium to quiet the audience; his successor, Serge Koussevitzky, simply stood silently with folded arms and waited until the commotion subsided. Walter Damrosch of the New York Symphony and Leopold Stokowski of the Philadelphia Orchestra would stop the music, turn to the audience, and lecture them on their various faults. When an unhappy audience erupted in hisses during a performance of Schoenberg, Stokowski demanded it accord him his right to freedom of expression. During a similar outburst in the midst of Villa-Lobos's Choro No. 8, Stokowski told the disrupters to go outside "and smoke the classic cigarette."[23]

The thrust of the conductors' efforts was to render audiences docile, willing to accept what the experts deemed appropriate rather than play a role themselves in determining either the repertory or the manner of presentation. When Theodore Thomas was warned that he was peppering his programs with too many compositions by Richard Wagner, which the people did not like, he replied, "Then they must hear them till they do." In the spring of 1897, at the close of the Chicago Orchestra's sixth season, the Chicago cultural journal, the *Dial*, applauded Thomas for eschewing "any attempt to win the applause of the multitude by concessions to vulgar prejudice or meretricious tastes," and asserted that the way to deal with the "average Philistine" was to say firmly: "This masterpiece deserves your attention . . . for it has the power to raise you to a higher spiritual level. If you do not like it now, pray that you may learn to like it, for the defect is yours." A year before his death Thomas was asked why he had abolished the traditional "request" programs, which had characterized his nineteenth-century concerts, and replied, "Because it is no longer necessary. My audiences no longer request. They are satisfied with what satisfies me."[24]

The very establishment of permanent orchestras of professional musicians in the late nineteenth century was in itself an important step in the direction of creating passive audiences. The elimination of part-time musicians from orchestras and the drastic reduction of what had been an abundance of voluntary amateur choral societies, which often collaborated with the orchestras, signaled the final destruction of a bridge over which members of the lay public, in the language of the music historian John Mueller, "had shuttled rather easily back and forth across the footlights." Those footlights now became a barrier between audience and performer that was fortified, as Paul DiMaggio has argued, by the importation of large numbers of European musicians without roots in the community who were of necessity largely dependent on the conductors and directors of their orchestras and with whom the audiences had difficulty either empathizing or communicating. To all of these developments were added a series of regulations that capped the transformation of practices which had dominated expressive culture for most of the nineteenth century.[25]

Concertgoers were increasingly lectured on the elements of proper behavior. In 1892 Edward Baxter Perry told them they had "no right" to sit through a concert "stolid and indifferent," to think about business or domestic affairs, to read the old letters accumulated in their pockets, to trim their finger nails, to crunch peanuts, "or even to take a nap." Attention, he announced, "is a rigid rule of the concert-room." Silence, he reminded them, "is to music what light is to painting." He even added a new commandment to the Decalogue: "Thou shalt not whisper!" Gradually, such injunctions became an integral part of the rules and mores governing audience behavior. Intermissions were introduced to allow the audience to stretch, talk, promenade, and then presumably to subside into reflective quiescence when the music resumed. Beginning in Baltimore and spreading to Boston and other cities, lights were dimmed in concert halls to further focus attention on the performers rather than on the audience. The incessant injunctions to be prompt were by the 1920s finally translated into rules barring latecomers from taking their seats until the first number on the program was completed. At the other end of the concert, from the 1880s to the beginning of the new century, constant pressure was put on members of the audience to refrain from leaving while the orchestra was performing. No one, the Boston Symphony's Concert Notes stipulated in 1885, "will disturb both audience and orchestra by leaving the hall during the performance." In 1908 an editorial in the *New York Times* denounced the "intolerable selfishness" of those operagoers "who spoil the aesthetic pleasure of others by rudely leaving the opera while the last act is in progress" and suggested a class difference by asking: "Has any sufferer noticed that these folks are generally the least tastefully dressed and worst-looking folks in the audience?" The eager perusal of concert notes, which were first distributed to concertgoers in the closing decades of the century, created a rustling of pages that added to the undercurrent of noisy inattention. "We may read and we may listen, but not both, dear friend, at the same time," John Sullivan Dwight admonished his readers.[26]

A greater and more persistent annoyance were the fashionably large women's hats of the period. In some places, such as Ohio, where the state legislature adopted a law banning large hats from theaters, the offending apparel was legally proscribed. In other places, there were campaigns of education. The *New York Times* urged those "very selfish and inconsiderate" hat-wearing members of the "ornamental sex" to act voluntarily, arguing that manners and morals "must be in a bad way when laws are really needed to enforce the principles of ordinary courtesy." When in the early days of 1909 Mrs. William Ellis Corey, whom the *Times* described as "the wife of the steel magnate," appeared at the Manhattan Opera House wearing a hat that measured three feet across, she received a personal note from the impresario, Oscar Hammerstein, requesting her to remove the hat. Her refusal led Hammerstein to find new seats for those whose view was blocked and to vow, "It will not occur again." At the beginning of the 1900–1 season the programs of the Boston Symphony announced a new city regulation prohibiting "any person to wear upon the head a covering which obstructs the view of the exhibition or performance." Higginson and his associates added to this note their hope that "gracious women with musical taste can be depended upon to wear hats, if they wear any, against which the meanest man on earth could find no indictment." Evidently the hope proved illusory for eight years later, in October 1908, the Boston Symphony again attempted to effect what the *Boston Evening Transcript* termed "a little revolution in the manners and customs" of the concerts, by announcing that women must either check their hats at the door or hold them in their laps. "Many hats were removed willingly," the *Evening Transcript* reported; "some were laid aside reluctantly; a considerable number remained obstinately fixed in their places . . . There were audible retorts of feminine petulance, selfishness and self-will. There was wordy protest—and gradual submission which after all was the main thing . . . At no afternoon concert in years have the orchestra and the soloist been so generally and easily visible." Although most women concertgoers seemed ready to conform to what one correspondent called "civilized custom," the refusal of a number of defiant women to comply led Mayor Fitzgerald to set a deadline of November 19, 1908. Despite threats of widespread civil disobedience, on the target day all the women in the audience dutifully removed their hats, save one lonely lady who marched to the box office and demanded her money back, and another who had received permission to stand against the wall with her hat on.[27]

Nothing seems to have troubled the new arbiters of culture more than the nineteenth-century practice of spontaneous expressions of pleasure and disapproval in the form of cheers, yells, gesticulations, hisses, boos, stamping of feet, whistling, crying for encores, and applause. By the middle of the twentieth century polite applause and occasional well-placed "bravos" were all that remained of this panoply of reactions, and there were some who seriously proposed abolishing even this small remnant. In 1895 George Gladden compared applause to the clashing together of spears, shields, and battle axes by primitive savages. Applause was neither appropriate nor logical. People who would not dream of making noise after "a beautifully worded prayer" would destroy the mood created by a Chopin Nocturne by banging their hands together. Although more than a quarter of a century later Leopold Stokowski asked for a referendum on whether to abolish applause, which he called "a relic of the dark ages," at concerts of the Philadelphia Orchestra, audiences were allowed to retain this one vestige of participation. Even more vigorous— and more successful—was the campaign against the nineteenth-century practice of treating arias or movements of symphonies as individual units that could be responded to separately. Conductors from Theodore Thomas on struggled against the demand for encores in operas and symphonic concerts. "When his audience relapses into barbarism on the subject of encores," a contemporary wrote of Thomas in 1872, "he quietly but firmly controls them. I have seen him . . . leave the stand and quietly take a seat in a corner of the orchestra, remaining there until he had carried his point." The New York music critic W. J. Henderson characterized the "encore habit" as "a shameful and stupid exhibition of greed" and called upon the artists to break it by refusing to comply. In 1899 the manager of the Sunday night Metropolitan Opera concerts complained that the previous Sunday's concert "was doubled in length by encores" and announced that "no more encores will be permitted." During the 1930s such conductors as Stokowski, Toscanini, and Koussevitzky successfully demanded that symphonies be treated as an integral whole and applauded only at the end.[28]

Total order, of course, was not achieved; audiences were never reduced to automatons. But the contrast between what they had been for most of the nineteenth century and what they were becoming was marked. In 1894 Theodore Thomas expressed delight at how much had been accomplished since he arrived in Chicago three years earlier:

> Our audience . . . has discovered that there is a deeper joy and a nobler spirituality to be gained from familiarity with the higher art forms than it ever dreamed of seeking in the lower . . . And having learned to value and appreciate the music, our audience now wishes to hear it all. The late comers are much fewer, and are content to wait for a pause in the music before disturbing others by taking their seats. Talking has almost wholly ceased, and only those leave early who are obliged to take suburban trains.

In 1897 *Harper's Weekly* worried that the change might have gone too far. The Astor Place Riot, it argued, "is long out of date."

> Indeed, American audiences are only too indulgent. We could save ourselves much poorish and worse musical art were our audiences more disposed to use time-honored 'privileges.' How much we endure unprotesting! We sit patiently through bad singing and playing, through dozens of compositions that we don't like . . . We do not hiss or cat-call . . . We do not send cabbages and cats in parabolas if a manager's good faith is not kept with us.

Not only did American audiences no longer manifest their displeasure, Karleton Hackett in 1894 complained that they had also stopped displaying their enthusiasm. "Let us now drop some of our vaunted Anglo-Saxon self-containedness," he pleaded, "and when we are pleased send out a few ringing bravos."[29]

In 1836 the *New York Mirror* had expressed its dismay at the extent to which Americans incessantly ignored rules and regulations in public places, and urged its countrymen to behave more like Europeans. By the turn of the century the situation was quite reversed. In 1881 Joseph Hatton, a British visitor, observed theaters in various cities and concluded that compared with the English, American audiences are "more easily pleased. They certainly behave better. They are more respectful to the actors. However bad the play they never hiss . . . On the first night of a new piece there are no running comments on the play . . . If it is particularly bad they leave before the last act. But they make no noisy protests . . . They are dignified and quiet." When the Metropolitan Opera Company's new director, Giulio Gatti-Casazza, was asked in 1908 to compare audiences at the Metropolitan and La Scala in Milan, he held Americans up as a paradigm of good behavior: "In Europe audiences are accustomed to express approval rather more sparingly than here, and to be vehement in expressions of disapproval. This is by no means the case in New York. The audience at the Metropolitan is most generous in applause when anything done on the stage pleases it; when, on the other hand, it sees or hears something not to its liking, it gives no expression whatever of its disapproval." In 1909 the *New York Times* noted that when what it called the "Italian contingent" vociferously clamored for an encore in *L'Elisir d'Amore,* the tenor Alessandro Bonci ignored it. The *Times* could not help thinking nostalgically of the 1880s and 1890s when "such a tenor as Bonci would have repeated 'Una furtiva lagrima' two or three times and the fact would have been duly chronicled as a great artistic triumph." Nevertheless, the *Times* pronounced the change "all for the good of art." Two years later the *Times* recalled the days when actors like Macready and Edmund Kean were hissed, and announced that the "time when hissing was regarded, by coarse natures, as a fair alternative to applause . . . has passed in this country . . . the body of playgoers will not tolerate it, as it disturbs their comfort, and destroys the decorum which they believe should be preserved in the theatre." Hissing, the *Times* concluded, "is not liked here, even when a performance deserves it."[30]

Throughout these years the audience was being transformed, in Richard Sennett's phrase, into "a spectator rather than a witness" and in the process "lost a sense of itself as an active force, as a 'public.'" With important exceptions—particularly in the areas of sports and religion—audiences in America had become less interactive, less of a public and more of a group of mute receptors. Art was becoming a one-way process: the artist communicating and the audience receiving. "Silence in the face of art," was becoming the norm and was helping to create audiences without the independence to pit their taste, publicly at least, against those of critics, performers, and artists.[31] Americans at the turn of the century were learning to defer to experts in a wide range of activities that had been relatively open during the nineteenth century and that were being professionalized and codified at its close. This development is familiar to us by now. What is less familiar is the fact that the same process was at work in the arts as well with crucial implications for the structure of culture and the manner in which it was perceived in the new century. The desire of the promoters of the new high culture to convert audiences into a collection of people reacting *individually* rather than collectively, was increasingly realized by the twentieth century. This was achieved partly by fragmenting and segregating audiences so that it was more and more difficult in the twentieth century to find the equivalent of the nineteenth-century theater audience that could serve as a microcosm of the entire society. Partly it was achieved by taming audiences, so that once again it is necessary to look to the athletic arena to find the equivalent of the nineteenth-century audience in which the spectators feel like participants, manifest a sense of immediacy and at times even of control, and articulate their opinions and feelings vocally and unmistakably.

The transition I have been describing was not confined to concert halls, museums, and opera houses. The standards of these emporia of high culture extended to what was quickly becoming the world of popular entertainment, which witnessed a less complete but still significant change. "The character of the vaudeville audience has notably improved in recent years," B. F. Keith wrote in 1898. The improvement had not a little to do with entrepreneurs of entertainment like F. F. Proctor and Keith himself, who built circuits of handsome vaudeville theaters, the largest of them resembling palaces, operated on the policy of "cleanliness and order," where, as Keith put it "the stage show must be free from vulgarisms and coarseness of any kind," so that the theater would be "as 'homelike' an amusement resort as it was possible to make it." If Keith and his associates promised audiences unprecedented comfort and courtesy, they demanded order and decorum in return. During the first performance at Keith's new theater in Providence, the gallery gods engaged in noisy demonstrations. Keith responded immediately:

> I stepped out onto the stage and explained to this portion of the audience that it would not be allowed to continue these demonstrations any longer. I said, "You can't do that here . . . I know that you mean no harm by it, and only do it from the goodness of your hearts, but others in the audience don't like it, and it does not tend to improve the character of the entertainment, and I know you will agree with me that it is better to omit it hereafter." As I walked off, I received a round of applause from the whole house including the gallery. And that was the last of the noise from the gallery gods.

Though it was doubtless not quite this easy, Keith worked diligently at establishing the kind of conduct he found appropriate, using ushers and police to carry out his will. Men who lit up cigars against the rules of the house were required to extinguish them. If a woman wore her hat in the theater, "Our rule was to have the party approached by the usher first, second by the assistant head usher, then by the head usher, and lastly by the management, who would request the party to leave if the hat could not be removed." When a woman did remove her hat, "there would be a round of applause, showing that the audience appreciated it as much as we did." A reporter who covered the opening of Keith's New Boston Theatre in 1894, praised the order and observed that "there is a pleasant avoidance of the encore nuisance." The public, Keith observed, simply "needed to be educated in these matters." Their teachers were the ushers, who, in all of the leading vaudeville theaters, were armed with a variety of printed notices that they freely dispensed:

> Gentlemen will kindly avoid carrying cigars or cigarettes in their mouths while in the building, and greatly oblige. THE MANAGE-MENT

Gentlemen will kindly avoid the stamping of feet and pounding of canes on the floor, and greatly oblige the Management. All applause is best shown by clapping of hands. Please don't talk during acts, as it annoys those about you, and prevents a perfect hearing of the entertainment. THE MANAGEMENT

In their published assessment of the amusement scene in Boston, the Drama Committee of the Twentieth Century Club in 1910 chided audiences at Boston's "better class" vaudeville houses not for their unruliness but for being "too good-natured, too easily satisfied."[32]

The passive politeness that came to characterize audiences in American theaters and vaudeville houses after the turn of the century became familiar as well in the new movie houses that soon dotted the nation. As early as 1909 Jane Addams was calling the movie theater a "veritable house of dreams," in which young people sat quietly drinking in filmed fantasies that became "infinitely more real than the noisy streets and the crowded factories." Thus though Addams was disturbed that movie houses purveyed "a debased form of dramatic art, and a vulgar type of music," she was even more distressed at what she considered to be the overwhelming passivity it inculcated in its audiences. Addams called for recreational opportunities in which youths' "sense of participation" would be more complete and meaningful. Addams's fellow social worker Mary Kingsbury Simkhovitch also surveyed the "5-cent [movie] theatre" and concluded that it had "revolutionised the theatre for working people" because of its low price and its ability to rerun its offerings almost infinitely, thus adapting to the busy schedules of urban folk. But there was one great drawback: "It is passive . . . in character. It is fed out to the auditors, whose reaction is but slight. No concentration or sustained interest is demanded. It is a good way of instilling facts, but a poor way of elevating the emotions or stimulating the attention."[33]

As movie theater owners attempted to attract middle-class people to what in its nickelodeon phase had been largely a working-class entertainment, movie houses, like vaudeville houses before them, began to ape the physical trappings of high culture. As Adolph Zukor put it, "theaters replaced shooting

galleries, temples replaced theaters, cathedrals replaced temples."
This process of emulation was not confined to architecture or
furnishings; if the eclectic audiences of movie houses resembled
the democratic mix that had characterized audiences of nineteenth-century theaters, their behavior patterns diverged markedly. These were far from the raucous, independent audiences of
the nineteenth century. In 1913 Walter Prichard Eaton wrote
that "motion picture audiences sit hour after hour without smil-
ing, without weeping, without applauding. They sit in solemn
silence in a dim dark room." That same year Olivia Howard
Dunbar observed, "Rarely does such an audience betray anima-
tion, scarcely ever awareness. Its posture is indifferent and relaxed; its jaws moving unconcernedly in tune with the endlessly
reiterated ragtime ground out by some durable automaton." The
movie audience gave "mysteriously few" signs of active enjoyment or of displeasure. "To watch it is to discover that it is
infinitely tolerant; completely and blessedly immune to boredom." Of course many of these accounts were written by those
who bemoaned the effects of movies on their audiences, and in
fact movie houses were neither as dreary nor audiences as passive
as they liked to picture. Audiences often engaged in sing-alongs
with the organ or piano that accompanied the films; they would
on occasion cheer heroes and hiss villains as as they had in the
plays of the nineteenth century, and there were theaters that
were, as Lewis Palmer observed, "genuine social centers where
neighborhood groups may be found any evening of the week;
where the 'regulars' stroll up and down the aisles between acts
and visit friends." But though limited participatory behavior was
still possible, and sometimes even encouraged, the undisciplined,
raucous behavior that had been so dominant during most of the
nineteenth century was seldom encountered.[34]

The relative taming of the audience at the turn of the century
was part of a larger development that witnessed a growing bifurcation between the private and the public spheres of life.
Through the cult of etiquette, which was so popular in this
period, individuals were taught to keep all private matters strictly
to themselves and to remain publicly as inconspicuous as possible. Norbert Elias has shown that with the new societal complexities and differentiation of social functions, an entire range

of intimate activities—eating, coughing, spitting, nose blowing, scratching, farting, urinating—were firmly removed from the public sphere to that of the private. Such activities were now restricted to special "temporal and spatial enclaves." People were similarly taught to remove from the public to the private universe an entire range of personal reactions. "A lady or gentleman should conduct herself or himself on the street so as to escape all observation," an etiquette book advised in 1892. "A shrill voice, a loud laugh, . . . occupying the center of the sidewalk are all very bad form." Or as another guide put it, "Never look behind you in the street, or behave in any way so as to attract attention. Do not talk or laugh loudly out of doors, or swing your arms as you walk. If you should happen to meet some one you know, take care not to utter their names loudly." As John Kasson has recently put it, the individual mirrored the increasing segmentation of society in a segmentation of self. Reactions and emotions had to be carefully governed. In the sense that theaters, opera houses, symphony halls, and art galleries, as well as the larger movie theaters and vaudeville houses, reflected this process they were mirrors of society. But they were more than that; they were active agents in teaching their audiences to adjust to the new social imperatives, in urging them to separate public behavior from private feelings, in training them to keep a strict reign over their emotional and physical processes.[35]

Just a week before Christmas 1914, Boston concertgoers were introduced to Schoenberg's *Five Pieces for Orchestra*, whose concepts of harmony and melody were largely foreign to them. The critic Olin Downes, who characterized the music as "not only intricate in its rhythms and in its polyphony, but also, for the most part, very ugly," felt that Karl Muck conducted it out of a sense not of admiration but of duty, and at its close "marched off the stage, apparently in an unamiable frame of mind." Yet the audience accepted it all without a murmur. "Nothing was thrown at Dr. Muck and the orchestra," the critic Philip Hale reported. "There was no perturbation of Nature to show that Schönberg's pieces were playing; the sun did not hasten its descent; there was no earthquake shock. It was as it should have been in Boston."[36] He might have added that this was the way it was rapidly becoming in the United States as a whole: culture and order, order and culture locked together in harmonious union.

In 1874 an anonymous journalistic poet had a dialogue with Culture and confronted it with serious charges: "'Culture!' I cried, . . . 'Thy narrow cliques have thrown the toiling mob . . . [and given] the earth's fatness to the fool and snob!'" Culture responded calmly that its work was all the more necessary as people's rights and opportunities grew without an accompanying increase in their sense of duty.

> I hold the faith while social forms are bending
> Instructed by the clamor,—not befooled.[37]

To "hold the faith while social forms are bending" sums up succinctly what the champions of culture in the late nineteenth century felt their function was. It was not merely the audiences in the opera houses, theaters, symphonic halls, museums, and parks that they strove to transform; it was the entire society. They were convinced that maintaining and disseminating pure art, music, literature, and drama would create a force for moral order and help to halt the chaos threatening to envelop the nation.

In 1870 John Sullivan Dwight called music a "civilizing agency," a "beautiful corrective of our crudities," and argued that a democratic people, "a great mixed people of all races," whose normal impulse was centrifugal, desperately needed the harmonizing, humanizing influence of fine music. "Our radicalism will pull itself up by the roots . . . unless it be restrained by a no less free, impassioned love of order." The year before, George Templeton Strong, his wife, and some friends went for a drive in Central Park and stopped in at one of Theodore Thomas's summer evening concerts. "This seems a civilizing institution," Strong noted. "I dare say Theodore Thomas has kept a good many young clerks and others out of mischief." In 1875 a critic for *Century Magazine* watched the vast crowds "that drink in the harmonies" of such orchestras as Thomas's and mused, "it is pleasant to think that many in that assembly might, without such opportunities, be sitting in desolate moodiness in narrow city apartments, and slowly laying up the seeds of a disordered brain." That same year Louisa Cragin maintained that if trade unions were transformed into choral societies and good music were brought to workers and their children, in a generation "there will be fewer strikes, the grimy faces will be less haggard; under the unconscious influence of beauty, harmony, and rhythm, labor will be more cheerfully, more faithfully performed." In 1893 George P. Upton looked forward to the day when wage workers "will experience in their too barren lives the uplifting influences of inner contact with the ideal, the orderly, and the celestial—all of which music is." For Charles Edward Russell two generations of symphonic music "might in the end scourge us of materialism. Is this fantastic? Not if what we believe about the power and the ethics of art has any foundation."[38]

The fine arts offered the same glorious prospects as music. During a meeting at New York's Union League Club in 1869, called to found what was to become the Metropolitan Museum of Art, the poet William Cullen Bryant assured some three hundred influential citizens that the labyrinths of villainy which inevitably scarred the streets of great cities could be countered by the "wholesome, ennobling, instructive" influence of works of art which were instrumental in "the cultivation of the sense of beauty . . . the perception of order, symmetry, proportion of parts." Eleven years later, Joseph Choate, one of the founders of the Metropolitan Museum, dedicated its new building in Central Park by urging the assembled millionaires "to convert pork into porcelain, grain and produce into priceless pottery, the rude ores of commerce into sculptured marble, and railroad shares and mining stocks . . . into the glorified canvases of the world's masters, that shall adorn these walls for centuries," assuring them that the diffusion of art "in its higher forms of beauty would tend directly to humanize, to educate, and refine a practical and laborious people." In its campaign to open the Metropolitan Museum on Sundays so working people could visit it, the *New York Times* observed that liquor stores were open on Sundays "and it is from these that the museum would attract a very large share, if not the majority, of its Sunday visitors." The very existence of the Metropolitan Museum, the *Times* observed in 1894, was "a most effective anti-Tammany comment," for nobody who visits the museum "can come away without feeling more ashamed than before that a city of which the good citizenship has produced so inspiring a result should be under the political dominion of the ignorant and vulgar."[39]

John Pintard, secretary of the Academy of Arts and Sciences in New York, warned that "gross dissipation always prevails where refinement is not cultivated," and urged that "the growth of vice and immorality" be stunted and "proper direction" be given to "young minds" by the creation of such "sources for occupation & killing time," as "Theatres, Operas, Academies of Arts, Museums &c." Frederick Law Olmsted would have added public parks to Pintard's list. In designing New York's Central Park, Olmsted was convinced that he had created "a distinctly harmonizing and refining influence upon the most unfortunate and most lawless classes of the city—an influence favorable to courtesy, self-control, and temperance." In 1873 his Park-Keepers were informed that "every foot of the Park's surface, every tree and bush, as well as every arch, roadway and walk had been fixed where it is *with a purpose*." The park, they were reminded, "is not simply a pleasure-ground," but a place meant to improve those who came to it. An observer noted in 1869 that under the influence of the park, "rude, noisy fellows . . . become hushed, moderate, and careful." Olmsted attempted to create and preserve a pastoral ethos by sinking the transverse roads that cut through the park at Sixty-fifth, Seventy-ninth, Eighty-fifth, and Ninety-seventh streets. This had the effect of doing for the park what others were accomplishing for the concert hall, opera house, and art museum: elevating it above the ordinary run of life, separating it from common influences, marking it—as definitively as neoclassical architecture marked the museum, opera house, and concert hall—as an oasis of order and culture, as what Olmsted called "a class of opposite conditions" from those prevailing in the city. "We want," Olmsted insisted, "the greatest possible contrast with the streets and the shops and the rooms of the town which will be consistent with convenience and the preservation of good order and neatness. We want . . . to completely shut out the city from our landscapes." Accordingly, Olmsted spent much of his tenure as the park's landscape architect fighting—often futilely—plans for invading his tranquil green spaces with such outside intrusions as auditoriums, restaurants, burial grounds, trotting tracks, playgrounds, athletic fields, zoos, statues, even museums.[40]

Olmsted was not alone in viewing parks as more than recreational centers. Boston's park commissioners expected Arnold Arboretum to function as a "public educator," and a speaker at Fanueil Hall in 1876 declared that "there will be less gambling, drinking, and quarreling in Boston when the mass of its inhabitants shall be allowed to partake of the blessing and beauty of a public park." In San Francisco a designer of Golden Gate Park argued in 1873 that parks were really part of the educational system since they served as "cultivators of public taste." Amid the harmony of such a park as San Francisco's, a report declared in 1890, even "the rudest boy forgets his jack-knife and his heedless vandalism." In his influential book, *The Dangerous Classes of New York* (1872), Charles Loring Brace observed that "one of the best modes of driving out low tastes in the masses is to introduce higher." He pointed to galleries, museums, and parks as "the most formidable rivals of the liquor-shops," and argued, "Whenever in the evening a laboring-man can saunter in a pleasant park, or, in company with his wife and family, look at interesting pictures, or sculpture, or objects of curiosity, he has not such a craving for alcoholic stimulus." The problem went deeper than combating the numerous dens of vice that cities provided; oases of culture were necessary because disorder was embodied in the very structure and appearance of the nation's cities. In 1874, while he was designing the landscaping on Capitol Hill, Olmsted complained that the public buildings in Washington, D.C., presented a "broken, confused, and unsatisfactory" image. "The Capitol of the Union," he wrote, "manifests nothing so much as disunity." Architects and planners like Olmsted and Daniel Hudson Burnham struggled to reorder society, to fight chaos, to create meaning out of what they conceived to be the frightening anarchy of urban life.[41]

More and more culture seemed to be a life raft in an unpredictable and turbulent sea. In the fall of 1878 the *Atlantic Monthly*, whose editor at the time was William Dean Howells, explored what it called "Certain Dangerous Tendencies in Amer-

Pastoral order in Central Park, 1894.

ican Life," and warned that "we are in the earlier stages of a war upon property, and upon everything that satisfies what are called the higher wants of civilized life." Workers were being taught to regard "works of art and instruments of high culture, with all the possessions and surroundings of people of wealth and refinement, as causes and symbols of the laborer's poverty and degradation, and therefore as things to be hated." If America was not to succumb to the "peril of democracy" and become mired in "a general mediocrity," those "who believe in culture, in property, and in order, that is in civilization, must establish the necessary agencies for the diffusion of a new culture," a "better culture," a "culture of a higher order," and work for "the moral education of the people." In 1886 Henry Lee Higginson adopted the same tone in requesting that one of his relatives donate $100,000 to Harvard College:

THE CENTRAL PARK.

A delightful resort for toil-worn New Yorkers.

Olmsted's vision for Central Park did not win universal approval, as illustrated by this cartoon from *Frank Leslie's Illustrated Newspaper*, 1869.

My reasons are that you, a public-spirited and educated gentleman, owe it to yourself, to your country, and to the Republic. How else are we to save our country if not by education in all ways and on all sides? . . .

. . . Our chance is *now*—before the country is full and the struggle becomes intense and bitter.

Educate and save ourselves and our families and our money from mobs![42]

None of this is meant to argue that culture at the turn of the century was primarily a mechanism for social control. Culture is too variegated, too complex, too human to be tied to one explanatory device. Those who believed in art, music, drama, and parks championed them for a complex of reasons which can only be trivialized by a reductionist view that links them to a single agenda. Concepts of social control, as Gareth Stedman Jones has argued, tend to explain both too much and too little. Indeed, one would be hard put to find an institution that could not, to some degree or another, be seen as an agency of social control.[43] I have emphasized the quest for order because it was an urge common to so wide a range of cultural leaders that it helped to shape the very manner in which people conceived of culture at the turn of the century. That is, it served as a bridge tying together the endeavors of a variety of people with a diversity of motives who labored in a number of cultural areas. But as important as the motif of order was, it was never an end in itself; it was a necessary means to the creation and maintenance of standards that would permit the establishment and appreciation of true culture in the United States: culture free of intrusion, free of dilution, free of the insistent demands of the people and the marketplace; culture that would ennoble, elevate, purify; culture that would provide a refuge from the turmoil, the feelings of alienation, the sense of impotence that were becoming all too common. But if order was a necessary prerequisite for culture it was also one of culture's salutary by-products. If without order there could be no pure culture, it was equally true that without culture there could be no meaningful order. In late nineteenth-century thought the two were so intricately interwoven, so crucial to one another, the circle they formed was so complete, that they could not be easily distinguished.

It is important to recognize the degree of tension in this relationship, which led the arbiters of culture on the one hand to insulate themselves from the masses in order to promote and preserve pure culture, and on the other to reach out to the masses and sow the seeds of culture among them in order to ensure civilized order. For every Frederick Law Olmsted who envisioned Central Park as a great nurturing, transforming medium of culture and civilization, there was doubtless a Henry James who resented the fact that the charming early summer afternoons he spent amid the park's vernal beauty were disrupted by the "hum of that babel of [immigrant] tongues," by "the fruit of the foreign trees as shaken down there with a force that smothered every-thing else." For all the talk about utilizing the institutions of high culture to transform the American people, there were a significant number of those whose desire to spread their culture was offset by the fancy they took to the notion of theaters without gallery gods, opera houses without encore-fiends, parks without proletarians, museums without crowds of meandering, gawking spectators. In 1914 an article in the *Atlantic Monthly* expressed the hope that through the great popularity of the movies "the art of the stage may escape from the proletariat, and again truly belong to those who in a larger, finer sense are 'the great ones of the earth.'" Culture thus could be used as a force with which to proselytize among the people or as an oasis of refuge from and a barrier against them. The ambivalence that these conflicting urges created runs like a thread through the prolonged discussion of culture that became so prominent in the late nineteenth and early twentieth centuries.[44]

This discussion took place in the context of a phenomenon we have already observed. Everywhere in the society of the second half of the nineteenth century American culture was undergoing a process of fragmentation, which prompted Henry Adams and Henry James to issue their complaints about multi-plicity. This multiplication, or fragmentation, was manifest in the rise of professionalization, which left the nation with a be-wildering multiplicity of distinctive professional organizations that gave testimony to the increased specialization, complexity, and atomization of life. It was manifest in residential patterns, which saw people who had once inhabited common ground—albeit not necessarily common conditions—increasingly sepa-rated, as the century progressed, into discrete neighborhoods determined by a combination of economic, social, and ethnic factors. It was manifest in the new immigration, which made an already heterogeneous people look positively homogeneous in comparison to what they were becoming. It was manifest too in the relative decline of a shared public culture, which in the second half of the nineteenth century fractured into a series of discrete cultures that had less and less to do with one another. Theaters, opera houses, museums, auditoriums that had once housed mixed crowds of people experiencing an eclectic blend of expressive culture were increasingly filtering their clientele and their programs so that less and less could one find audiences that cut across the social and economic spectrum enjoying an expressive culture which blended together mixed elements of what we would today call high, low, and folk culture.

There was no better symbol of the growing fragmentation than Chicago's slightly tardy celebration of the quadricentennial of Columbus's voyage. "Since Noah's Ark," Henry Adams commented after spending two weeks at the fair, "no such Babel of loose and ill-joined, such vague and ill-defined and unrelated thoughts and half-thoughts and experimental outcries as the Exposition, had ever ruffled the surface of the Lakes." The World's Columbian Exposition of 1893 was divided into two separate universes: the first was the Court of Honor, or White City, consisting of magnificent classical buildings and monuments gleaming with an impressive facade of plaster constructed to look like marble. The decision of the fair's planners to ignore the modern urban architecture of Chicago and opt for what one critic called a "reactionary and academic neoclassicism," was an accurate reflection of the direction in which the high culture of the period was moving. The second and contrasting universe consisted of the Midway Plaisance, a 600-foot-wide, mile-long avenue that embodied the spirit of a sideshow lined with popular entertainments from around the world including Oriental theaters, German beer gardens, and a Cairo street with veiled Egyptian dancers; villages from Ireland, Japan, Java, Dahomey, and Austria; George Ferris's first great towering wheel, which was to become a recurring feature of fairs and amusement parks; and a multitude of such other popular entertainments as acrobatics, beauty shows, and shopping bazaars. If visitors to the White City heard Paderewski performing Chopin, those on the Midway heard Scott Joplin playing ragtime.[45]

The "common" pleasures of the Midway helped to define the rarified atmosphere of the White City, which became the physical embodiment of the longing of those who looked to culture for relief from American materialism. "As soon as you become a

The ethereal monuments of the Columbian Exposition's White City, 1893.

The more worldly pleasures of the Midway Plaisance, dominated by the industrial presence of the Ferris Wheel. The Moorish Palace, billed as the "greatest show on the grounds," is on the right.

day-inhabitant of the White World, you are emancipated from the troubles of earth," Mary Hartwell Catherwood confessed. But her exultation was laced with concern: "One question I dare not face: What shall we do when this Wonderland is closed?— when it disappears—when the enchantment comes to an end." Richard Watson Gilder's ode to "The Vanishing City" expressed a similar blend of celebration and lament:

> O joy almost too high for saddened mortal!
> O ecstasy envisioned! Thou shouldst be
> Lasting as thou art lovely; as immortal
> . . . . .
> Then vanish, City of Dream, and be no more;
> Soon shall this fair Earth's self be lost on the unknown
>   shore.

The Midway constituted the antithesis to this Citadel of Art. According to the president of the exposition's Board of Directors, the White City was physically separated from the Midway in order to prevent "jarring contrasts" between "the beautiful buildings and grounds and the illimitable exhibits" of the former and "the amusing, distracting, ludicrous, and noisy attractions" of the latter. "To the layman not interested in the arts and sciences," *Frank Leslie's Weekly* commented, the Midway "will remain the great attraction of the fair." The language was revealing: a "layman,"—someone not schooled, not trained, not disciplined in the intricate ways of the arts and sciences—would clearly be better off devoting himself or herself to the simpler pleasures of the Midway. The White City contained the greatest collection of paintings, murals, frescoes, and sculpture ever assembled in the United States, and those who wanted to benefit from the arts so amply available had better be devoted, M. G. Van Rensselaer warned in the *Century Magazine*:

> I know whereof I speak, for I went to [the Paris World's Fair] in 1889 with an insistent need to acquaint myself with modern art. I stayed five weeks . . . I tried to do my duty and I did devote myself especially to the art galleries . . . I left Paris with a sense of shame and defeat . . . I did not really learn about modern art.
>
> Nor, at Chicago, will you learn about the things which are dear to you unless you are very wise and steady, patient and self-denying.[46]

Christopher Lasch has argued that the new professions, which another historian has called the "consensus of the competent," came into being "by reducing the layman to incompetence." A similar development occurred in the realm of high culture, which paralleled the formation of the professions in the late nineteenth century and which, like the new professions, was involved in a quest for cultural authority. Culture had become a manifestly serious and intricate endeavor that few could hope to master. Just as Shakespeare was increasingly portrayed as a complex writer whom readers could comprehend only if they armed themselves with a plethora of study aids, so too was the sophistication and difficulty of all aspects of culture driven home continually. The rural Georgian who attends his first opera in Mary Tucker Magill's short story warns others not to do the same "without bein' prepared by readin' a library . . . Maybe if I had studied it when I was a new born infant, and kept at it stiddy till now, I might like the Grand Opery. As it is it is too much for me." In 1890 the music critic H. E. Krehbiel wrote in exasperation of those many people who willingly admitted that they did not know enough to speak about music. There was a time, he commented, when such an admission "would place the brands of illiteracy and boorishness on the speaker. A cultured Greek of the classical period would as little have dared to say, 'I know nothing about music,' as we would dare to proclaim inability to read our own language." To emulate cultured Greeks proved to be no small task. In 1892, W. J. Henderson addressed a public letter "To Persons Desiring to Cultivate a Taste in Music," which stressed the fact that listening was not enough. One required knowledge of the theory of music, a knowledge of musical form, as well as an understanding of the history of music. "A year of sincere study ought to lift the student far above the level of the commonplace, and enable him to stand where he will hear with the mind as well as the sense. He will not be completely equipped, but he will no longer be of the number of those who, having ears, hear not." Because "people do not turn naturally to the best," Norman Hapgood advised the readers of *Collier's Weekly*, "education is necessary to the appreciation of art." In her ode to "Art's Devotees," Helen Noe warned that "the way of art, beginning smooth and wide" soon "narrows as we go."

> And many falter, faint and sick and weary;
> 　　And many down diverging pathways turn

For those who steadfastly hewed to the True Path, life took an increasingly sober turn:

> No more light laughter leaps in mirthful flurry—
> 　　We are too tired, we only work and pray
> · · · · ·
> With steadfast eyes, with white, set, fearless faces,
> 　　We reach unto the laurel leaves of art.[47]

　　This equation of high art and high seriousness made it difficult for some to consider an irreverent humorist like Mark Twain a cultured writer. Brander Matthews recalled that "the average public opinion" had classified Twain as "a professional humorist . . . a writer whose sole duty it was to make us laugh, and to whom therefore we need never give a second thought after the smile had faded from our faces." Following his lecture tours of the United States, Matthew Arnold wrote in 1888 that the American "addiction to the funny man" illustrated the lack of "the discipline of awe and respect" necessary to the creation of "distinction" in American culture. As late as the 1920s Van Wyck Brooks wrote *The Ordeal of Mark Twain* to demonstrate that "in Mark Twain, the making of the humorist was the undoing of the artist. It meant the suppression of his aesthetic desires, the degradation of everything upon which the creative instinct feeds."[48]

　　In the first chapter we accompanied George William Curtis in 1863 as he took a visiting friend to a play starring the popular actor Edwin Forrest, after one act of whose exuberant, melodramatic style the friend whispered, "I have had as much as I can hold," and they departed for more rarified entertainments. Thirty years later the writer Hamlin Garland, then living in Chicago, visited the Columbian Exposition and was so "amazed at the grandeur of 'The White City'" that he wrote his family on their Dakota farm, "Sell the cookstove if necessary and come. You *must* see this fair." His parents followed his advice and Garland has described the effects of the White City upon his mother.

Stunned by the majesty of the vision, my mother sat in her chair, visioning it all yet comprehending little of its meaning. Her life had been spent among homely small things, and these gorgeous scenes dazzled her, overwhelmed her, letting in upon her in one mighty flood a thousand stupefying suggestions of the art and history and poetry of the world . . .

At last utterly overcome she leaned her head against my arm, closed her eyes and said, "Take me home, I can't stand any more of it."[49]

In the impatient "I have had as much as I can hold," of Curtis's friend and the exhausted "I can't stand any more of it," of Garland's mother, we can catch a glimpse of cultural worlds moving farther and farther apart; worlds with less and less tolerance for or understanding of each other.

This cultural gulf was reflected in and deepened by the preoccupation with discussing, defining, and categorizing culture that characterized the period. The Civil War was over for only two years when the New England man of letters and former Union colonel Thomas Wentworth Higginson issued "A Plea for Culture," a term he defined in a resolutely classical and European-oriented manner and often used with the adjective "high" appended. For Higginson culture involved "the training and finishing of the whole man," the pursuit of science and art as objects of "intrinsic worth," the elevation "of the fine arts above the useful arts," for "carpentry and upholstery, good as a beginning, are despicable as an ending." What cultivated person, he asked, "would not prefer poorer lodgings and better galleries," would not choose "nobler living" over material comforts? Higginson offered a bleak portrait of his nation's contemporary cultural state: "American literature is not yet copious, American scholarship not profound, American society not highly intellectual, and the American style of execution, in all high arts, yet hasty and superficial . . . Our brains as yet lie chiefly in our machine-shops." "What we need," Higginson asserted, "is the opportunity of high culture somewhere." Culture required training. Our "leaders of public affairs" might be self-made men but our literary leaders had usually "tumbled about in a library" as children and were "college-bred." Because America had the wealth and human material necessary for a cultured state, Higginson predicted that only an interval of time "lies between the America of toil and the America of art."[50] In all but his staunch optimism, Higginson's plea was an accurate forecast of the discussion that followed.

It was a discussion based upon the conviction that a genuine American culture had not yet emerged. "There is no such thing as a distinctively American art," *Frank Leslie's Illustrated Newspaper* complained in 1883. "Our art, like our literature and drama, halt before the foreigners, and an American opera has yet to be written." Some felt this was the case because of the nation's youth: "The American soil is not yet rich enough to grow a luxuriant plant," *Appleton's Journal* declared in 1869. "The vital forces of American growth do not tend, as yet, in the direction of culture; nor is it well they should. We have first to complete our triumphs over the material." In 1880 the *New York Times* asked, "Why should we flatter what is known as the general American taste? It is too young yet . . . let it rather be supposed to be as a sheet of wax, quite ready to receive any impressions." Such evolutionary analyses tended to be optimistic. George Templeton Strong was convinced that "in the course of time . . . we shall have our poets, and that we have as fair a chance of producing the next Dante or Milton or Shakespeare as any other nation."[51]

Others were less optimistic, agreeing with Henry James's litany of American deficiencies: "no cathedrals, nor abbeys, nor little Norman churches; no great Universities nor public schools—no Oxford, nor Eton, nor Harrow; no literature, no novels, no museum, no pictures . . . ," and with his devastating conclusion that Americans had "the elements of modern man with *culture* quite left out."* It was quite left out because as a people Americans lacked refinement and their democratic society militated against their remedying the deficiency. Charles Eliot Norton echoed James in 1889, asserting that "of all civilized nations,"

---

*James's 1879 list of American deficiences was reminiscent of the Reverend Sydney Smith's famous acerbic statement, printed in the *Edinburgh Review* more than half a century earlier, which began: "In the four quarters of the globe, who reads an American book? or goes to an American play? or looks at an American picture or statue?"

the United States was "the most deficient in the higher culture of the mind, and not in the culture only but also in the conditions on which this culture mainly depends." In 1843 James Fenimore Cooper felt very much in the minority when he maintained that "This is no country for arts or letters . . . Public opinion drags every thing to its own level, up or down, forming a very reputable mediocrity, but a mediocrity after all." By the late nineteenth century, Cooper's lament was widely heard. Wealth was sufficient to create "art of the mere decorative kind," O. B. Frothingham wrote in 1882, but "art of an ideal, imaginative kind it originates not." True art required standards and authority of a kind that was difficult to find in a country with America's leveling, practical tendencies. If America wanted culture it needed to encourage "the man of high aesthetic nature and cultivation" who, the Boston music critic William F. Apthorp wrote in 1875, "has an almost divine right to exercise and nourish his superior faculties in what most transcendent manner he can. Let the mediocre majority feed after him, even on the crumbs that fall from his table, if need be." The worst thing that could happen would be to harness these cultured individuals to "the yoke of public instruction" and force them to become mere teachers for the benefit of "plodding mankind."[52]

In the first half of the nineteenth century it was common to find such central cultural figures as the publisher George Putnam or the historian George Bancroft arguing vigorously that it was the artist's obligation to be a teacher and actively communicate with the people. As we have seen in the career of Theodore Thomas, this emphasis upon popular education diminished toward the end of the century. Increasingly it was asserted that cultivated people were needed not as educators but as leaders, as examples. Each Cultured Man would in effect become his own City on a Hill. The society's real obligation was to do everything in its power to enhance the already enlightened few. "Let our leaders in opinion be as perfect as possible," Apthorp argued. "Culture is infectious. Where the most highly cultivated nucleus exists, there will be the highest general cultivation. Nothing is more fatal to general culture than that intellectual and aesthetic communism which would have the foremost wait until those who lag behind shall have caught up with him." The real peril

America faced, *The Outlook* declared in 1893, was not a dearth of art but the acceptance of inferior standards. "We are in danger of exalting the average man, and rejoicing in . . . mediocrity." The true American is "he who demands the best in life, manners, and art, and who will rest satisfied with nothing less than the best." Americans, a writer in the Chicago journal the *Dial* lamented in 1914, had deceived themselves into believing they were "good enough," had become "neglectful of the best in human thought, the highest in human endeavor," and "contemptuous of those strenuous paths which lead us towards, though never quite to, a rounded perfection of mind and soul." Americans had to learn that the only real test of worth was "centered in authority,—the authority of the trained judgment of the wisest and the best." In his plea for elevating the American theater, T. R. Sullivan charged that "the general public is an ass, and will as tenderly be led by the nose as asses are. The one thing needful is to lead it in the right direction." "We are not a critical people," Aline Gorren wrote in 1898. "We have need of the philosopher-critic to cultivate in us, finally, a deep feeling for . . . art and literature." Arguing that American civilization "is a crowd civilization," Gerald Stanley Lee then proceeded logically: "The only beauty of art or life that such a civilization can produce must be produced by making the crowd beautiful. The crowd can only be made beautiful by the great man in it. A man can only be great by being . . . an artist . . . He sees so much that he makes us all see. He is the lifter of the horizons in which we live our lives . . . He is the playwright over us all. He shall master the crowd and make it beautiful."[53]

For the *New York Times'* music critic, W. J. Henderson, the first step toward such mastery was the suppression of the unworthy. When a reader asked him how the standard of music in the United States might best be improved, his answer was simple: "The way to elevate is to elevate," to keep the people face to face with the best by eradicating everything less than the best:

> First of all, abolish the music halls in which vulgar tunes set to still more vulgar words provide the musical milk upon which the young of the masses are reared. Abolish the diabolical street pianos and hand organs which disseminate these vile tunes in all directions and which reduce the musical taste of the children in the residence streets to the level of that of the Australian bushman, who thinks

noise and rhythm are music. Abolish the genuine American brand of burlesque . . . and the genuine American "comic opera" . . . Abolish the theatre orchestra which plays the music hall stuff . . . Abolish those newspapers which degrade art by filling their columns with free advertising of so-called musical performers who are of the genus freak.

There were doubtless many who agreed with Henderson. In 1900 Harry Thurston Peck spent several pages of *Cosmopolitan* arguing that the *opera bouffe* of Offenbach played a vital role in creating the moral and social decadence that undermined the France of Napoleon III and warned that the United States faced a similar peril. "I have often wondered whether some kind of a censorship could not be established in this country; for there is no country in the world which needs a censorship so much." Ultimately, neither Henderson, nor Peck, nor anyone else produced a viable plan for the wholesale abolition or censorship of popular culture. Reliance, therefore, remained on steadfastly upholding the ideal in the face of a Philistine majority. Courtenay Guild, who was elected president of Boston's Handel and Haydn Society in 1915, spoke with dismay of the new "talking machines," which were becoming substitutes for attending concerts and which helped to spread the "mania for dancing and syncopated time" that cultivated "a taste for a sort of barbarous sequence of sounds that is more worthy of savages than of civilization." However disheartened he was, Guild's belief that such "depraved musical taste" could not conceivably be more than ephemeral, convinced him that "there is an especial responsibility on us to hold fast to the highest musical and artistic standards in the performance of the class of music to which we devote our energies."* [54]

---

*Although this cultural Utopianism may have been the creation of conservative elites, it became part of the intellectual equipment of many on the left later in this century. David Horowitz, who was the child of members of the Communist Party, recalled what his father taught him about music in the 1940s: "I remember him saying that the saxophone is not a real instrument . . . There was a right music, and jazz, and certainly popular music, were all capitalistic expressions. In my adolescent mind there was a day when the Revolution would come, and there would be no popular music. This music would be gone. Everybody would listen to Beethoven."

Thus in spite of the flood of rhetoric embracing the task of converting the unwashed masses to true culture, the spokesmen for culture at the turn of the century were less missionaries than conservators, less bent upon eradicating the cultural gap between themselves and the majority than on steadfastly maintaining that gap as they came increasingly to subscribe to a Gresham's Law of Culture, convinced that without taking every precaution, the bad would inevitably drive out the good. In 1877 the *Atlantic Monthly* distinguished between "false culture" and "real culture" and reminded its readers that not everyone had the capacity to acquire culture: "Any wood may be varnished, but not every sort receives polish; and so it is with men and women." Such distinctions were ubiquitous during these decades. John Sullivan Dwight labored to teach his readers to distinguish between "pure art" and "skill," between "mere music and the art of music." W. J. Stillman attempted to distinguish between journalism and literature, observing that "men are divided into journalists and eternalists, ephemera and immortals . . . the ephemera have the immense majority, and until human nature changes are likely to have." James Ford warned of the dangers of "imitation culture," which he called "culterine," and its subproducts, "artine, prosaline, and versaline," all of which were defined by being too fashionable and too accessible. In 1895 the *Independent* urged its fellow "quality magazines" not to compete with such periodicals as *Cosmopolitan*, which had just reduced its price to ten cents, but instead to maintain their "higher, purer" literary standards: "The fit audience in an educated country like ours is not few, but it is not yet unlimited; nevertheless, it is the only audience worth addressing, for it contains the thinking people." Peering into a shop window displaying the sheet music of such popular songs as "Everybody Works but Father," and "Keep a Little Cosey Corner in Your Heart for Me," a *Collier's* editorial writer in 1905 thought immediately of Sir Edward Fry's aphorism: "Whatever popularizes vulgarizes." Culture, Katharine Fullerton Gerould admitted without apology in 1915, "is not a democratic achievement, because culture is inherently snobbish. 'Contact with the best that has been said and thought in the world' makes people intellectually exclusive, and makes them draw distinctions." As long as democracy was confined to politics "culture is left free to select its groups and proclaim its hierarchies," but once extend the "I am as good as you are" formula beyond politics, "and culture, with its eternal distinction-making will naturally die" for culture induces "a mighty scorn of those who do not know enough to be humble before the Masters."[55]

INEVITABLY, in a heterogeneous nation in which the working classes were more and more composed of recent immigrant groups and migrant blacks, the ideology of culture assumed ethnic and racial dimensions. Indeed, as early as Jenny Lind's triumphant tour of the United States in the 1850s, racial factors began to play a role in the reception of music. According to the *New York Herald*, Lind's wonderful voice "never could be fed on anything warmer than cold air . . . Her organization is suited to please the people of our cold climate. She will have triumphs here that never would attend her progress through France or Italy." "The wand of civilization" the *Herald* proclaimed, had passed to "the hardy northern races." The Swedish soprano's appeal to Americans, John Sullivan Dwight speculated, was based not only on her magnificent talent but also on her northern European origins. "The South has had its turn; it has fulfilled its mission; the other end of the balance now comes up. The Northern Muse must sing her lesson to the world. Her fresher, chaster, more intellectual, and . . . colder strains come in due season to recover our souls from the delicious languor of a music which . . . has degenerated into mere sensibility, and a very cheap kind of superficial, skin-deep excitability." The mood established by Lind's visit survived her departure. The narrator of Gail Hamilton's short story "Camilla's Concert" (1863) stood by her window listening to an Italian organ-grinder whose lilting music transported her to moonlit Venetian waterways. Such romantic visions, she realized, were not natural to the "Vikings of this frigid Norseland." America's musical needs and tastes were those of a rising not a fading civilization. "Go away . . . from my window, Giuseppe," she commanded the street musician, "the air is growing deep and chilly, and I do not sleep in the shadows of broken temples."[56]

Italian opera, which had been dominant in the first half of the century, came under attack in the second. In 1857 the *Atlantic Monthly* claimed that Italian opera, promoted by a group of "musical Jew-brokers," constituted not an art but "merely a few singers lifted up on the cheapest platform of an opera." A year later the *Atlantic* asserted that "the passionate music of Italy" was the music of "hand organs," which "electrifies our cooler blood, but it does not express our feelings nor in any way represent our character." Writing of America's "Italophobia" in 1879, William Francis Allen spoke "not for myself alone, but as one of a class," in maintaining that Italians "have by no manner of means reached so high a degree of development in the art of musical composition as the Germans have." The German masters, he insisted, "appeal to the feelings in a far higher way than the Italians." In 1884 the *New York Daily Tribune* dismissed Italian opera as "the sweetmeats of the hurdy-gurdy repertory." "Say Highbrow," wrote Simeon Strunsky in 1915, "and you think at once of German music." From 1884 to 1891 the Metropolitan Opera Company presented German-language opera exclusively, performing all operas, including French and Italian, in German. In the first twenty years after its opening season of 1883–84, more than a third of its presentations were Wagnerian operas. During its first fifty years, the company continued to perform Wagner more frequently than any of the Italian masters. Although John Sullivan Dwight could never reconcile himself to Wagner's music, which he attacked regularly, most of the Guardians of Culture hailed Wagner as a force for civilizing America, moderating its crude materialism, and countering the naive power of wealth with the cosmopolitan power of Culture. "Musical history," Mabel Dodge proclaimed, with Wagner very much in mind, "is the history of the race."[57]

The attempt to downgrade Italian music was related to the even firmer insistence that the music of Asia, Africa, Eastern Europe, and of the North American Indian peoples, hardly qualified as culture. In 1918 the *New Orleans Times-Picayune* denied the widely accepted notion that people were either musical or non-musical. In fact, there were "many mansions in the houses of the muses." There was the "great assembly hall of melody" where "most of us take our seats." There were the "inner sanctuaries of harmony" where a lesser number enjoyed "truly great music." Finally, there was still one more apartment

> down in the basement, a kind of servants' hall of rhythm. It is there we hear the hum of the Indian dance, the throb of the Oriental tambourines and kettledrums, the clatter of the clogs, the click of Slavic heels, the thumpty-tumpty of the negro banjo, and, in fact, the native dances of the world.

Rhythm, though often associated with melody and harmony, "is not necessarily music," the *Times-Picayune* instructed its readers. Indeed, when rhythm took such forms as ragtime or jazz it constituted an "atrocity in polite society, and . . . we should make it a point of civic honor to suppress it. Its musical value is nil, and its possibilities of harm are great."[58]

The crusade for culture in America, then, was to a significant extent a struggle to bring into fruition on a new continent what the crusaders considered the traditional civilization from which the earliest Americans sprang and to which all Americans were heir. The primary obstacle to the emergence of a worthy American music, Frederick Nast asserted in 1881, "lies in the diverse character of our population . . . American music can not be expected until the present discordant elements are merged into a homogeneous people." It was obvious under whose auspices the "merger" was to take place. In 1898 Sidney Lanier argued that it was time for Americans to move back "into the presence of the Fathers" by adding the study of Old English to that of Greek and Latin, and by reading not just *The Odyssey* but *Beowulf.* "Our literature needs Anglo-Saxon iron; there is no ruddiness in its cheeks, and everywhere a clear lack of the red corpuscles." American society, Henry Adams observed in his autobiography, "offered the profile of a long, straggling caravan, stretching loosely towards the prairies, its few score of leaders far in advance and its millions of immigrants, negroes, and Indians far in the rear, somewhere in archaic time."[59]

It should hardly surprise us that such attitudes informed the adjectival categories created in the late nineteenth century to define types of culture. "Highbrow," first used in the 1880s to describe intellectual or aesthetic superiority, and "lowbrow," first used shortly after 1900 to mean someone or something neither "highly intellectual" or "aesthetically refined," were derived from the phrenological terms "highbrowed" and "lowbrowed," which were prominently featured in the nineteenth-century practice of determining racial types and intelligence by measuring cranial shapes and capacities. A familiar illustration of the period depicted the distinctions between the lowbrowed ape and the increasingly higher brows of the "Human Idiot," the "Bushman," the "Uncultivated," the "Improved," the "Civilized," the "Enlightened," and, finally, the "Caucasian," with the highest brow of all. The categorization did not end this broadly, of course, for within the Caucasian circle there were distinctions to be made: the closer to western and northern Europe a people came, the higher their brows extended. From the time of their formulation, such cultural categories as highbrow and lowbrow were hardly meant to be neutral descriptive terms; they were openly associ-

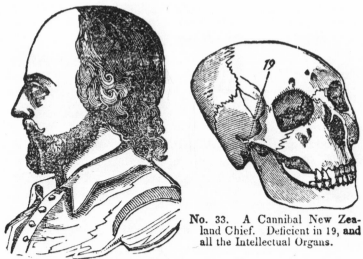

No. 33.   A Cannibal New Zealand Chief.   Deficient in 19, and all the Intellectual Organs.

No. 32.   Portrait of Shakspeare.

This typical illustration from *Coombs' Popular Phrenology*, 1865, demonstrates the widespread interest in the shape and measurement of brows. The high brows of such figures as Shakespeare, Milton, and Dickens, especially when contrasted with the pitifully low brows of alien races, became emblematic of culture and intelligence.

ated with and designed to preserve, nurture, and extend the cultural history and values of a particular group of peoples in a specific historical context.[60]

Increasingly, in the closing decades of the nineteenth century, as public life became everywhere more fragmented, the concept of culture took on hierarchical connotations along the lines of Matthew Arnold's definition of culture—"the best that has been thought and known in the world . . . the study and pursuit of perfection." The Englishman Arnold, whose critical writings preceded his trips to America in 1883 and 1886, did not discover a *tabula rasa* in America; he found many eager constituents here from the very beginning. Two years before Arnold's *Culture and Anarchy* was published, *Harper's* maintained that certain authors were "not only tests of taste but even of character." If a man gave himself to Shakespeare or Chaucer, "we have a clew to the man."

> The man who among all Operas prefers Don Giovanni, or Fidelio, or the Barber of Seville, or Robert le Diable, involuntarily unveils himself as he makes his preference known. He rises or falls, he is near or far in our regard just as he instinctively likes or rejects what you feel to be best.

Nevertheless, Arnold was perhaps the single most significant disseminator of such attitudes and had an enormous influence in the United States.* The Arnold important to America was not Arnold the critic, Arnold the poet, Arnold the religious thinker, but Arnold the Apostle of Culture. "I shall not go so far as to say of Mr. Arnold that he invented" the concept of culture, Henry James commented in 1884, "but he made it more definite than it had been before — he vivified and lighted it up." Arnold had his detractors. Walt Whitman dismissed him as "one of the dudes of literature," and complained to Horace Traubel that Arnold

---

*In his scholarly assessment of Arnold's influence in the United States, John Henry Raleigh concluded that "Arnold's success in America was immediate, far-reaching, and lasting. In the academic world in particular he has become a fixed star. It would not be an overstatement to say, as several nineteenth century admirers of Arnold did say, that he had perhaps more readers in America than he had in England itself."

brought to the world what the world already had a surfeit of—
"delicacy, refinement, elegance, prettiness, propriety, criticism,
analysis: all of them things which threaten to overwhelm us."
Whitman was in the minority. More typical was William H.
Dawson, who proclaimed in 1904, sixteen years after Arnold's
death, "There is today a cult of Matthew Arnold; it is growing;
it must grow. It will grow." "Why does nobody any more mention Arnold's name?" Ludwig Lewisohn asked in 1927 and
replied that it was because Arnold's views had become completely
absorbed in the mainstream of American thought.[61]

The ubiquitous discussion of the meaning and nature of culture, informed by Arnold's views, was one in which adjectives
were used liberally. "High," "low," "rude," "lesser," "higher,"
"lower," "beautiful," "modern," "legitimate," "vulgar," "popular," "true," "pure," "highbrow," "lowbrow" were applied to such
nouns as "arts" or "culture" almost *ad infinitum*. Though plen-
tiful, the adjectives were not random. They clustered around a
congeries of values, a set of categories that defined and distinguished culture vertically, that created hierarchies which were to
remain meaningful for much of this century. That they are categories which to this day we have difficulty defining with any
precision does not negate their influence. Central terms like
"culture" changed their meaning, or at least their emphasis, in
the second half of the nineteenth century. In early nineteenth-
century editions of Webster's dictionary the primary definition
of *culture* was agricultural: "The act of tilling and preparing the
earth for crops; cultivation; . . . The application of labor or other
means in producing; as the *culture* of corn, or grass." By the
second half of the nineteenth century, while the agricultural
definitions held, *culture* was defined as "the state of being cultivated . . . refinement of mind or manners." Words like "enlightenment," "discipline," "mental and moral training," and "civilization," cropped up freely in the definitions. The word *cultivate*,
in addition to its agricultural meaning, was defined as "to civilize;
as to *cultivate* the untamed savage." In 1898 *The People's Webster
Pronouncing Dictionary and Spelling Guide*, a pocket dictionary of
23,000 words with single-word definitions, defined "culture"
simply as "refinement." By 1919 *Webster's Army and Navy Dictionary* and an elementary school edition of *Webster's New Stan-*

dard Dictionary armed American servicemen and school children with precisely the same succinct definition.[62]

It was this concept of culture that Henry James had in mind when, some thirty years after the Astor Place Riot, he pronounced it a manifestation of the "instinctive hostility of barbarism to culture." The new meanings that became attached to such words as "art," "aesthetics," and "culture" in the second half of the nineteenth century symbolized the consciousness that conceived of the fine, the worthy, and the beautiful as existing apart from ordinary society. In 1894 Hiram M. Stanley defined the "masses" as those whose sole delight rested in "eating, drinking, smoking, society of the other sex, with dancing, music of a noisy and lively character, spectacular shows, and athletic exhibitions." Anyone demonstrating "a permanent taste for higher pleasures," Stanley argued, "ceases, *ipso facto*, to belong to the 'masses.'" This practice of distinguishing "culture" from lesser forms of expression became so common that by 1915 Van Wyck Brooks concluded that between the highbrow and the lowbrow "there is no community, no genial middle ground." "What side of American life is not touched by this antithesis?" Brooks asked. "What explanation of American life is more central or more illuminating?" The process that had seen the noun "class" take on a series of hierarchical adjectives—"lower," "middle," "upper," "working"—in the late eighteenth and early nineteenth centuries was operative for the noun "culture" a hundred years later. Just as the former development mirrored the economic changes brought about by the Industrial Revolution in England so the latter reflected the cultural consequences of modernization.[63]

Walt Whitman consistently fought this new cultural hierarchy. He insisted that culture should not be "restricted by conditions ineligible to the masses," should not be created "for a single class alone, or for the parlors or lecture-rooms," and placed his hopes for the creation of a classless, democratic culture in the leadership of the new "middling" groups—"men and women with occupations, well-off owners of houses and acres, and with cash in the bank." The groups to which Whitman turned were neither willing nor able to fulfill his expectations. The emergence of the new middle and upper-middle classes, created by rapid industrialization in the nineteenth century, seems to have accelerated rather than inhibited the growing distinctions between elite and mass culture. When, in the waning years of the century, Thorstein Veblen constructed his concept of conspicuous consumption, he included not only the obvious material possessions but also "immaterial" goods—"the knowledge of dead languages and the occult sciences; of correct spelling; of syntax and prosody; of the various forms of domestic music . . . of the latest proprieties of dress, furniture, and equipage"; of the ancient "classics"—all of which constituted a conspicuous culture that helped confer legitimacy on the newly emergent groups. This helps explain the vogue during this period of manuals of etiquette, of private libraries and rare books, of European art and music displayed and performed in ornate—often neoclassical—museums and concert halls.[64]

When the Englishman Henry Brougham maintained in 1835 that "learning and improvement make their way in society . . . in one way, and that downwards," he was putting forth a doctrine that many in the United States would embrace by the turn of the century. "You begin by making the upper classes aware of the value of certain kinds of knowledge," Brougham argued, then "the middle parts of the middle class get well acquainted with the subject and feel its importance . . . and they try, by their exertions and their money . . . to spread to the class below them a little of the same feeling, the same love of learning, which they possess themselves; and so that lower class gets by degrees impregnated itself."[65] It was a comforting notion; one that many Americans came to indulge themselves in: that by pursuing their own cultural pleasures and creating institutions after their own fashion, they would in the long haul benefit all classes of society. It was the cultural version of a financial doctrine that such reformers as William Jennings Bryan would label the "trickle down" theory: take care of those on top and those on the bottom would ultimately prosper while the entire society blossomed. The problem, of course, was that the trickle-down theory was no less simplistic in the cultural arena than it was in the financial. It masked the ambivalences of those that espoused it even from themselves.

Elsewhere I have argued that the master class in the antebellum South had an unconscious stake in seeing their African slaves maintain much of their cultural distinctiveness since it was far more difficult to justify the enslavement of a kindred folk than of a people whose behavior patterns were sufficiently different to allow them to be branded with such commonly used epithets as "primitive," "barbaric," and "childlike."[66] A similar argument might be advanced concerning cultural differences in the late nineteenth century. Once again we can find an elite group with a vested interest—unconscious though it may have been—in welcoming and maintaining the widening cultural gaps that increasingly characterized the United States. Despite all of the rhetoric to the contrary, despite all of the laments about the low state of mass culture, there were comforts to be derived from the situation as well. Lift the people out of their cultural milieu, wipe them clean, elevate their tastes, and where in this world of burgeoning democracy was one to locate distinctiveness? How could one justify any longer the disparate conditions in which the various classes lived and worked? This concern was by no means a monopoly of the old genteel classes. Indeed, the culture they prized and approved of offered much to the newly rich— who, while themselves mostly from the solid middle classes, were nevertheless distinguished from the larger mass less by pedigree than by their life style, manners, and cultural artifacts—and was equally attractive to significant segments of the new professional and middle classes who lacked any bedrock of security and needed to distance themselves, culturally at least, from those below them on the socioeconomic scale. The cloak of culture— approved, sanctified, conspicuous culture—promised to become a carapace impervious to assault from above or below.

This is not to say that there were no aesthetic factors involved in the shaping of high culture; of course there were, and they were of central importance, as I trust this book makes clear. There is little to be gained from giving historical legitimacy to a familiar caricature: corpulent millionaires sleeping while their overdressed wives chat in opulent boxes to the background noise of opera singers and symphonic performers who were appreciated primarily by a handful of the gentility and some educated professionals. Such scenes may have taken place, but falsity does not reside only in what never happened at all; it is often more pernicious when it is sheltered in those events that did take place but that explain too little. Some of those who helped to build the impressive array of artistic and musical institutions in late nineteenth-century America may have come initially to play but many of them stayed to pray. They were converted to the substantial structures they helped to erect; they came to care about, and give themselves to, the institutions and the performances they joined together with the older gentry to create and sustain. The roots of the new high culture cannot be explained exclusively by the quest for legitimacy on the part of the newer groups and the drive for continued hegemony on the part of the older elites who were losing their grip on political and economic authority; there were also aesthetic questions and attitudes that were fundamental. But aesthetics by themselves cannot account for the nature of the mores and the institutions that accompanied the developing high culture; these were shaped by the entire context—social, cultural, and economic—in which that development took place. It should not really surprise us that the thrust of the Mugwumps—those independent Republicans whose devotion to the cause of orderly and efficient civil service reform led them to desert their own party in the election of 1884—was not confined to the political sphere. Once we understand that the drive for political order was paralleled by a drive for cultural order, that the push to organize the economic sphere was paralleled by a push to organize the cultural sphere, that the quest for social authority ("the control of action through the giving of commands") was paralleled by a quest for cultural authority ("the construction of reality through definitions of fact and value"),* we can begin to place the cultural dynamics of the turn of the century in clearer perspective.[67]

The British historian Eric Hobsbawm has demonstrated that the period from 1870 to 1914 was a particularly prolific one for

---

*The definitions are those of the sociologist Paul Starr who goes on to write: "Though they are often combined, social authority need not entail cultural authority. Subjects may obey a government while privately rejecting its claims as untrue or unjust. And cultural authority need not always entail authority over conduct. The priest or scientist may be authoritative about morals or nature, but may be restricted by convention from addressing, much less regulating, specific choices and actions."

what he and his associates have called "invented tradition," a set of symbolic ritual practices that function to inculcate values and behavior patterns signifying continuity with the past. Nineteenth-century America, of course, was a fertile ground for these attempts to fix certain aspects of the shifting landscape of modernity into an unchanging relationship with a symbolic past. One thinks almost automatically of the political icons that illustrate this process: the Pilgrim Fathers, George Washington and the cherry tree, the Liberty Bell, the Great Rail Splitter, the Fourth of July, Uncle Sam, the Statue of Liberty. The invention of tradition was not confined to the political arena. I have attempted to illustrate the process by which a familiar cultural syndrome was invented, and institutions designed to maintain and perpetuate it. Hobsbawm has observed that "the crucial informal device for stratifying a theoretically open and expanding system was the self-selection of acceptable social partners." There were, of course, many ways to achieve this, especially in a country like the United States, where fraternal and religious organizations were so abundant and so important. But there can be little doubt that the creation of the institutions and criteria of high culture was a primary means of social, intellectual, and aesthetic separation and selection. Here one learned not only how to appreciate art but also how to behave while doing so. Here one became part of a long-standing cultural tradition that linked one not only to the eras of Bach, Mozart, Haydn, Shakespeare, and Beethoven, but—through the art museums—to the classical epochs of Rome, Greece, and beyond.[68]

This linkage was real enough; people actually did experience aspects of those eras by learning to appreciate their expressive culture. What was invented in the late nineteenth century were the rituals accompanying that appreciation; what was invented was the illusion that the aesthetic products of high culture were originally created to be appreciated in precisely the manner late nineteenth-century Americans were taught to observe: with reverent, informed, disciplined seriousness. The Mozart who wrote his father in 1787, after attending a ball, that he had witnessed "with the greatest pleasure all these people flying about with such delight to the music of my *Figaro* transformed into quadrilles and waltzes," the Mozart who commented in another letter to his father, referring to his opera *Idomeneo*, "As for what is called popular taste, do not be uneasy, for in my opera there is music for every class, except the long-eared," the Mozart who observed that his concertos were "a happy medium between what is too easy and what is too difficult," that Mozart was dead. The Mozart who had become a symbol of divine artistic genius and a purveyor of cultivated taste was firmly in place by the late nineteenth century.[69]

Max Weber observed that one of the consequences of what he called a "status order" was the constant attempt to hinder the free development of the market; to withhold certain goods from free exchange by monopolization, "which may be effected either legally or conventionally."[70] Whatever validity this observation may have for economic history, it does help us to understand what happened to culture toward the turn of the century. When Shakespeare, opera, art, and music were subject to free exchange, as they had been for much of the nineteenth century, they became the property of many groups, the companion of a wide spectrum of other cultural genres, and thus their power to bestow distinction was diminished, as was their power to please those who insisted on enjoying them in privileged circumstances, free from the interference of other cultural groups and the dilution of other cultural forms. As long as they remained shared culture, the manner of their presentation and reception was determined in part by the market, that is, by the demands of the heterogeneous audience. They were in effect "rescued" from the marketplace, and therefore from the mixed audience and from the presence of other cultural genres; they were removed from the pressures of everyday economic and social life, and placed, significantly, in concert halls, opera houses, and museums that often resembled temples, to be perused, enjoyed and protected by the initiated— those who had the inclination, the leisure, and the knowledge to appreciate them.

This was by no means an absolute monopoly. The symphony hall, opera house, and museum were never declared off limits to anyone. Admission to art museums was inexpensive and often free, and tickets to concerts, opera, and what became known as "legitimate" drama, while sometimes dear, were nonetheless available. But after the turn of the century there was one price that had to be paid: these cultural products *had* to be accepted on the terms proffered by those who controlled the cultural institutions. In that sense, while there was never a total monopoly of access, there was a tight control over the terms of access. The taste that now prevailed was that of one segment of the social and economic spectrum which convinced itself and the nation at large that its way of seeing, understanding, and appreciating music, theater, and art was the only legitimate one; that *this* was the way Shakespeare, Beethoven, and Greek sculpture were meant to be experienced and in fact *had* been experienced always by those of culture and discernment. The accomplishment of the patrons of culture at the turn of the century was not only that they were now able to experience the expressive culture they appreciated, performed, and presented in ways they thought proper, but that everyone had to experience them in these ways as well. They became both the promoters and the arbiters of this corner of the cultural world and gradually appropriated the term "culture" itself, which in the popular parlance came more and more to signify the high arts.

I N 1912 the editor of *Harper's Magazine*, arguing against school authorities in Massachusetts who wanted to censor movies because they corrupted youth, maintained "there is no high, no low," but then thought better of it and added, "or if not quite that, there is nothing too high or too low"—a very different proposition. Movies, the editor maintained, though superior to musical comedies or commercial plays, remained a low form of popular entertainment that might through imaginative use become a force for education, though obviously never a form of art. A year later the *Nation* indulged in a similar reversal. It opened its article on the film with praise, observing that while in the world of the theater the subject of "technique" was one for "professionals and highbrows," in the world of the movie it was a subject for the masses:

> The crowd discusses the technique of the moving-picture theatre
> with as much interest as literary salons in Paris or London discuss

the minutiae of the higher drama. The crowd knows how the films are made, and what it costs to make them, and who the leading actors in the show are. The producers of these shows have achieved an extraordinary triumph. They have converted their entire audience into first-nighters.

Significantly, the *Nation* concluded by negating the interesting point it had just made, reminding readers that movies were "not a very high art," that they revealed "the common predilection of the popular taste for the lurid and the fantastic," and required "no thought and little attention." The straining for complexity engaged in by these and many other commentators was frustrated by the rigid orthodoxies already well established.[71]

The exaggerated antithesis between art and life, between the aesthetic and the Philistine, the worthy and the unworthy, the pure and the tainted, embodied in the host of adjectival categories so firmly established at the turn of the century, has unquestionably colored our view of culture ever since. Still, it is important not to commit the error of accepting this antithesis literally and assuming that everything vaguely called "cultural" was now monopolized by one class, by one group in the society. People have as much difficulty existing in a cultural or aesthetic limbo as in any other kind. When the art forms that had constituted a shared culture for much of the nineteenth century became less accessible to large segments of the American people, millions of them satisfied their aesthetic cravings through a number of the new forms of expressive culture that were barred from high culture by the very fact of their accessibility to the masses: the blues, jazz or jazz-derived music, musical comedy, photography, comic strips, movies, radio, popular comedians, all of which, though relegated to the nether world culturally, in fact frequently contained much that was fresh, exciting, innovative, intellectually challenging, and highly imaginative. If there is a tragedy in this development, it is not only that millions of Americans were now separated from exposure to such creators as Shakespeare, Beethoven, and Verdi, whom they had enjoyed in various formats for much of the nineteenth century, but also that the rigid cultural categories, once they were in place, made it so difficult for so long for so many to understand the value and importance of the popular art forms that were all around them. Too many of those who considered themselves educated and cultured lost for a significant period—and many still have not regained—their ability to discriminate independently, to sort things out for themselves and understand that simply because a form of expressive culture was widely accessible and highly popular it was not therefore necessarily devoid of any redeeming value or artistic merit.

For most of the nineteenth century a number of forms of artistic expression—Shakespearean dramas, *bel canto* operas, novels by authors like Dickens and Twain, poems by Longfellow and Lowell, certain forms of painting and sculpture—were able to enjoy simultaneously high cultural status and mass popularity. By the twentieth century this was less and less true. This is not to suggest the existence of an idyllic era when the American people experienced a cultural unity devoid of tensions. In the nineteenth century folk paintings of Edward Hicks, the wolf and the lamb, the lion and the fatling, the leopard and the kid, might occupy the same territory in harmony, but reality was more complex—as Hicks and his countrymen well knew. Still, the United States in the first half of the nineteenth century did experience greater cultural sharing in the sense that cultural lines were more fluid, cultural spaces less rigidly subdivided, than they were to become. When George Templeton Strong sat down with his diary to record his reactions to the death of Charles Dickens in 1870, he found no ready-made cultural category sufficient to sum up the novelist and was forced to deal with the kaleidoscopic, complex strands of Dickens's work and following: "His genius was unquestionable; his art and method were often worthy of the lowest writer of serials for Sunday papers . . . Few men since Shakespeare have enriched the language with so many phrases that are in everyone's mouth . . . I feel Charles Dickens's death as that of a personal friend, though I never even saw him and though there was so much coarseness and flabbiness in his style of work." Compare this with Virgil Thomson's reaction to George Gershwin in 1935: "I don't mind his being a light composer, and I don't mind his trying to be a serious one. But I do mind his falling between two stools."[72]

Certainly, what I have called a shared public culture did not disappear with the nineteenth century. Twentieth-century Americans, especially in the palaces they built to the movies and in their sporting arenas, continued to share public space and public culture. But with a difference. Cultural space became more sharply defined, more circumscribed, and less flexible than it had been. Americans might sit together to watch the same films and athletic contests, but those who also desired to experience "legitimate" theater or hear "serious" music went to segregated temples devoted to "high" or "classical" art. Cultural lines are generally porous and there were important exceptions: Caruso made best-selling records, Shakespeare's works were offered on the movie screen, Toscanini was featured on commercial radio and television and his final orchestra was sponsored by and named for the National Broadcasting Company. But these were conscious exceptions to what normally prevailed. The cultural fare that was actively and regularly shared by all segments of the population belonged *ipso facto* to the lower rungs of the cultural hierarchy. As we gradually come to the realization that Fred Astaire was one of this century's fine dancers, Louis Armstrong one of its important musicians, Charlie Chaplin one of its acute social commentators, we must remember that for most of this century they could be shared by all of the people only when they were devalued and rendered non-threatening as "popular" art.

Martin Jay has recently written that "so-called high culture has been and will continue to be renewed from below, just as popular or even mass culture derives much of its energies from above. The boundaries shift and dissolve, the categories harden and soften . . . Esoteric art is not forever superior to exoteric, whatever its present function may be." What needs to be added to this quite accurate observation is that exoteric or popular art is transformed into esoteric or high art at precisely that time when it in fact *becomes* esoteric, that is, when it becomes or is rendered inaccessible to the types of people who appreciated it earlier. Thus a film like D. W. Griffith's *Birth of a Nation*, which was popular or lowbrow culture when it was released in 1915, is transformed into high culture when time renders its "language"—its acting styles, technology, kinetics—archaic and thus less familiar and accessible to the masses. Accessibility, as I have tried to demonstrate earlier, becomes a key to cultural categorization and thus a key to help us comprehend how the categories functioned and what they signified.[73]

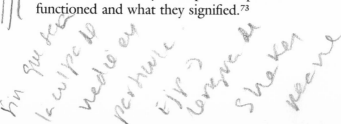

In the late nineteenth century, and well into the twentieth, culture became an icon as never before. Even while anthropology was redefining the concept of culture intellectually, aesthetically it proved remarkably impervious to change; it remained a symbol of all that was fine and pure and worthy. Whatever Franz Boas and Ruth Benedict might have meant by culture, and however influential their meaning ultimately was, Charlie Chaplin knew what the *society* meant by Culture and he and the Marx Brothers and a legion of other popular comedians built parodies of that meaning into the very heart of their humor: they created a rapport with their audiences that generated a sense of complicity in their common stand against the pretensions of the patrons of high culture. Thus when Chaplin, clad in his rags and twirling a cane, mocked cultured gentility as he selected, with meticulous deliberation, a butt from his sardine-tin cigarette case and lit it while strictly observing all the proper forms, he was speaking for his audience as well as himself. So too were the Marx Brothers when they created havoc in the opera house—which ironically had become the very citadel of high culture in the popular imagination—by tricking the orchestra into playing "Take Me out to the Ball Game" in the middle of the overture to *Il Trovatore*, giving Groucho the opportunity to ply the aisles dispensing the snacks of common folk to the cry of "Peanuts! Peanuts!"

Although the stated intention of the arbiters of culture was to proselytize and convert, to lift the masses up to their level, in fact their attitudes often had the opposite effect. The negative stereotypes of terms like "culture" and "cultivated" took hold early; the term "highbrow" was still young when it became a term of popular derision. When Harvard President Charles W. Eliot spoke to the National Educational Association on the definition of the "Cultivated Man," in 1903, he was quick to point out, "I propose to use the term cultivated man in only its good sense—in Emerson's sense. In this paper he is not to be a weak, critical, fastidious creature, vain of a little exclusive information or of an uncommon knack in Latin verse or mathematical logic." True culture, Eliot assured his listeners, "is not exclusive, sectarian or partizan, but the very opposite." Such assurances did not seem to penetrate very deeply into the society. For much of this century significant segments of the American population remained at best ambivalent about and often hostile toward the "high" cultural categories and definitions that were established at the turn of the century. It is common to attribute this to some deeply rooted anti-intellectualism, and certainly there is more than a little validity in the notion, but as Martin Green has observed it is frequently "not so much intellectualism as intellectual authority which is resisted and resented."[74]

This insight returns us full circle to the origins of these cultural categories, which were after all rooted in a quest for intellectual and cultural authority to begin with. The tendency to accept these relatively recent categories as natural products of long standing has obscured their genuine origins and purpose. This myopia, which continues to affect us, was not universal among those who experienced the actual shift in the meaning of culture. Walt Whitman understood what was transpiring as early as 1871. With "this word Culture, or what it has come to represent," he charged in *Democratic Vistas,* "we find ourselves abruptly in close quarters with the enemy." Whitman was not alone. Six years later, Charles Dudley Warner cautioned the alumni of Hamilton College against embracing that culture which was a "kind of fetish," a "mere fastidiousness of taste," a "dainty intellectualism." He focused on the ironic figure of the college graduate who was "able to read all the Greek authors, and yet to have gone, in regard to his own culture, very little deeper than a surface reading," and he warned the assembled alumni "that you cannot stand aloof in a class isolation." Even as Frederick Jackson Turner was speaking for that side of ourselves which yearned to believe that the break with the Old World had been clean and definitive, another historian, and politician, Theodore Roosevelt, was worrying that we had not yet achieved true independence. Even as Turner offered his countrymen a historical rationale for assuming the existence of a frontier crucible continually melting feudal European manners and beliefs into democratic American patterns of thought and culture, Roosevelt was deeply troubled by the many influential men of letters who continued to occupy a colonial status, looking to Europe for their cultural standards, dismissing their nation's culture as "crude and raw," and displaying "that flaccid habit of mind which its possessors style cosmopolitanism." In 1894 he wrote of those "over-civilized, over-sensitive, over-refined" classes that "still retain their spirit of colonial dependence on, and exaggerated deference to, European opinion," and criticized their willingness to "throw away our birthright, and, with incredible and contemptible folly, wander back to bow down before the alien gods whom our forefathers forsook."[75]

In the first chapter we saw that Shakespeare did not simply lose his popularity in twentieth-century America; his appropriation by certain groups and the manner of his presentation in theaters and schools often converted him into an alienating force: a symbol of irrelevant, impractical, pretentious, effete learning fit only for what the Tammany Hall politician George Washington Plunkitt called "the name-parted-in-the-middle aristocrats." A similar fate awaited other forms of expressive culture that underwent the same symbolic transformations Shakespearean drama did. In his autobiography, John Philip Sousa indicated how often he was forced to explain his decision to mix musical genres and defend his penchant for marches and familiar tunes. Though he usually did so with good humor, one can sense his patience straining at the frequency with which he had to justify himself. "Notwithstanding the credo of musical snobs," he asserted, "'popular' does not necessarily mean 'vulgar' or 'ephemeral.'" To touch "the public heart" required inspiration and the "stamp of genius." "Artistic snobbery is so ridiculous!" he complained. "Many an immortal tune has been born in the stable or the cotton-field. *Turkey in the Straw* is a magic melody; anyone should be proud of having written it, but, for musical highbrows, I suppose the thing is declassée. It came not from a European composer but from an unknown negro minstrel." Surveying his career near its close, Sousa explained it as a conscious attempt to "cater to the many rather than the few." Theodore Thomas, Sousa observed, "gave Wagner, Liszt, and Tchaikowsky, in the belief that he was educating his public; I gave Wagner, Liszt, and Tchaikowsky with the hope that I was entertaining my public." Sousa not only had no apologies for the choices he had made, he came to aggressively reject the alternatives: "Believing then and—even more strongly now [1928]—that entertainment is of more real value to the world than technical education in music appreciation, I would not accept the symphonic orchestra as my medium." Sousa's anger at the orthodoxies that threatened to box him in and demean the significance of his art was not always contained. In 1893 he told a New York reporter that wearing "long hair, goggles, an air of mystery and . . . always smelling of Dutch cheese," did not necessarily connote talent. Ten years later he went even further in helping to fix a negative stereotype of the classical musical style when he told a Houston reporter, "The people who frequent my concerts are the strong and healthy. I mean healthy both of mind and body. These people like virile music. Longhaired men and shorthaired women you never see in my audience. And I don't want them." This same aggressive pride, which included overt or implicit rejection of high culture, was often typical of Sousa's admirers. "All the way through a Sousa program you can see the old flag waving, hear the clothes flapping on the line in the back yard, and smell the pork and beans cooking in the kitchen," the *Topeka Daily Capital* declared in 1902. "The principal soloist was born in St. Joseph, Mo., and the average man can pronounce the names of the members of the organization." Sousa's band, the paper concluded, "is for Tom Jones and John Smith and their families."[76]

Sousa's insistence that the artistic route he followed was the result not of limited vision or talent but of a positive choice, was not unique. Neither was Sousa's tendency to counter the stereotypes and simplicities of the apostles of high culture with stereotypes and simplicities of his own. The increasingly antagonistic portrait of European art music that emerged from Sousa's writings was endemic in American films in which it became common for classical musicians to be portrayed as silly, pretentious, and archaic. *Gold Diggers of 1933* was typical. Its hero, the son of a Boston Brahmin family, defends his decision to compose and perform in Broadway musicals by telling his proper banker brother: "Music is my career, you know that! I mean the kind of songs sung in shows and over the radio and on record, I don't mean the kind of music played by the Boston Symphony Orchestra. You have to be half dead to compose that!" In his autobiography, the jazz musician Mezz Mezzrow characterized a symphonic orchestra as "one-hundred-men-with-a-fuehrer, a musical battalion hypnotized by a dictator's baton." Mezzrow insisted that jazzmen were actually superior to symphonic musicians for while the latter were primarily performers, jazzmen were also creators: "To us the two things are one, a guy composed *as* he played, the creating and performing took place at the same time—and we kept thinking what a drag it must be for any musician with spirit to have to sit in on a symphonic assembly-line . . . Symphony means slavery in any jazzman's dictionary. Jazz and freedom are synonyms."[77]

Similar counterstereotypes were conjured up in the fight over the nature of Central Park. To be sure, there were some who felt that Olmsted had not gone far enough in creating an oasis of refinement. *Appleton's Journal*, for example, bemoaned the presence of disreputable men and women, which made the park unpleasant for "the better sort of people," and advocated the imposition of a charge for seats in the park as a means of clearing it of undesirables. Most frequently, however, opposition to Olmsted's plans came from those New York politicians and their journalistic allies who were uncomfortable with his aesthetic imperatives and envisioned a broader use of Central Park more in keeping with the tastes and habits of the mass of New Yorkers. Newspapers commonly advocated the inclusion of a parade ground, atheletic fields, a trotting track, a grove of chestnut trees for little boys to climb. "A footrace a week . . . would do something toward the physical improvement of the race; and a wholesome game of baseball would not be deserving of contempt," one newspaper advised. "Let us not," implored another, "restrict the privilege [of using the park] with any miserable rules about breaking a twig or grazing the bark." Olmsted and his associates were frequently ridiculed as overly delicate and effete. In 1877 the *New York Evening Express* characterized Olmsted's supporters as "Miss Nancies" who "babble in the papers and in Society Circles, about aesthetics and architecture, vistas and landscapes, the quiver of a leaf and the proper blendings of light and shade."* There has, then, been persistent opposition to the imposition and exercise of the new cultural authority, opposition

---

*It was this conflict that ultimately led to Olmsted's dismissal as Central Park's landscape architect in 1878, furnishing further proof to Olmsted's peers that the cultural institutions they were creating must be kept as free from governmental control as possible.

that scholars and intellectuals have tended to misunderstand by labeling it simple Philistinism or anti-intellectualism. It is in fact a more complex and interesting phenomenon that deserves a study of its own.[78]

In 1955 the historian John William Ward entitled a book *Andrew Jackson—Symbol for an Age*. His choice of words was deliberate and important. Andrew Jackson was not the symbol *of* an age but *for* it because, as Ward demonstrated, the prevailing symbol of Jackson was not the creation of Jackson or of the Democratic Party, it was the creation of the times. "To describe the early nineteenth century as the Age of Jackson," Ward concluded, "misstates the matter. The age was not his. He was the age's."[79] So it is with all expressive culture. An age constructs, or reconstructs, the symbols of culture into something it can be comfortable with, something in which it can locate meaning. The composer who wrote an aria in part designed to utilize the gifts of a particular contralto or a concerto crafted for the pyrotechnics of a specific violinist, did not necessarily intend that his work become either the common property of any performer who desired to alter it to fit his or her own gifts, on the one hand, or that it become a frozen and inalterable exhibit in a classical museum of supreme and sacred compositions, on the other. Yet that is precisely how various ages have transformed their compositions. Nineteenth-century Americans tended to alter the works of such creators as Shakespeare and Mozart, twentieth-century Americans to revere and preserve them. Once we have understood this process—and only then—can we utilize the composers' work, or what people have *made* of their work, as a valuable indicator of the spirit of an age.

We have to remind ourselves that although we inherited much of our culture from nineteenth-century Americans, our sense of that culture, our ways of using it, are not theirs. What we make of a Beethoven symphony, a Shakespearean play, a Sousa march, a color lithograph, a Rossini aria, a melodrama, a minstrel show, is not necessarily what nineteenth-century Americans made of, or how they used, these forms of expressive culture. We tend to forget too easily the truth that precisely the same forms of culture can perform markedly distinct functions in different periods or among different groups. It is in the ways they receive and utilize culture that people exert far more control over their lives and their societies than historians often acknowledge. That panoply of cultural creations, attitudes, and rituals which we have learned to call high culture was not the imperishable product of the ages but the result of a specific group of men and women acting at a particular moment in history. The reason why we have had such difficulty defining categories like "high" and "popular" culture and distinguishing with any kind of precision or consistency the boundaries between them is because we have insisted upon treating them as immutable givens rather than what the sociologist Paul DiMaggio has called "historically evolved systems of classification" whose boundaries have varied constantly; "ideological classifications embodied in organizational forms."[80]

It is interesting to reflect upon the difficulty we have had in receiving this truth. What happened to the notion of culture at the turn of the century occurred in other aspects of American life as well. Professions, for example, fragmented into a myriad of new organizations and specialties that, like the institutions of high culture, attempted to create and exercise cultural authority. The difference is that we accept this; we understand that the worlds of doctors, lawyers, professors, engineers, and scientists. as they are presently constituted, are not ancient classifications but are the constructs of modernity and were established as we know them just about a century ago. Our perception of the cultural categories we have inherited, by contrast, has not been illuminated by the same comprehension. Here we have tended to take relatively recent developments and invest them with the mystique of age. Here we have indulged in the process of inventing tradition and have become the prisoners of our own constructs. Scholars have not merely described and tried to understand the cultural classifications created around the turn of the century as products of that specific era which help to illuminate it, we have accepted them as truths and perpetuated them. The continual pleas that Shakspearean drama or opera or classical music finally be extended to the masses *for the first time*, betrays a lack of historical memory or understanding of the contours of culture in nineteenth-century America. When Paul Whiteman observed in 1926 that "good" music "has never had a chance to reach the multitudes in America," he was merely articulating what had become by then an orthodoxy.[81]

Categories and classifications are not simply inevitable but also useful as long as they sharpen our vision and free us to rethink and redefine them. The cultural categories we live with can become vehicles of comprehension not mystification only insofar as we remember just how human and fragile, how recent and porous they have been and continue to be. To confine something as variable and dynamic as culture within rigid hierarchical divisions, which are then projected back into a past in which they did not yet exist, is to risk misunderstanding not merely our history but ourselves.

Epilogue

LIKE ALL CULTURAL CHANGES, the transformations described in this book are themselves subject to change. In our own day the perimeters of culture have altered once again, becoming more expansive, more all-embracing. The anthropological notion that culture encompasses all genres and modes of a people's expressive life has since the Great Depression and the Second World War become familiar throughout our society. Above the words "CULTURE! CULTURE! READ ALL ABOUT IT," the *New York Times* in 1985 listed examples of the cultural diet available in its pages seven days a week:

> American Ballet Theatre * Norman Mailer * Cannes Film Festival * Kiss * New York Shakespeare Festival * . . . Santa Fe Light Opera * The Big Chill * Warren Beatty * . . . Diane Arbus * Leonard Bernstein * Rocky IV * . . . Meryl Streep * Miles Davis * Nora Ephron * Steven Spielberg * Thelonious Monk * . . . Kiri Te Kanawa * Eugene O'Neill * Stephen Sondheim * . . . Claude Monet * Woody Allen * Mostly Mozart.

If the *Times'* concept of culture was not all-inclusive, it certainly incorporated far more than it would have in the early years of this century or indeed only a relatively few years ago. Similarly, in 1986 Connecticut's Stamford Center for the Arts advertised itself by picturing hands applauding Mel Torme, James Galway, Leontyne Price, Andres Segovia, Peter, Paul, and Mary, PDQ Bach, and Sarah Vaughan. "Beethoven would like what we're doing in Stamford," it announced. "So would Louis Armstrong. And James Dean. And Edith Bunker. And Nijinsky."[1]

Evidence of what appears to be a growing cultural eclecticism and flexibility is everywhere at hand. The conductor Michael Tilson Thomas was hardly a lonely voice when he proclaimed in 1976: "There has been altogether too much separation of different types of music, such as so-called 'classical' and 'rock.' In the future, people will have to open up their ears and their souls to many kinds of sounds. There's no reason why a person can't be ardently into rhythm-and-blues and chamber music as well— they're so different, yet beautiful human realities." Thomas was echoing what a number of jazz artists had been saying for some time. "Soon it'll all be just music," Duke Ellington predicted. "'Jazz' is only a word and really has no meaning," he declared. "To keep the whole thing clear, once and for all, I don't believe in categories of any kind." When the saxophonist Charlie Parker was asked about the differences between jazz and European "art" music, his answer was characteristic: "There is no boundary line to art." "We never labeled the music," the drummer Kenny Clarke told an interviewer. "It was just modern music . . . We wouldn't call it anything, really, just music." In his memoirs, Dizzy Gillespie was willing to recognize only two categories of music: "there's only good and bad."[2]

The overlapping of cultural categories became so common that it was hardly surprising to find former opera singer and actress Maria Fisher, founder of the Washington, D.C., Beethoven Society, raising funds for the Thelonious Monk Foundation, named in honor of the late jazz pianist. No more surprising was a 1987 recording by San Francisco's Kronos Quartet that included a scherzo by Charles Ives, an arrangement of the jazz saxophonist Ornette Coleman's "Lonely Woman," a modernist version of the American hymn "Amazing Grace," and Bela Bartok's Quartet No. 3. "At this late date in our musical history," the critic John Rockwell wrote, "interesting new compositions can come from any source, conventionally classical or otherwise." In terms of quality and innovation, he concluded, "genre distinctions mean next to nothing." In her essay "One Culture and the New Sensibility," Susan Sontag attempted to sum up the cultural shift:

> One important consequence of the new sensibility (with its abandonment of the Matthew Arnold idea of culture) has already been alluded to—namely, that the distinction between "high" and "low" culture seems less and less meaningful . . . For it is important to understand that the affection which many younger artists and intellectuals feel for the popular arts is not a new philistinism (as has so often been charged) or a species of anti-intellectualism or

some kind of abdication from culture . . . It reflects a new, more open way of looking at the world and at things in the world, our world. It does not mean the renunciation of all standards . . . The point is that there are new standards, new standards of beauty and style and taste. The new sensibility is defiantly pluralistic.[3]

It is perhaps too early to assess the dimensions of the "defiance" or the full extent to which this rhetoric has been translated into action. But there can be little doubt that it is more than mere rhetoric. The pluralism described by Sontag has been practiced for decades by those jazz musicians who have reached out, with a minimum of fuss or comment, to embrace the themes, the techniques, the idioms of any music they found appealing. As early as the second decade of this century, the stride pianist James P. Johnson, who was to have a major influence upon Fats Waller and Duke Ellington, was paying little attention to the boundary lines: "From listening to classical piano records and concerts . . . I would learn concert effects and build them into blues and rags . . . When playing a heavy stomp, I'd soften it right down, then I'd make an abrupt change like I heard Beethoven do in a sonata." When the pianist Earl Hines discussed the formative influences upon his music, he included both the Baptist church and Chopin. When Gil Evans was asked if the *Sketches of Spain* score he wrote for Miles Davis, which was influenced by the Spanish composers Joaquin Rodrigo and Manuel de Falla, was classical or jazz music, he responded: "That's a merchandiser's problem, not mine." In recent years such nominally "classical" composers and performers as Gunther Schuller and the Kronos Quartet have followed the same pattern.[4]

The blurring of cultural classifications has been accompanied by the efforts of producers and performers of drama, symphonic and operatic music, and other forms of high culture, to reach out to their audiences in ways not known since the nineteenth century. Although there have been intermittent attempts throughout the twentieth century to make Shakespeare accessible once more to a larger public, the endeavor first gained force in the productions of such directors as Joseph Papp in the 1960s. By the 1980s a production of *The Comedy of Errors* featuring juggling, acrobatics, rope walking, tap dancing, unicycling, and baton twirling was greeted by critics not with disdain but with enthusiasm. When Randy Nelson, one of the featured actor-jugglers, insisted that "Shakespeare would have been pleased by what we're doing," the *New York Times* consulted the English Elizabethan scholar A. L. Rowse, who agreed, observing that "it's a play that needs to be filled out with acrobatic fun, juggling and the like . . . The thing we must remember about Shakespeare is that he was so very open-minded. He was very much interested in production, and I think he would be quite sympathetic to an acrobatic version of 'The Comedy of Errors.'"[5]

In the world of opera the attempt to attract the heterogeneous audiences of the past has taken the form of "supertitles"—translations or paraphrases of the libretto projected onto a stage screen to allow audiences greater access to foreign-language operas. The financial difficulty many symphony orchestras have experienced in recent years has led to an enhanced understanding of the need to reach out to more people. "We did a survey recently and the average age of our audience was well over 50 years," Edward Q. Moulton, the general manager and president of the Columbus, Ohio, Symphony Orchestra revealed. "We're either fast becoming a dinosaur or we'd better get to the yuppies pretty fast. I think we've been a little smug." In the 1980s the New York Philharmonic began a community outreach program with concerts in such Harlem locations as the Abyssinian Baptist Church and the Apollo Theater. "It's a part of our mandate and policy to be a cultural institution for all of the city and its inhabitants," the philharmonic's director of educational activities announced. "Historically, people have not come, perhaps because it's unfamiliar territory or they may have felt they were not wanted. Those perceptions are pretty longstanding, and it's up to the institution to try to break down those barriers."[6]

Similarly, Edward Kresky, vice chairman of the New York State Council on the Arts, insisted that museums had to become more responsive as well. "Our museums have to reach out more into ethnic arts than they have in the past. There has to be more of a move into the community . . . We have had a great growth in numbers of institutions. We need equal growth in the numbers of audiences if the organizations are going to survive. Some of the people we're seeking to reach have never had the experience of taking their children to concerts or museums. There are economic hurdles, but if they'll go and feel comfortable with things they are attuned to ethnically, hopefully they will broaden their interests into other areas." Interestingly, the urge to reach out to a broader audience has led some museums to focus on the very objects that museums at the turn of the century rejected with such finality. The Metropolitan Museum of Art's extensive collections of plaster casts, which had been slowly crumbling into decay in a storehouse under Manhattan's West Side Highway, were rediscovered by such institutions as the Queens Museum in New York, which in the 1970s and 1980s began to restore and exhibit them along with Princeton and Carnegie Mellon Universities and the New York Academy of Art. Ironically, since the casts were made before the effects of pollution took their toll on the originals, they contain more detail than the genuine works of art. Beginning with the exhibitions of industrial products and machines in the Museum of Modern Art in the 1930s and culminating most forcefully in the work of such artists as Andy Warhol since the 1960s, the once firm line between the unique products of high art and those of industrial or mass art grew less and less distinct. "Painting a soup can is not a radical act," the critic Robert Hughes wrote in 1971. Warhol's radicalism resided in his adaptation of "the means of production of soup cans to the way he produced paintings, turning them out *en masse*— consumer art mimicking the process as well as the look of consumer culture." As John Russell observed after the artist's death in the winter of 1987, Warhol embraced kitsch "and walked away with all that it had to give," turned his back on the idea of art as something unique, and "was interested above all in the demystification of art." The art historian Kirk Varnedoe, appointed head of the Museum of Modern Art's department of painting and sculpture, announced an exhibition entitled "High and Low: Modern Art and Popular Culture," scheduled for the spring of 1991. The purpose of the show, Varnedoe declared, would be to examine the close relationship of such expressive forms as comics, graffiti, and advertising to modernist innovation: "The founding premise of Modernism was to call into question the distinction between high and low art, from Cubist collage on. The show cuts the distinction between modern and contemporary, and raises basic issues of the relationship of modern art to society. Built into our charter is the notion of crossing borders and beating down standard hierarchies."[7]

An examination of university curricula from the 1960s on reveals the same picture of change. Courses and studies in history, for example, began to include groups and subjects formerly ignored or at least largely neglected: workers, immigrants, women, blacks, popular and mass entertainment, leisure activities, the culture of the home, workplace, and public arena. Movies, radio, popular novels and magazines, even comic strips, became part of the materials studied by students and scholars endeavoring to understand American culture. When Professor E. D. Hirsch and his associates compiled the list "What Literate Americans Know," for Hirsch's 1987 book, *Cultural Literacy,* they included Saint Thomas Aquinas and Fred Astaire, Beethoven and the Beatles, Chaucer and Ty Cobb, classical music and Currier and Ives, Dante and Disney, $E = mc^2$ and Duke Ellington, Goethe and Grandma Moses, Hamlet and "Home Sweet Home," Henry James and Jesse James, King Lear and King Kong, Henry Wadsworth Longfellow and Joe Louis, Karl Marx and the Marx Brothers, Mozart and Mother Goose, Othello and "O, Susanna," Picasso and Pinocchio, the Renaissance and Babe Ruth, Socrates and swing, Tchaikovsky and Tarzan, William Wordsworth and Mae West. The argument was not that all of these were of equal aesthetic worth but that all of them were part of a cultural matrix that defined "culturally literate" Americans at the close of the twentieth century.[8]

As cultural categories softened and overlapped, formally despised genres began to be conceived and spoken of in tones once limited to more ethereal expressive forms. Thus when computer technology made it possible to transform old black-and-white movies into color movies, a coalition of outraged directors, screen writers, theatrical unions, cinematographers, and critics denounced the development as "barbarism." "God knows every motion picture is not a work of art," the director Sydney Pollack declared, "but if we are to say that motion pictures are an art form, it seems only logical that there is an artist responsible, and I can't see why that artist should be afforded less protection than an artist in any other field." Testifying before Congress, the actor, writer, and director Woody Allen rejected the notion that public preference was a valid argument in favor of "colorization." "It would be clearly irrelevant if every person in the United States wanted *The Maltese Falcon* in color. The moral here is, you should not be able to take an artist's work and change it without his approval." The analogies used reveal the changes that have taken place in conceptions of culture. If the public wanted Hamlet to live at the end, Allen asked, should Shakespeare's play be changed? "It's so absurd. You can't have a culture like that." When the businessman Ted Turner defended his right to "color-ize" by remarking, "The last time I checked I owned those films," a columnist quickly rejoined, "If Ted Turner . . . bought the Mona Lisa and painted a mustache on it, would it be enough for him to say, 'Last time I checked I owned that painting?'"[9]

Even this brief and inadequate summary of current trends makes it evident that the transformation examined in this book has not been all-encompassing. Culture remains a dynamic process, a constant interchange between the past and the present. Nevertheless, as significant as these recent developments have been, it would be premature to announce the arrival of the Age of Cultural Ecumenism. It would be a mistake to conclude that the cultural transformation described here was merely one point in an ever-revolving cycle of change which we have by now—happily or unhappily—moved well beyond. In fact, for all of the recent developments, the major transformation that took place at the turn of the last century helped to shape attitudes and establish categories which continue to affect profoundly our understanding of and our reactions to culture. If the cultural values and attitudes traced in this study are no longer as dominant as they were, their presence continues to be felt whenever and wherever culture is discussed.

This certainly has been evident in the reaction to Allan Bloom's *The Closing of the American Mind*. It is possible to evaluate Bloom's work in terms of the author's reading—or misreading—of classical philosophy, as Martha Nussbaum has done, or in terms of his documentation in and knowledge of American cultural history, which are so perfunctory and shallow that one is tempted to appropriate the phrase a historian of an earlier generation once employed in criticizing a book for having been written "without fear and without research." Such judgments, however, risk missing the truth that Bloom's book is less a scholarly work than a cultural phenomenon which has found deep resonance in contemporary society. Bloom has in effect written a largely autobiographical account permeated by an angst shared by enough readers to have made it the second best selling hard-cover nonfiction book of 1987.[10]

What is particularly striking and most significant about Bloom's book is how closely his message at the end of this century approximates the jeremiad of the close of the last century. There is the same ethereal, sacred sense of culture, which Bloom defines in Arnoldian terms as "everything that is uplifting and edifying," as "the peak expression of man's creativity," as "something high, profound, respectable," as that which "restores 'the unity in art and life' of the ancient polis."[11]

There is the same sense of America's cultural deterioration, the same conviction that our culture, indeed, our entire civilization, is experiencing "an intellectual crisis of the greatest magnitude," which for Bloom is symbolized by the state of our young people: "Today's select students know so much less, are so much more cut off from the traditions, are so much slacker intellectually, that they make their predecessors look like prodigies of culture."[12]

There is the same sense of the absolute qualitative distinctiveness of cultural genres, which makes cultural degeneration easy to spot. "There is no relation between popular culture and high culture," Bloom tells us unequivocally as he laments that "the former is all that is now influential on our scene." Classical music, which once functioned as "the only regularly recognizable class distinction between educated and uneducated in America," as the only remaining "class distinction between high and low," is "dead among the young." It has been replaced by rock music, which Bloom assures us contains "nothing noble, sublime, profound, delicate, tasteful or even decent," and has "room only for the intense, changing, crude and immediate, which Tocqueville warned us would be the character of democratic art." This "junk food for the soul," this "gutter phenomenon," this "voyage to the underworld," is produced and disseminated by an industry that Bloom asserts "has all the moral dignity of drug trafficking" and has helped convert the lives of our youth "into a nonstop, commercially prepackaged masturbational fantasy," which has effectively removed them from their heritage: "As long as they have the Walkman on, they cannot hear what the great tradition has to say. And after its prolonged use, when they take it off, they find they are deaf."[13]

There is the same sense that culture is less something that *is* than something that *was*; something created for eternity in an age before the dominance of specialists, when individuals with vision—"the best minds"—could debate on the highest level "a unified view of nature and man's place in it." What is essential about the Platonic dialogues, Bloom insists, "is reproducible in almost all times and places." Thus the only serious solution to the problem occasioned by "the undeniable fact" that our young people "are uncivilized, and that the universities have some responsibility for civilizing them," is to turn once more to the wisdom of the past,

> the good old Great Books approach, in which a liberal education means reading certain generally recognized classic texts, just reading them, letting them dictate what the questions are and the method of approaching them—not forcing them into categories we make up, not treating them as historical products, but trying to read them as their authors wished them to be read.[14]

There is, as the statement above indicates, the same sense that we can somehow become privy to how the great minds of the past "wished" their works to be read, or heard, or performed, for all time, by all people, in all circumstances. In spite of the evidence we possess that so many enduring works of art were created for specific performers by artists perfectly willing to see them altered or interpreted by other performers; in spite of our increased understanding of the difficulty, if not impossibility, of performing a play or a concerto without infusing it with the spirit and perception of the performing artist; in spite of our recognition of the insurmountable complexities involved in knowing precisely how painters, musicians, or writers desired us to experience their works and our comprehension of how many producing artists harbored no such concrete desires in the first place, this cult of the sacred inalterable work of art continues into our own time.

There is the same sense, so well articulated at the turn of the century by Henry James and Henry Adams, that unity has been replaced by multiplicity. "Liberal education flourished when it prepared the way for the discussion of a unified view of nature and man's place in it," Bloom informs us. The contemporary student finds no such unity: "He finds a democracy of the disciplines which . . . is really an anarchy . . . he finds a bewildering variety of courses . . . Nor does he usually find readily available examples, either among students or professors, of a unified use of the university's resources . . . So the student must navigate among a collection of carnival barkers, each trying to lure him into a particular sideshow." Bloom assures us that his grandparents, though uneducated by current standards, had the untold benefits of the Bible, with its unified faith and philosophies. In spite of their M.D.'s and Ph.D.'s, later generations, who have had to find their way through the "technical smorgasbord" of contemporary school systems, cannot talk about the human condition without uttering "clichés, superficialities, the material of satire." The difference is obvious—his grandparents' generation possessed the unified vision of "the real nature of things," the "great revelations, epics and philosophies" provided by "the Book," which Bloom is quick to say need not be the Bible, "but without a book of similar gravity, read with the gravity of the potential believer," there is "nothing to see out there, and eventually little left inside." This conflation of education and revelation, of discriminating choice and blind acceptance, proceeds from still another conviction Bloom shares with the older jeremiad: that only the minority can fruitfully investigate and discuss the nature of the cultural authority which the majority needs to accept.[15]

There is, finally, the same sense that culture is something created by the few for the few, threatened by the many, and imperiled by democracy; the conviction that culture cannot come from the young, the inexperienced, the untutored, the marginal; the belief that culture is finite and fixed, defined and measured, complex and difficult of access, recognizable only by those trained to recognize it, comprehensible only to those qualified to comprehend it:

The real community of man, in the midst of all the self-contradic-
tory simulacra of community, is the community of those who seek
the truth, of the potential knowers, that is, in principle, of all men
to the extent they desire to know. But in fact this includes only a
few, the true friends . . .[16]

Bloom's is not an isolated voice. We have been hearing it for
some time now. Historians are told that they should diminish,
if not abandon, their studies of that multiplicity of ethnic mi-
norities, workers, immigrants, and women, about whose culture
and role we still have so much to learn if we are to truly comprehend the American past, and that they should turn again to
the sweeping politically focused narratives that once supposedly
gave us a sense of the unified whole, although in fact they focused
overwhelmingly upon a decided minority of the population in
terms of class, ethnicity, region, and gender. Students of literature
are told that they must stop tampering with the canon and
confine their energies once more to the small list of those worthy
of study and perpetuation. Indeed, the *Washington Post* critic
Jonathan Yardley is so convinced that the pantheon of writers
worth studying is absolutely finite that he can only attribute
ignoble motives to those who would go beyond it:

> A central fact of life in the humanities departments, the English
> departments in particular, is that all the really good subjects for
> study already have been taken—have, in fact, been studied right
> into the ground. If there is anything left to be said about Haw-
> thorne or Hemingway, Melville or Crane, Longfellow or Frost, it
> could only be said by a person of such originality of mind as to
> border on genius . . . With the good subjects for study already
> taken, they [professors of literature] have done the perfectly sen-
> sible thing and invented new subjects around which to construct
> their careers. This means that they must invest those subjects with
> academic legitimacy: Hence the rush to cover with glory writers
> and books that previously had been properly regarded as of minor
> scholarly interest.

In a February 1988 speech before four hundred university presidents and deans, Secretary of Education William Bennett referred to the reconsideration of the cultural canon as "curricular
debasement" and accused faculty of "trashing" Plato and Shake-

speare. All of this furor often obscures the cultural conservatism of the many universities in which American art history continues to be neglected, entire genres of American music are totally ignored, and non-European culture in general tends to be suspect.[17]

It also obscures the fact that a great many influential voices continue to advocate the values and standards that prevailed at the beginning of this century. Classical music, the critic Will Crutchfield recently charged, "is more accessible than it ought to be already, because we already have gone fairly far down the road of cheapening and diluting it in order to make it accessible." When the ballet dancer Rudolph Nureyev was questioned about his superb athletic abilities, he interrupted the reporter and declared, "I am not an athlete. I am a great artist." Asked to define "artistry," the violinist Yehudi Menuhin responded, "I would say that it is a subtle reaction to barbarism and crudity . . . Art, true art, opposes such reactions in the way that I suppose real religion would oppose them, and teaches instead humility, tolerance, honor, respect." This sacred spirit animates not only artists of an older generation like Menuhin but younger ones like the pianist, conductor, and musical director James Levine of the Metropolitan Opera, who in the mid-1980s adamantly opposed the use of the increasingly popular English supertitles: "Over my dead body will they show those things at this house. I cannot imagine not wanting the audience riveted on the performers at every moment." But, as Levine was to learn, in the universe of sacralized culture even the defenders of purity have difficulty being pure enough. Levine soon found himself under attack by the critic Donal Henahan for placing the artistic fortunes of the Metropolitan Opera in the hands of the "spectacle merchants," by presenting opera not primarily as a musical art form but as "sumptuous stage designs," "empty spectacle," and "conspicuous consumption" of an "artistically dubious sort." The opera world was in trouble, the tenor Jon Vickers insisted in 1987, "because it's being invaded by those techniques that are corrupting our society—big PR, the personality cult, techniques that create hysteria but do not elevate man. They degrade our art . . . We cannot compromise . . . We mustn't smear the line between art and entertainment." "You cannot bring art to the masses," he proclaimed. "You never will."[18]

The debate, then, goes on, and it is important to understand that it is not primarily between those with standards and those whose rampant relativism has robbed them of all discrimination, as the defenders of "Culture" would have it. The debate, of course, can deteriorate into a mere battle of vanities. The aficionados of any cultural genre—no matter how lowly a place it is accorded in the hierarchy of culture—can become stubbornly elitist and insular in their conviction that the sun shines brightest in their own cultural backyards. Nevertheless, it is possible to close one's ears to this parochial cacophony of competing elites and focus upon the real debate, which is between those on one side who "know" what culture is and what it is not, who have a map of its fixed perimeters and a profile of the identity of its creators and its followers, who perceive culture to be something finite and fragile, which needs to be conserved and protected from the incessant Philistinism that threatens it, and those on the other side who, possessing no map and little liking for fixed and unmovable fences and boundaries, believe that worthy, enduring culture is not the possession of any single group or genre or period, who conceive of culture as neither finite nor fixed but dynamic and expansive, and who remain unconvinced that the moment an expressive form becomes accessible to large numbers of people it loses the aesthetic and intellectual criteria necessary to classify it as culture. To say that there is both nonsense and wisdom being articulated by both camps is to state the obvious, but that should not blur the crucial distinctions between their positions.

We have in recent decades begun to move gradually but decisively away from the rigid, class-bound definitions of culture forged at the close of the nineteenth century. The contemporary debate is a reaction—often an extremely angry one—to this development. If the debate is to be fruitful it needs to be rooted not merely in the web of our immediate aesthetic and social predilections but in the matrix of history, which can allow us to perceive more clearly what shapes culture has assumed in the American past, which may in turn allow us to understand better both the possibilities and the effects of the types of cultural boundaries we embrace. More than two decades ago the novelist Ralph Ellison worried that the chance for empathy and identification with those of other backgrounds was being "blasted in the interest of specious political and philosophical conceits." Those writers and scholars who constructed "prefabricated Negroes," which they then superimposed upon the black community, Ellison maintained, were shocked and even indignant "when someone thrusts his head through the page and yells, 'Watch out there, Jack, there're people living under here.'" The identical point can be made concerning culture. Here too "political and philosophical conceits" have erected prefabricated and stereotyped categories that transform complexity into banality. Thus the Nobel Laureate Saul Bellow can demonstrate the limits of his own education by issuing his ignorant—or arrogant—challenge to those who would expand the corpus of the cultural curriculum: "Who is the Tolstoy of the Zulus? The Proust of the Papuans? I'd be glad to read them." Thus Professor Bloom, who speaks so feelingly of "the community of those who seek the truth," can harshly dismiss an entire genre of music as worthless and harmful without giving us the slightest indication that he has made any serious effort to study or understand it.[19]

In defining and redefining the contours of culture, we are not merely dealing with intellectual abstractions; we are dealing with lives and minds, we are dealing with people, and we owe them more than the hubris of narrow self-defense; we owe them no less than the adoption of an open search for and a careful understanding of what culture has been in our past and can become in our future.

Notes

Prologue

1. Gerald Nachman, "Take All You Want off the Top, Figaro," *San Francisco Chronicle Datebook,* October 4, 1987.

2. Raymond Carney, *American Vision: The Films of Frank Capra* (Cambridge, England, and New York, 1986), xii.

3. Stuart Levine, "Arts, Values, Institutions and Culture: An Essay in American Studies Methodology and Relevance," *American Quarterly,* 24 (May 1972), 131–32.

4. Marc Bloch, *The Historian's Craft* (New York, 1962), 87.

5. Russel Blaine Nye, *Society and Culture in America, 1830–1860* (New York, 1974), 148.

6. See, for example, Dwight Macdonald, "Masscult and Midcult," in Macdonald, *Against the American Grain* (New York, 1962), 3–75, and the debate in Bernard Rosenberg and David Manning White, eds., *Mass Culture: The Popular Arts in America* (New York, 1957), 3–110.

7. Richard Chase, *The American Novel and Its Tradition* (1957; repr., New York, 1978), 9–10.

8. *American Historical Review,* 89 (February 1984), 34–66.

One · William Shakespeare in America

1. Mark Twain, *The Adventures of Huckleberry Finn* (New York, 1884), 190.

2. Laurence Hutton, *Curiosities of the American Stage* (New York, 1891), 157, 181–186; Stanley Wells, ed., *Nineteenth-Century Shakespeare Burlesques,* V (London, 1978), xi–xii; Charles Mathews, *Trip to America* (Baltimore, 1824), 9, 25; Charles Haywood, "Negro Minstrelsy and Shakespearean Burlesque," in Bruce Jackson, ed., *Folklore and Society: Essays in Honor of Benj. A. Botkin* (Norwood, Pa., 1976), 88; and Ray B. Browne, "Shakespeare in America: Vaudeville and Negro Minstrelsy," *American Quarterly,* 12 (Fall 1960), 381–382. For examples of parodies of *Hamlet,* see *An Old Play in a New Garb: Hamlet, Prince of Denmark,* in Wells, ed., *Nineteenth-Century Shakespeare Burl-*

esques, V; and *Hamlet the Dainty,* in Gary D. Engle, ed., *This Grotesque Essence: Plays from the Minstrel Stage* (Baton Rouge, 1978). For the popularity of parodies of *Hamlet* in the United States, see Ralph Leslie Rusk, *The Literature of the Middle Western Frontier,* 2 vols. (New York, 1925), II, 4n; Louis Marder, *His Exits and His Entrances: The Story of Shakespeare's Reputation* (Philadelphia, 1963), 295–296, 316–317; and Esther Cloudman Dunn, *Shakespeare in America* (New York, 1939), 108–112, 215–216.

3. For examples, see Wells, ed., *Nineteenth-Century Shakespeare Burlesques,* V, and Engle, ed., *This Grotesque Essence.* For a contemporary view of nineteenth-century parodies, see Hutton, *Curiosities of the American Stage,* 145–204. Also see Marder, *His Exits and His Entrances,* 316–317; Alice I. Perry Wood, *The Stage History of Shakespeare's King Richard the Third* (New York, 1909), 158; Browne, *"Shakespeare in America,"* *American Quarterly,* 12 (Fall 1960), 380, 385–390; David Grimsted, *Melodrama Unveiled: American Theater and Culture, 1800–1850* (Chicago, 1968), 240; Constance Rourke, *Troupers of the Gold Coast* (New York, 1928), 221; Russell Nye, *The Unembarrassed Muse* (New York, 1970), 172; and Charles B. Lower, "Othello as Black on Southern Stages, Then and Now," in Philip C. Kolin, ed., *Shakespeare in the South: Essays on Performance* (Jackson, Miss., 1983), 211.

4. Haywood, "Negro Minstrelsy and Shakespearean Burlesque," in Jackson, ed., *Folklore and Society,* 80, 86–87; and Browne, "Shakespeare in America," *American Quarterly,* 12 (Fall 1960), 376–379.

5. Adams to James H. Hackett, printed in Hackett, *Notes and Comments upon Certain Plays and Actors of Shakespeare, with Criticisms and Correspondence* (New York, 1864), 229. See Alfred Van Rensselaer Westfall, *American Shakespearean Criticism, 1607–1865* (New York, 1939), 45–46, 50–55; Wood, *The Stage History of Shakespeare's King Richard the Third,* 134–135; Charles H. Shattuck, *Shakespeare on the American Stage: From the Hallams to Edwin Booth* (Washington, D.C., 1976), 3, 15–16; and Hugh Rankin, *The Theater in Colonial America* (Chapel Hill, 1960), 191–192.

6. Arthur Hobson Quinn, *A History of the American Drama* (New York, 1943), 162; Dunn, *Shakespeare in America,* 133, 171–172; and Carl Bode, *The Anatomy of American Popular Culture, 1840–1861* (Berkeley and Los Angeles, 1960), 16–17. For the reception of Shakespeare in specific eastern and southern cities, the following are useful: T. Allston Brown, *A History of the New York Stage from the First Performance in 1732 to 1901,* 3 vols. (New York, 1903); James H. Dorman, Jr., *Theater in the Ante-Bellum South, 1815–1861* (Chapel Hill, 1967); W. Stanley Hoole, *The Ante-Bellum Charleston Theatre* (Tuscaloosa,

Ala., 1946); Reese Davis James, *Cradle of Culture, 1800–1810: The Philadelphia Stage* (Philadelphia, 1957); Martin Staples Shockley, *The Richmond Stage, 1784–1812* (Charlottesville, Va., 1977); Eola Willis, *The Charleston Stage in the Eighteenth Century* (Columbia, S.C., 1924); Joseph Patrick Roppolo, "Hamlet in New Orleans," *Tulane Studies in English*, 6 (1956), 71–86; and the essays in Kolin, ed., *Shakespeare in the South*. For tables showing the popularity of plays in the first half of the nineteenth century, see Grimsted, *Melodrama Unveiled*, apps. 1–2. Towle's observation was made in his *American Society*, II (London, 1870), 22. The migration of English stars to America is demonstrated throughout Shattuck's *Shakespeare on the American Stage: From the Hallams to Edwin Booth*.

7. Bernard, *Retrospections of America, 1797–1811* (New York, 1887), 263; Tocqueville, *Democracy in America*, pt. 2 (Vintage edn., New York, 1961), 58; Knortz, *Shakespeare in Amerika: Eine Literarhistorische Studie* (Berlin, 1882), 47. For Bridger and Lincoln, see James G. McManaway, "Shakespeare in the United States," *Publications of the Modern Language Association of America*, 79 (December 1964), 514; and Bernard DeVoto, *Mark Twain's America* (Boston, 1932), 142–143.

8. Rusk, *The Literature of the Middle Western Frontier*, I, 398–400, 411–414; Louise Taylor, "Shakespeare in Chicago, 1837–1900" (Ph. D. diss., 2 vols., Northwestern University, 1981), I, 5–12; William Bryan Gates, "Performances of Shakespeare in Ante-Bellum Mississippi," *Journal of Mississippi History*, 5 (January 1943), 28–37; Ashley Thorndike, "Shakespeare in America," in L. Abercrombie et al., eds., *Aspects of Shakespeare* (Oxford, 1933), 116–117; Westfall, *American Shakespearean Criticism*, 59; William G. B. Carson, *The Theatre on the Frontier: The Early Years of the St. Louis Stage* (1932; repr., New York, 1965); West T. Hill, Jr., *The Theatre in Early Kentucky, 1790–1820* (Lexington, Ky., 1971); Joseph Gallegly, *Footlights on the Border: The Galveston and Houston Stage before 1900* (The Hague, 1962); Sol Smith, *Theatrical Management in the West and South for Thirty Years* (New York, 1868); and Noah Ludlow, *Dramatic Life as I Found It* (St. Louis, 1880).

9. Rourke, *Troupers of the Gold Coast*, 33, 44, 101–102, George R. MacMinn, *The Theater of the Golden Era in California* (Caldwell, Idaho, 1941), 23–24.

10. Leman, *Memories of an Old Actor* (San Francisco, 1886), 212–213, 260–262, 276–277; Ludlow, *Dramatic Life as I Found It*, 89–90, 113, 116, 242–243, 256, 258, 303; and Smith, *Theatrical Management in the West and South for Thirty Years*, 90–91.

11. Joseph S. Schick, *The Early Theater in Eastern Iowa: Cultural*

Beginnings and the Rise of the Theater in Davenport and Eastern Iowa, 1836–1863 (Chicago, 1939). Schick's appendixes contain a list of all plays performed in either English or German in Iowa during these years. Place is quoted in Dormon, *Theater in the Ante-Bellum South,* 257n.

12. James Fenimore Cooper, *Notions of the Americans,* II (London, 1828), 100, 113. The dedication of Shakespeare's memorial was covered in the *New York Times,* May 24, 1872. Bayard Taylor's poem was printed in the *New York Tribune,* May 23, 1872.

13. Playbill, American Theatre, Philadelphia, May 13, 1839, Folger Shakespeare Library, Washington, D.C. For the prevalence of this format in the eighteenth century, see Rankin, *The Theater in Colonial America,* 150, 193–194; Kenneth Silverman, *A Cultural History of the American Revolution* (New York, 1976), 62; and Garff B. Wilson, *Three Hundred Years of American Drama and Theatre* (Englewood Cliffs, N.J., 1973), 19–27.

14. Playbills, St. Charles Theatre, New Orleans, November 30, 1846, Alexandria, Virginia, July 12, 1799, and Arch Street Theatre, Philadelphia, March 2, 1857, Folger Shakespeare Library.

15. Playbills, American Theatre, Philadelphia, August 30, 31, 1838, September 1, 11, 1838, June 24, 1839, Walnut Street Theater, Philadelphia, November 30, 1821, Military Hall, Newark, N.J., August 15, 1852, Montgomery Theatre, Montgomery, Ala., March 21, 1835, and American Theatre, Philadelphia, June 25, 1839, December 14, 1837, Folger Shakespeare Library. See also Arnold Aronson, "Shakespeare in Virginia, 1751–1863," in Kolin, ed., *Shakespeare in the South,* 30; and MacMinn, *The Theater of the Golden Era in California,* 90. Davenport is quoted in Lloyd Morris, *Curtain Time: The Story of the American Theater* (New York, 1953), 205. For examples of *Catharine and Petruchio* being used as an afterpiece, see playbills, American Theatre, New Orleans, April 20, 1827, American Theatre, Philadelphia, September 26, 1838, and St. Charles Theatre, New Orleans, March 25, 1864, Folger Shakespeare Library. *Catharine and Petruchio* also served as an afterpiece when plays other than Shakespeare's were presented; see playbills, American Theatre, New Orleans, April 20, 1827, and American Theatre, Philadelphia, September 26, 1838, December 8, 1838, Folger Shakespeare Library.

16. John S. Kendall, *The Golden Age of the New Orleans Theater* (Baton Rouge, 1952), 210; Hudson, *Lectures on Shakespeare,* I (New York, 1848), 1–41; and Smith, *The Sentinel and Other Plays,* ed. Ralph H. Ware and H. W. Schoenberger (Bloomington, Ind., n.d.), 101–114.

17. Power, *Impressions of America*, 2 vols. (London, 1836), II, 189–192. Shakespeare's contemporary is quoted in Alfred Harbage, *Shakespeare's Audience* (New York, 1941), 84–85. The *Times Picayune* quote comes from Joseph Patrick Roppolo, "Shakespeare in New Orleans, 1817–1865," in Kolin, ed., *Shakespeare in the South*, 126n7. For an excellent discussion of theater audiences in the first half of the nineteenth century, see Grimsted's indispensible *Melodrama Unveiled*, chap. 3. For a comparison with audiences in eighteenth-century England, see James T. Lynch, *Box, Pit and Gallery: Stage and Society in Johnson's London* (New York, 1971). Claudia Johnson deals with a neglected part of the American audience in "That Guilty Third Tier: Prostitution in Nineteenth-Century Theaters," *American Quarterly*, 27 (1975), 575–584.

18. *The Autobiography of Joseph Jefferson*, ed. Alan S. Downer (Cambridge, Mass., 1964), 286; Benjamin McArthur, *Actors and American Culture, 1880–1920* (Philadelphia, 1984), 171; Whitman, "The Old Bowery," in Justin Kaplan, ed., *Walt Whitman: Poetry and Prose* (New York, 1982), 1189–90; and Irving, *Letters of Jonathan Oldstyle*, ed. Bruce I. Granger and Martha Hartzog (Boston, 1977), 12–25.

19. Trollope, *Domestic Manners of the Americans*, 2 vols. (London, 1832), I, 179–184, and II, 87–88, 194–195; Power, *Impressions of America*, I, 171–174; also see I, 62–66, 87–89, 123–126, 210–211.

20. Irving, *Letters of Jonathan Oldstyle*, 14; *New York Mirror*, June 8, 1833; the Virginia and New York editors are quoted in Grimsted, *Melodrama Unveiled*, 63–64; the French reporter's account is reprinted in Barnard Hewitt, *Theatre U.S.A., 1665 to 1957* (New York, 1959), 164–166; and the account of Salvini's *Hamlet* appeared in "The Old Cabinet," *Scribner's Monthly*, 9 (January 1875), 379.

21. Smith, *Theatrical Management*, 137–138; Rourke, *Troupers of the Gold Coast*, 149–150, 209–210; *Sacramento Daily Union*, December 8, 1856.

22. For an example of the warning of law enforcement, see playbill, Walnut Street Theatre, Philadelphia, November 30, 1821, Folger Shakespeare Library; the gentleman is quoted in Nancy Webb and Jean Francis Webb, *Will Shakespeare and His America* (New York, 1964), 84; Fullerton's suicide is described and the American critic is quoted in James S. Bost, *Monarchs of the Mimic World, or, The American Theatre of the Eighteenth Century through the Managers—The Men Who Made It* (Orono, Me., 1977), 84–85, 103; the *San Francisco Chronicle*, January 1854, is quoted in MacMinn, *The Theater of the Golden Era in California*, 100.

23. The Bowery Theatre scenes are described in *New York Mirror*, December 29, 1832. Edwin Forrest portrayed the Iago who so infuri-

ated the canal boatman; see William Rounseville Alger, *Life of Edwin Forrest, the American Tragedian,* 2 vols. (1877; repr., New York, 1972), I, 477. Constance Rourke's anecdote is contained in her *American Humor: A Study of the National Character* (1935; repr., New York, 1953), 96–97. The other examples of audience engagement and interference, can be found in Grimsted, *Melodrama Unveiled,* 60, and *Harper's New Monthly Magazine,* 28 (December 1863), 133.

24. Nachman, "Break a Leg, Willy," *San Francisco Chronicle,* November 30, 1979; Alfred Harbage, *Theatre for Shakespeare* (Toronto, 1955), 1–3, 8. Papp is quoted in Gerald M. Berkowitz, *New Broadways: Theatre across America, 1950–1980* (Totowa, N.J., 1982), 37.

25. Young, *The Community Theatre and How It Works* (New York, 1957), 126; George McManus, *Bringing up Father,* ed. Herb Galewitz (New York, 1973), 37; Plunkitt, *Plunkitt of Tammany Hall: A Series of Very Plain Talks on Very Practical Politics,* recorded by William L. Riordon (1905; repr., New York, 1963), 52, 71; Richardson, *The Long Day: The Story of a New York Working Girl* (1905), reprinted in its entirety in William L. O'Neill, ed., *Women at Work* (Chicago, 1972), chap 6, see p. 300.

26. Playbills, American Theatre, San Francisco, May 29, 1855, Varieties Theatre, New Orleans, December 30, 1869, California Theatre, San Francisco, April 4, 1873, Mechanics Hall, Salem, Mass., February 12, 1868, San Jose Opera House, August 22, 1870, Roberts Opera House, Hartford, Conn., November 1869, Academy of Music, Providence, R.I., November 24, 1969, Leland Opera House, Albany, N.Y., September 27, 1880, April 15, 1882, Opera House, Albany, N.Y., January 21, 22, 1874, Piper's Opera House, Virginia City, Nevada, July 29, 1878, Walnut Street Theatre, Philadelphia, November 5, 1875, Duquesne Theatre, Pittsburgh, December 23, 24, 25, 1890, Murray Hill Theatre, New York, May 4, 1903, Garden Theatre, New York City, December 24, 1900, Forty-fourth Street Theatre, New York City, February 22, 1915, Schubert Memorial Theatre, St. Louis, November 9, 1914, Olympic Theatre, St. Louis, January 6, 1902, May 6, 1907, and National Theatre, Washington, D.C., October 2, 1939, Folger Shakespeare Library.

27. White, "Opera in New York, II," *Century Magazine,* 23 (April 1882), 869; Mark Twain, "About Play-Acting," *Forum,* 26 (October 1908), 150–151; Marder, *His Exits and His Entrances,* 317–318.

28. Dormon, *Theatre in the Ante-Bellum South,* 256–259; Dunn, *Shakespeare in America,* 133–135, 142–145, 175; Robert Bridges, *The Influence of the Audience* (New York, 1926), 3, 23.

29. Hudson, *Lectures on Shakespeare,* I, 54; "Observations on Some

of the Male Characters of Shakespeare," *American Monthly,* 7 (February 1836), 129–130; Kenneth S. Lynn, *William Dean Howells: An American Life* (New York, 1971), 67–68.

30. Whitman, *Specimen Days,* in Kaplan, ed., *Whitman: Poetry and Prose,* 702–703; Twain, *Is Shakespeare Dead?* (New York, 1909), 4–7; William S. McFeely, *Grant: A Biography* (New York, 1982), 29; George Templeton Strong, *The Diary of George Templeton Strong,* ed. Allan Nevins and Milton Halsey Thomas, 4 vols. (New York, 1952), II, 18; Robert N. Reeves, "Abraham Lincoln's Knowledge of Shakespeare," *Overland Monthly,* 43 (April 1904), 336–342; David Saville Muzzey, *James G. Blaine: A Political Idol of Other Days* (1934; repr., Port Washington, N.Y., 1963), 296–297; Roppolo, "Shakespeare in New Orleans, 1817–1865," in Kolin, ed., *Shakespeare in the South,* 112–113; Westfall, *American Shakespearean Criticism,* 227–229, and Henry W. Simon, *The Reading of Shakespeare in American Schools and Colleges: An Historical Survey* (New York, 1932).

31. Ludlow, *Dramatic Life as I Found It,* 234, 690–691, 694–695; Richard Moody, *America Takes the Stage: Romanticism in American Drama and Theatre, 1750–1900* (Bloomington, Ind., 1955), 195–196; Whitman, "The Old Bowery," in Kaplan, ed., *Whitman: Poetry and Prose,* 1187–88; Alger, *Life of Edwin Forrest,* II, 786.

32. For Whitman's musings about the effects of Shakespeare's "aristocratic perfume," see his "A Thought on Shakespeare" and "A Backward Glance o'er Travel'd Roads," in Kaplan, ed., *Whitman: Poetry and Prose,* 1150–52, 663–664. Eighteenth-century depictions of Shakespeare as a moral playwright are described in Bernard, *Retrospections of America,* 270–271; Westfall, *American Shakespearean Criticism,* 30–31; and Shattuck, *Shakespeare on the American Stage: From the Hallams to Edwin Booth,* 16. Jefferson, is quoted in Lawrence A. Cremin, *American Education: The Colonial Experience, 1607–1783* (New York, 1970), 438, and Lincoln is quoted in Alan Bloom, *Shakespeare's Politics* (New York, 1964), 5. For Adams's views see his essays "The Character of Desdemona," and "Misconceptions of Shakespeare upon the Stage," in Hackett, *Notes and Comments,* 234–249, 217–228.

33. Hudson, *Lectures on Shakespeare,* I, 79; playbill, Varieties Theatre, New Orleans, January 3, 4, 1870, Folger Shakespeare Library. Also see Ruth Miller Elson, *Guardians of Tradition: American Schoolbooks of the Nineteenth Century* (Lincoln, Neb., 1964), 242, 283; and Simon, *The Reading of Shakespeare in American Schools and Colleges,* 19, 26, 44.

34. *The Autobiography of Joseph Jefferson,* 166–167; Hudson, *Lectures on Shakespeare,* I, 69; Martha Baker Dunn, "My Shakespeare Progress," *Atlantic Monthly,* 98 (October 1906), 528–533.

35. For the New York reaction to Sophocles, see Doris M. Alexander, "Oedipus in Victorian New York," *American Quarterly,* 12 (Fall 1960), 417–421.

36. Grimsted, *Melodrama Unveiled,* chap. 6; George C. Branam, *Eighteenth-Century Adaptations of Shakespearean Tragedy* (Berkeley and Los Angeles, 1956), chap. 1; Rankin, *The Theater in Colonial America,* 83–84, 191–192; Charles B. Lower, "Othello as Black on Southern Stages, Then and Now," in Kolin, ed., *Shakespeare in the South,* 199–208.

37. Cibber, *The Tragical History of King Richard III,* in Christopher Spencer, ed., *Five Restoration Adaptations of Shakespeare* (Urbana, Ill., 1965), 275–344. For an excellent discussion of Cibber's adaptation, see Wood, *The Stage History of Shakespeare's King Richard the Third,* chaps. 4, 6; also see Frederick W. Kilbourne, *Alterations and Adaptations of Shakespeare* (Boston, 1906), 107–112. For the longevity of Cibber's version, see Wood, *The Stage History of Shakespeare's King Richard the Third,* 133, 165; Arthur Colby Sprague, *Shakespearian Players and Performances* (1953; repr., New York, 1969), 151, 212n3; and Roger Marvell, *Shakespeare and the Film* (New York, 1971), 48.

38. Tate, *The History of King Lear,* in Spencer, ed., *Five Restoration Adaptations of Shakespeare,* 201–274. Also see Kilbourne, *Alterations and Adaptations of Shakespeare,* 157–172. The exchange between Kean and Hackett is in Hackett, *Notes and Comments,* 227n; the contemporary critic is quoted in Grimsted, *Melodrama Unveiled,* 119–120. For Booth's "restored" *Lear,* see Charles Shattuck, *Shakespeare on the American Stage: Booth and Barrett to Sothern and Marlowe* (manuscript), chap. 1, pp. 6–7.

39. A. C. Wheeler, "The Extinction of Shakespeare," *Arena,* 1 (March 1890), 423–431.

40. *The Diary of Philip Hone,* I, 305; *New York Times,* March 14, 1909, section 6. For Bryan's decline, see Lawrence W. Levine, *Defender of the Faith: William Jennings Bryan, the Last Decade, 1915–1925* (New York, 1965). For interesting personal reflections on the changes in audiences' tolerance for oratory, see Thomas Wentworth Higginson, "American Audiences," *Atlantic Monthly,* 95 (January 1905), 38–44.

41. The foreign press statistics are from Joshua A. Fishman, *Language Loyalty in the United States* (1966; repr., New York, 1978), 59. Louise Taylor's assertion is in her unpublished dissertation, "Shakespeare in Chicago" (Northwestern University, 1981), I, 26–27. For a condescending but valuable contemporary description of the theater created by Italian and Jewish immigrants in New York City, see John Corbin, "How the Other Half Laughs," *Harper's New Monthly Maga-*

zine, 98 (December 1898), 30–48. For Shakespeare in the Yiddish theater, see Hutchins Hapgood, *The Spirit of the Ghetto* (New York, 1902), 126–127; Irving Howe, *World of Our Fathers* (New York, 1976), 466, 470; Lulla Rosenfeld, *Bright Star of Exile: Jacob Adler and the Yiddish Theatre* (New York, 1977), 265–267, 274–275, 303–305; and Ronald Sanders, *The Downtown Jews: Portraits of an Immigrant Generation* (New York, 1969), 310–314.

42. For Denney's phrase, see his essay "The Discovery of Popular Culture," in Robert E. Spiller and Eric Larrabee, eds., *American Perspectives: The National Self-Image in the Twentieth Century* (Cambridge, Mass., 1961), 164–165. Dewey's remark appeared in *Frank Leslie's Illustrated Weekly*, 42 (October 21, 1876), 103. The relationships between recitation of the King James Bible and performances of Shakespeare and between the transformation of nineteenth-century religious style and the transformation of Shakespeare need further thought and research.

43. Higham, "The Reorientation of American Culture in the 1890s," in John Weiss, ed., *The Origins of Modern Consciousness* (Detroit, 1965), 25–48; Olive Logan, "The Grand Days of Histrionics," *Harper's New Monthly Magazine*, 59 (June 1879), 50. The critics' advice to Power is quoted in Rourke, *American Humor*, 100. For Booth's statement about his father, see Otis Skinner, *Footlights and Spotlights: Recollections of My Life on the Stage* (Indianapolis, 1924), 93, 213. For evidence of Booth's influence, see Hutton, *Curiosities of the American Stage*, 293–294; Henry Austin Clapp, *Reminiscences of a Dramatic Critic* (1902; repr., Freeport, N.Y., 1972), chap. 15; and Charles H. Shattuck, *The Hamlet of Edwin Booth* (Urbana, Ill., 1969).

44. Shattuck, *Shakespeare on the American Stage: Booth and Barrett to Sothern and Marlowe* (manuscript), chap. 4, pp. 143–144, and chap. 5, pp. 40, 47; McArthur, *Actors and American Culture*, 177; Hackett, "After the Play," *New Republic*, 22 (March 24, 1920), 122.

45. Gance is quoted in Walter Benjamin, "The Work of Art in the Age of Mechanical Reproduction," in Benjamin, *Illuminations*, ed. Hannah Arendt, trans. Harry Zohn (New York, 1969), 221–222. The American critic was P. W. Wilson, "Hollywood Tries out Mr. Shakespeare," *New York Times Magazine*, October 13, 1935, 9, 19. For the suitability of Shakespeare to modern media, see Manvell, *Shakespeare and the Film*, 9–10; Jan Kott, *Shakespeare, Our Contemporary*, trans. Boleslaw Taborski (Garden City, N.Y., 1964), 231–235; John Wain, *The Living World of Shakespeare* (London, 1978), 2–7; and Brian Hooker, "Shakespere and the Movies," *Century Magazine*, 93 (December 1916), 298–304.

46. *Montgomery Ward & Company Catalogue and Buyers' Guide,* no. 57 (Spring and Summer 1895), p. 59.

47. *New York Times,* October 10, 1935; *Time,* 26 (October 21, 1935), 44–45; *New Yorker,* October 19, 1935, 67; *New Republic,* 84 (October 16, 1935), 272. For Shakespeare on radio, see Erik Barnouw, *The Golden Web: A History of Broadcasting in the United States, 1933–1953,* (New York, 1968), 70–71. Tapes of the Barrymore series exist in the Motion Picture, Broadcasting, and Recorded Sound Division, Library of Congress. Five of the CBS Shakespearean series were released on Murray Hill Records 898667, *Hollywood Immortals Perform Shakespeare: Five Original Radio Broadcasts,* a copy of which exists in the Library of Congress.

48. Wheeler, "The Extinction of Shakespeare," *Arena,* 1 (March 1890), 429; "Burton's Last Performance," *San Francisco Chronicle,* August 19, 1984; *San Francisco Focus: The Public Broadcasting Magazine of KQED 9, KQEC 32, KQED-FM,* February 1979, 20.

49. Slason Thompson, ed., *the Humbler Poets: A Collection of Newspaper and Periodical Verse, 1870–1885* (Chicago, 1911), 449–450; *Savannah Morning News,* November 22, 1883; Bella C. Landauer, "When Advertisers Discovered Shakespeare: From the Collection of Bella C. Landauer" (1937), typescript in the New York Public Library; *Youth's Companion,* 66 (May 4, 1893).

50. These films and radio programs are available in the Motion Picture, Broadcasting, and Recorded Sound Division, Library of Congress.

51. Peter Finley Dunne, *Mr. Dooley's Philosophy* (New York, 1906), 223–228; *Leslie's Illustrated Weekly,* September 22, 1900, 206.

52. Goffman, *Encounters: Two Studies in the Sociology of Interaction* (Indianapolis, 1961); "Report of the Tremont Theatre Investigating Committee," *American Monthly,* 2 (December 1830), 586–592; 2 (February 1831), 764–770; Whitman, "Miserable State of the Stage," *Brooklyn Eagle,* February 8, 1847, reprinted in Montrose J. Moses and John Mason Brown, eds., *American Theatre as Seen by Its Critics* (New York, 1934), 70–72; Trollope, *Domestic Manners of the Americans,* II, 194–195; Power, *Impressions of America,* I, 141.

53. Curtis, "Editor's Easy Chair," *Harper's New Monthly Magazine,* 28 (December 1863), 131–133. For the contrast between the two actors portraying Hamlet, see Hutton, *Curiosities of the American Stage,* 281.

54. Payne is quoted in Grimsted, *Melodrama Unveiled,* 56–57. For descriptions of the new "legitimate" theaters and their audiences, see *Harper's New Monthly Magazine,* 40 (March 1870), 605–607; *Scribner's*

Monthly, 3 (January 1872), 378–379; 3 (March 1872), 632–633. The importance of space is discussed in Somer, *Personal Space: The Behavioral Basis of Design* (Englewood Cliffs, N.J., 1969), chap. 2; Bledstein, *The Culture of Professionalism: The Middle Class and the Development of Higher Education in America* (New York, 1976), 58–64, 80; and Taylor, "Public Space, Public Opinion, and the Origins of Mass Culture," paper presented to a joint meeting of the American Council of Learned Societies and the Hungarian Academy of Sciences, held in Budapest, August 1982.

55. *The Autobiography of Joseph Jefferson,* 41–42; William B. Wood, *Personal Recollections of the Stage* (Philadelphia, 1855), 118–119; Francis Courtney Wemyss, *Twenty-six Years of the Life of an Actor and Manager* (New York, 1847), 103–105.

56. Bost, *Monarchs of the Mimic World,* 87; Irving, *Letters of Jonathan Oldstyle,* 12.

57. Kean's tribulations in Boston are discussed in Wemyss, *Twenty-six Years of the Life of an Actor and Manager,* 97–99, 113–115, and Shattuck, *Shakespeare on the American Stage: From the Hallams to Edwin Booth,* 42–43; his experiences in Baltimore are described in Wood, *Personal Recollections of the Stage,* 321, and Christopher J. Thaiss, "Shakespeare in Maryland, 1752–1860," in Kolin, ed., *Shakespeare in the South,* 61–62.

58. Power, *Impressions of America,* I, 351–355.

59. *The Diary of Philip Hone,* I, 49–51; *New York Evening Standard,* October 13, 15, 1831; *New York Evening Sun,* October 14, 1831; *New York Evening Post,* October 17, 18, 1831.

60. *New York Herald,* May 7, 8, 9, 10, 11, 12, 13, 14, 15, 1849. In addition to the local press, my account of the Astor Place Riot is based on Richard Moody, *The Astor Riot* (Bloomington, Ind., 1958); William Toynbee, ed., *The Diaries of William Charles Macready,* 2 vols. (London, 1912), II, 404–429; *The Diary of Philip Hone,* II, 866–869; Lester Wallack, *Memories of Fifty Years* (New York, 1889), 131; and Peter G. Buckley, "The Astor Place Riot and Jenny Lind," paper presented at the Ninety-sixth Annual Meeting of the American Historical Association, held in Los Angeles, December 28–30, 1981, and 'A Privileged Place': New York Theatre Riots, 1817–1849," paper presented at the annual meeting of the Organization of American Historians, held in St. Louis, April 8–11, 1982. I am extremely grateful to Buckley for sharing these unpublished papers with me before his dissertation was completed. I have subsequently benefited greatly from his dissertation, "To the Opera House: Culture and Society in New York City, 1820–1860" (State University of New York at Stony Brook, 1984).

61. *New York Herald*, May 12, 1849; *New York Tribune*, May 12, 1849.

62. *Home Journal*, May 12, 1849, as quoted in Montrose J. Moses, *The Fabulous Forrest: The Record of an American Actor* (Boston, 1929), 262; *New York Tribune*, May 12, 1849; *New York Herald*, May 12, 1849; *Philadelphia Public Ledger*, May 16, 1849. For a useful compendium of newspaper opinion, see "Opinions of the Press on the Late Occurrences in Astor Place," *New York Herald*, May 16, 1849.

63. The speaker was quoted in the *New York Herald*, May 12, 1849. The relations between Forrest and Macready can be traced in Macready, *Diaries*, II, 228–231, 326–331, 334, 404–405, 420–421; Buckley, "To the Opera House" (Ph.D. diss., State University of New York at Stony Brook, 1984), chap 1; and Alan S. Downer, *The Eminent Tragedian: William Charles Macready* (Cambridge, Mass., 1966), chap. 7. Van Buren is quoted in Buckley, "To the Opera House," 303.

64. Herman Melville, *The Confidence Man: His Masquerade* (1857; repr., London, 1948), 219.

65. Arnold Aronson, "Shakespeare in Virginia, 1751–1863," in Kolin ed., *Shakespeare in the South*, 35–36.

66. Barnum's announcement and the speeches of Hackett and Bryant appeared in the *New York Times*, April 23, 24, 1864, May 24, 1872.

67. Melville is quoted in Buckley, "To the Opera House" (Ph.D. diss., State University of New York at Stony Brook, 1984), 289. Poe's comments came in the course of his caustic remarks concerning Carlyle's ideas on hero-worship in the *Democratic Review*, April 1846, reprinted in *Edgar Allan Poe: Essays and Reviews*, ed. G. R. Thompson (New York, 1984), 1392–93. White expounded his views in a four-part article, "The Anatomizing of William Shakespeare," *Atlantic Monthly*, 53 (May 1884), 595–612; 53 (June 1884), 815–837; 54 (August 1884), 257–267; 54 (September 1884), 313–326.

68. The poem was printed in the *New York Mirror*, June 1, 1839. Helena Modjeska, "Endowed Theatres and the American Stage," *Forum*, 14 (November 1892), 338–340; Israel Zangwill, "The Future of Vaudeville in America," *Cosmpolitan*, 38 (April 1905), 639–646; The Drama Committee of the Twentieth Century Club, *The Amusement Situation in the City of Boston: Based on a Study of the Theatres for Ten Weeks from November 28, 1909, to February 5, 1910* (Boston, 1910), 3–4; T. R. Sullivan, "A Standard Theatre," *Atlantic Monthly*, 75 (May 1895), 686–689.

69. Mark H. Liddell, "Botching Shakespeare," *Atlantic Monthly*, 82 (October 1898), 461–472; "Why Shakspere is Not Understood," *World's Work*, 5 (March 1903), 3249–51. James Russell Lowell's 1887

address was printed as "Shakespeare's Richard III," *Atlantic Monthly*, 68 (December 1891), 817–823. The ads appeared in *Collier's Weekly*, 32 (November 7, 1903), 19; 32 (November 28, 1903), 33; 32 (December 5, 1903), 42.

70. John Quincy Adams, "Personations of the Characters of Shakespeare," *American Monthly*, 7 (January 1836), 38–40; Charles Lamb, "On the Tragedies of Shakspere, Considered with Reference to Their Fitness for Stage Representation," in *Poems, Plays, and Miscellaneous Essays of Charles Lamb* (London and New York, 1888), 220–240; A. C. Wheeler, "The Extinction of Shakespeare," *Arena*, 1 (March 1890), 423–431; A. A. Lipscomb, "Uses of Shakespeare off the Stage," *Harper's New Monthly Magazine*, 65 (August 1882), 431–438. The attempted assassination of Booth was covered in great detail in the *Chicago Tribune*, April 24, 25, 26, 27, 1879.

71. Thomas J. Richardson, "Is Shakespeare Dead? Mark Twain's Irreverent Question," in Kolin, ed., *Shakespeare and Southern Writers*, 71–72.

72. Delia Bacon, "William Shakespeare and His Plays: An Inquiry Concerning Them," *Putnam's Monthly*, 7 (January 1856), 19; Appleton Morgan, "The Shakespearean Myth," *Appleton's Journal*, 6 (February 1879), 118; Ignatius Donnelly, "The Shakespeare Myth," *North American Review*, 145 (July 1887), 68. There were, of course, many defenders of Shakespeare. See, for example, Myron B. Benton, "Shakespeare and the Musical Glasses," *Appleton's Journal*, 6 (April 1879), 336–344; John Fiske, "Forty Years of Bacon-Shakespeare Folly," *Atlantic Monthly*, 80 (November 1897), 635–652; Charles William Wallace, "New Shakespeare Discoveries," *Harper's Monthly Magazine*, 120 (March 1910), 489–510. The debate over the authorship of Shakespeare's plays is summarized in R. C. Churchill, *Shakespeare and His Betters* (London, 1958); F. E. Halliday, *The Cult of Shakespeare* (New York, 1960); and H. N. Gibson, *The Shakespeare Claimants* (London, 1962).

73. Norman Hapgood, "The Actor of To-Day," *Atlantic Monthly*, 83 (January 1899), 120, and "The Upbuilding of the Theatre," *Atlantic Monthly*, 83 (April 1899), 421; Lewes is quoted in "The Upbuilding of the Theatre," 419. For the development of the term "legitimate" in England, see Ernest Bradlee Watson, *Sheridan to Robertson: A Study of the Nineteenth-Century London Stage* (1926; repr., New York, 1963), chap. 2. For the term in the United States, see the *Dictionary of American Slang* (New York, 1960), and *A Dictionary of American English on Historical Principles* (Chicago, 1942).

74. Hapgood, "The Upbuilding of the Theatre," *Atlantic Monthly*, 83 (April 1899), 421; James L. Ford, "Why Shakespeare Languishes,"

Munsey's Magazine 28 (January 1903), 629–631; "The Drama as Art," *Dial*, 25 (November 16, 1898), 333–335.

75. Walter Prichard Eaton, "Class-Consciousness and the 'Movies,'" *Atlantic Monthly*, 115 (January 1915), 49–51; Rollin Lynde Hartt, "The Home of Burlesque," *Atlantic Monthly*, 101 (January 1908), 68–78. The vaudeville actress is quoted in Gunther Barth, *City People* (New York, 1980), 192.

76. Alfred L. Bernheim, *The Business of the Theatre* (New York, 1932), which was prepared for and published by the Actor's Equity Association, contains an excellent detailed account of the rise of the new theatrical system. See also Shattuck, *Shakespeare on the American Stage: Booth and Barrett to Sothern and Marlowe*, Introduction; McArthur, *Actors and American Culture, 1880–1920*, chap. 1; Robert Grau, *The Business Man in the Amusement World* (New York, 1910), chap. 1; Norman Hapgood, *The Stage in America, 1897–1900* (New York, 1901), chap. 1.

77. Hapgood, "The Actor of To-Day," *Atlantic Monthly*, 83 (January 1899), 119; Grau, *The Business Man in the Amusement World*, Introductory.

78. The Drama Committee of the Twentieth Century Club, *The Amusement Situation in the City of Boston*; Booth to his daughter Edwina, September 25, 1890, December 3, 1890, in Edwina Booth Grossman, *Edwin Booth: Recollections by His Daughter and Letters to Her and to His Friends* (New York, 1894), 112–113.

79. Shattuck, *Shakespeare on the American Stage: Booth and Barrett to Sothern and Marlowe*, Epilogue. MacKaye's production was extensively covered in the *New York Times*, April 15, 1916, May 14, 17, 18, 20, 21, 22, 23, 24, 25, 26, 30, 1916.

80. Kate Field, "A Conversation on the Stage," *Atlantic Monthly*, 21 (March 1868), 270–277. McKellan is quoted in the *San Francisco Chronicle*, February 1, 1987.

Two · The Sacralization of Culture

1. Whitman, *Memoranda* in Kaplan, ed., *Whitman: Poetry and Prose*, 1288. For Whitman's relationship to opera and its effects upon his poetry, see Robert D. Faner, *Walt Whitman and Opera* (Philadelphia, 1951). For a still valuable overview of opera in nineteenth-century New York, see the four-part series by Richard Grant White, "Opera in New York," *Century Magazine*, 23 (March 1882), 686–703; "Opera in New York, II," *Century Magazine*, 23 (April 1882), 865–882; "Opera in

New York, III," *Century Magazine*, 24 (May 1882), 31–43; "Opera in New York, IV," *Century Magazine*, 24 (June 1882), 193–210. For eighteenth-century opera in America, see O. G. Sonneck, *Early Opera in America* (New York, 1915); Julian Mates, *The American Musical Stage before 1800* (New Brunswick, N.J., 1962); and Patricia H. Virga, *The American Opera to 1790* (Ann Arbor, Mich., 1982).

2. *The Diary of George Templeton Strong*, II, 59, 63, 85, 373, 445.

3. Whitman, *Proud Music of the Storm*, in Kaplan, ed., *Whitman: Poetry and Prose*, 525–530; *New York Times*, December 21, 1854. Whitman's *Brooklyn Daily Eagle* column is quoted in Faner, *Walt Whitman and Opera*, 6. In this period Buckley's Ethiopian Opera House was offering an entire series of burlesques of such popular operas as *La Cenerentola* and *Fra Diavolo*. See amusement columns of the *New York Times*, October 3, 1854. The *Times'* assertion of parenthood was made in its issue of October 11, 1859.

4. For opera in New Orleans, see Henry A. Kmen, *Music in New Orleans: The Formative Years, 1791–1841* (Baton Rouge, 1966), 56–200, and Ronald L. Davis, *A History of Opera in the American West* (Englewood Cliffs, N.J., 1965), chaps. 1–2.

5. Katherine K. Preston, "Travelling Opera Troupes in the United States, 1825–1860," (Ph.D. diss. in progress, City University of New York), chap. 4, and "Opera on the Road: The American Adventures of the Pyne and Harrison Opera Company, 1855–56," unpublished paper presented to a joint meeting of the Capital Chapter, American Musicological Society, and the Chesapeake Chapter, Music Library Association, Richmond, Virginia, October 4, 1986. For the variety of opera throughout the country, see also Howard Swan, *Music in the Southwest* (San Marino, Calif., 1952), and the two books by Ronald L. Davis, *Opera in the West*, and *Opera in Chicago* (New York, 1966).

6. Theodore Thomas, *A Musical Autobiography*, ed. George P. Upton, 2 vols. (Chicago, 1905), I, 24–25; *New York Times*, September 1, 1883.

7. Julius Mattfeld, *A Hundred Years of Grand Opera in New York, 1825–1925: A Record of Performances* (New York, 1927), 15.

8. This information was derived from Mattfeld's extremely useful alphabetical listing of the operas performed in New York between 1825 and 1925, *A Hundred Years of Grand Opera in New York*, 39–80, and Kmen, *Music in New Orleans*, 133–134, 175–178.

9. Mattfeld, *A Hundred Years of Grand Opera in New York*, 49, 52, 55.

10. *New Orleans Picayune*, May 23, 24, 1837.

11. See the alphabetical listings in Mattfeld, *A Hundred Years of*

Grand Opera in New York. See also *New York Times*, October 24, 1856, November 27, 1876, and *Philadelphia Public Ledger*, September 26, 1849, November 19, 1849, January 2, 1850.

12. Mattfeld, *A Hundred Years of Grand Opera in New York*, 60; Kmen, *Music in New Orleans*, 175; *New York Times*, October 5, 1858.

13. Charles Hamm, *Yesterdays: Popular Song in America* (New York, 1979), chap. 4, is particularly good on the popularity of opera in English translation. Richard Grant White attests to the lucrativeness of opera in English in his "Opera in New York," *Century Magazine*, 23 (March 1882), 699.

14. *The Diary of Philip Hone*, II, 103–104, 183. Hone's 1835 remarks, dated November 11, 1835, are excerpted in the Nevins edition of his diary: for the full quote see *The Diary of Philip Hone*, ed. Bayard Tuckerman (New York, 1889), I, 170. The *Chicago Daily Journal* is quoted in Davis, *Opera in Chicago*, 13. The *Mobile Daily Advertiser*, February 12, 1856, is quoted in Preston, "Opera on the Road" (unpublished paper, cited in n. 5 above), 11. The New Orleans incidents are in Kmen, *Music in New Orleans*, 194–196. Whitman's ambiguities concerning opera are traced in Faner, *Walt Whitman and Opera*, 36, 39, 43, 81n.

15. This paragraph is based largely on material in Preston's as yet unpublished pioneering work ("Travelling Opera Troupes in the United States, 1825–1860").

16. For the popularity of operatic arias in English translation, see Hamm, *Yesterdays*, chap. 4. White's recollections are in his "Opera in New York," *Century Magazine*, 23 (March 1882), 701.

17. Willis originally published these remarks in the *Home Journal* in the fall of 1850 and reprinted them in his *Memoranda of the Life of Jenny Lind* (Philadelphia, 1851), 144–145; the letter to the *Tribune* is also printed in Willis's *Memoranda*, 216–217. *New York Times*, July 17, 1883; *Frank Leslie's Illustrated Newspaper*, August 18, 1883, 414.

18. Hamm, *Yesterdays*, 88; Swan, *Music in the Southwest*, 77–78; Towle, *American Society*, II, 4. The Massachusetts soldier is quoted in Margaret Hindle Hazen and Robert M. Hazen, *The Music Men: An Illustrated History of Brass Bands in America, 1800–1922* (Washington, D.C., 1987), 155–156. Dwight quotes his friend in *Dwight's Journal of Music*, July 6, 1878, 263.

19. *Dwight's Journal of Music*, August 17, 1878, 287; *Lockport Daily Journal and Courier*, April 26, 1862, quoted in Louis Moreau Gottschalk, *Notes of a Pianist* (1881; repr., New York, 1964), 61n.

20. *Putnam's Magazine*, 1 (May 1853), 588–591; Thomas Whitney Surette, "The Opera," *Atlantic Monthly*, 117 (April 1916), 466–476.

21. Hamm, *Yesterdays*, 69, 87; Ronald L. Davis, *A History of Music in American Life*, 3 vols. (New York, 1980), I, 134; *San Francisco Chronicle*, March 3, 1885. For descriptions of wealthy operagoers in the early twentieth century, see Irving Kolodin, *The Metropolitan Opera, 1883–1966: A Candid History* (New York, 1967), 152, 211, 249, 265. For the situation in Los Angeles, see Swan, *Music in the Southwest*.

22. Matilda Despard, "Music in New York Thirty Years Ago," *Harper's New Monthly Magazine*, 57 (June 1878), 115; "Editor's Easy Chair," *Harper's New Monthly Magazine*, 68 (May 1884), 968–969; *The Diary of George Templeton Strong*, II, 13–14. Wagner's attitudes are discussed in Herbert Lindenberger, *Opera: The Extravagant Art* (Ithaca, 1984), chap. 5.

23. *Harper's New Monthly Magazine*, 74 (February 1887), 475; *New York Times Illustrated Magazine*, October 30, 1898, 12; *New York Times*, April 29, 1900.

24. Davis, *A History of Music in American Life*, I, 137; Lindenberger, *Opera: The Extravagant Art*, 251.

25. Raoul Camus, "Brass Bands in Community Life," unpublished paper presented to the conference "Music and Dance in Nineteenth Century America" at the State University of New York at Stony Brook, August 10, 1984; the statistics on the number of bands come from p. 7. See also Jonathan Elkus, *Charles Ives and the American Band Tradition: A Centennial Tribute* (Exeter, England, 1974). Robyn's career in St. Louis is chronicled in "The Autobiography of William Robyn," ed. Ernst C. Krohn, in Krohn, *Missouri Music* (New York, 1971), 239–255.

26. John Erskine, *The Philharmonic-Symphony Society of New York: Its First Hundred Years* (New York, 1943), 5; Gilbert Chase, *America's Music* (New York, 1966), 621–624; Thomas, *A Musical Autobiography*, I, 19–27. For Dodworth's concert, see the program reprinted facing p. 102 in John H. Mueller, *The American Symphony Orchestra: A Social History of Musical Taste* (Bloomington, Ind., 1951). Gilmore's National Peace Jubilee is treated in H. W. Schwartz, *Bands of America* (Garden City, N.Y., 1957), chap 3, and Marwood Darlington, *Irish Orpheus: The Life of Patrick S. Gilmore Bandmaster Extraordinary* (Philadelphia, 1950), chap. 5. For Dwight's reactions, see Irving Sablosky, ed., *What They Heard: Music in America, 1852–1861, From the Pages of Dwight's Journal of Music*, (Baton Rouge, 1986), 58–70. Gilmore is quoted in Neil Harris, "John Philip Sousa and the Culture of Reassurance," in Jon Newsom, ed., *Perspectives on John Philip Sousa* (Washington, D.C., 1983), 21.

27. Schwartz, *Bands of America*, 144; John Philip Sousa, *Marching*

Along: Recollections of Men, Women and Music (Boston, 1928), 133, 275; William Mason, *Memories of a Musical Life*, (New York, 1902), 187–188; M. A. DeWolfe Howe, *The Boston Symphony Orchestra, 1881–1931* (Boston, 1931), 5.

28. O. G. Sonneck, *Early Concert Life in America: 1731–1800* (Leipzig, 1907), is filled with examples of eighteenth-century musical eclecticism.

29. Davis, *A History of Music in American Life*, I, 101, 107–119; W. Porter Ware and Thaddeus C. Lockard, Jr., *P. T. Barnum Presents Jenny Lind: The American Tour of the Swedish Nightingale* (Baton Rouge, 1980); Ivor Guest, *Fanny Elssler* (London, 1970), 104–185; *The Diary of Philip Hone*, I, 481–482.

30. Mueller, *The American Symphony Orchestra* 33–34; Philip Hart, *Orpheus in the New World: The Symphony Orchestra as an American Cultural Institution* (New York, 1973), 7–8; *Dwight's Journal of Music*, October 29, 1853; Thomas, *A Musical Autobiography*, I, 26–27; Rose Fay Thomas, *Memoirs of Theodore Thomas* (New York, 1911), 12–13. Jullien's tour of the United States, which should be the subject of a penetrating cultural study, is treated rather perfunctorily in Adam Carse, *The Life of Jullien* (Cambridge, England, 1951), chap. 5.

31. Walter Damrosch, *My Musical Life* (New York, 1924), 30–33; Edwin T. Rice, "Personal Recollections of Leopold Damrosch," *Musical Quarterly*, 28 (July 1942), 269–275; Thomas, *A Musical Autobiography*, I, 88–91; Rose Fay Thomas, *Memoirs of Theodore Thomas*, 380–384; Joseph A. Mussulman, *Music in the Cultured Generation: A Social History of Music in America, 1870–1900* (Evanston, Ill., 1971), 183–184.

32. H. Earle Johnson, "The Germania Musical Society," *Musical Quarterly*, 39 (January 1953), 75–93; *Dwight's Journal of Music*, September 16, 1854, 187–189; Hart, *Orpheus in the New World*, 7. Apthorp is quoted in Howe, *The Boston Symphony Orchestra*, 4. Damrosch's recollections of his Oklahoma City concert can be found in his *My Musical Life*, 192–193.

33. Charles Edward Russell, *The American Orchestra and Theodore Thomas* (Garden City, N.Y., 1927), 1–6; Huneker, *The Philharmonic Society*, 10–11, 33.

34. Thomas, *A Musical Autobiography*, I, 3, 38–43, 50–51; William Mason, *Memories of a Musical Life*, 193–197. The Philharmonic member is quoted in Mueller, *The American Symphony Orchestra*, 330. The number of Philharmonic concerts is given in Johnson, "The Germania Musical Society," *The Musical Quarterly*, 39 (January 1953), 80n, and Henry Edward Krehbiel, *The Philharmonic Society of New York: A Memorial* (New York, 1892), 75–76.

35. Edwin T. Rice, "Thomas and Central Park Garden," *The Musical*

Quarterly, 26 (April 1940), 143, 144, 148, 149; Thomas, *A Musical Autobiography*, I, 66.

36. Thomas, *A Musical Autobiography*, I, 54.

37. Ibid., II, 3; Rose Fay Thomas, *Memoirs of Theodore Thomas*, 258, 333; C. Norman Fay, "The Theodore Thomas Orchestra," *Outlook*, January 22, 1910, 160.

38. Thomas, *A Musical Autobiography*, I, 103–104; Fay, "The Theodore Thomas Orchestra," *The Outlook*, January 22, 1910, 159–169.

39. Fay, "The Theodore Thomas Orchestra," *The Outlook*, January 22, 1910, 162–168; Thomas, *A Musical Autobiography*, I, 105, 107; Rose Fay Thomas, *Memoirs of Theodore Thomas*, 372. See the lists of officers, trustees, and members of the Chicago Orchestral Association from 1891 to 1924 in Philo Adams Otis, *The Chicago Orchestra: Its Organization, Growth and Development, 1891–1924* (Chicago, 1924), 391–414, also pp. 28–29. Otis, who for many years was a trustee and an officer of the Chicago Symphony, has an invaluable year by year account of the Chicago Symphony's financial condition. Thomas's remark about the three epochs was made at a private dinner attended by Otis, who recounts it on p. 97 of his book. Otis's detailed account of the orchestra's history to 1924 includes lists of their programs. For a complete list of all of the concert programs of Thomas from his days with the Mason-Thomas Quartette through his years with the Chicago Symphony, see the second volume of his *A Musical Autobiography*. For a copy of the program for Thomas's first "American Night" see Mueller, *The American Symphony Orchestra*, 275.

40. Thomas, *A Musical Autobiography*, I, 104–105.

41. Martin Green, *The Problem of Boston: Some Readings in Cultural History* (New York, 1966), 103. For Dwight's life, see George Willis Cooke, *John Sullivan Dwight: Brook-Farmer, Editor, and Critic of Music* (Boston, 1898); Field's anecdote is related on pp. 278–279. See also Edward N. Waters, "John Sullivan Dwight, First American Critic of Music," *Musical Quarterly*, 21 (January 1935), 69–88. Dwight's 1840 review is quoted in Howe, *The Boston Symphony Orchestra*, 2–3. The "John Sebastian Dwight" anecdote is mentioned in Jeanne Behrend's introduction to Gottschalk, *Notes of a Pianist*, xxvii (note).

42. *Dwight's Journal of Music*, October 4, 1873, 102.

43. Ibid., October 4, 1873, 102–103; October 31, 1874, 326; July 5, 1879, 110. Dwight's remark about the Germania Musical Society is quoted in Johnson, "The Germania Musical Society," *Musical Quarterly*, 39 (January 1953), 80.

44. *Dwight's Journal of Music*, September 11, 1880, 150; April 9, 1881, 58–59.

45. This sketch of Higginson's life is derived from Bliss Perry, *Life*

and Letters of Henry Lee Higginson (Boston, 1921); Higginson's lament is on p. 267. See chap. 9 for Perry's portrayal of Higginson's ambivalence about his business career. Adams's characterization of Higginson is in *The Education of Henry Adams* (1918; Modern Library ed., New York, 1931), 210.

46. Higginson's 1918 address is reprinted in Hart, *Orpheus in the New World*, 48–50. Aldrich is quoted in Howe, *The Boston Symphony Orchestra*, 127.

47. Higginson's letter outlining his original conditions of employment is reprinted in Howe, *The Boston Symphony Orchestra*, 39; see also pp. 28–29; for newspaper reaction, see pp. 40–45. Higginson's contracts with his musicians and his conductors can be found in Perry, *Life and Letters of Henry Lee Higginson*, 308n, and Hart, *Orpheus in the New World*, 57–58.

48. Gericke's account is printed in Howe, *The Boston Symphony Orchestra*, 62–66; for newspaper commentary, see pp. 72–73. For other examples of defections when Gericke and his successor Arthur Nikisch played Brahms's symphonies, see Mueller, *The American Symphony Orchestra*, 363, and Henry T. Finck, *My Adventures in the Golden Age of Music* (New York, 1926), 400.

49. Higginson, "*In re* the Boston Symphony Orchestra," reprinted in Howe, *The Boston Symphony Orchestra*, 16–20; Higginson to Eliot, July 9, 1917, in Perry, *Life and Letters of Henry Lee Higginson*, 482–483.

50. Higginson's address to his musicians is reprinted in Perry, *Life and Letters of Henry Lee Higginson*, 291–296. For Dwight's remarks, see Mussulman, *Music in the Cultured Generation*, 98. Higginson's defense came in the course of his farewell address to Gericke, reprinted in Howe, *The Boston Symphony Orchestra*, 84–87.

51. Higginson's 1889 address is reprinted in Howe, *The Boston Symphony Orchestra*, 84–87. His 1914 address is reprinted in Perry, *Life and Letters of Henry Lee Higginson*, 291–296.

52. *New York Times—Supplement*, October 18, 1896, 12; Huneker, *The Philharmonic Society of New York*, 25–26; Erskine, *The Philharmonic-Symphony Society*, 21; Mueller, *The American Symphony Orchestra*, 53. The San Francisco paper is quoted in Howe, *The Boston Symphony Orchestra*, 26. John Crerar's library bequest is quoted in Helen Lefkowitz Horowitz, *Culture and the City: Cultural Philanthropy in Chicago from the 1880s to 1917* (Lexington, Ky., 1976), 98–99.

53. Krehbiel, *Philharmonic Society*, 68–69; Mueller, *The American Symphony Orchestra*, 47–56. See also Stephen R. Couch, "Class, Politics, and Symphony Orchestras," *Society*, 14, (November/December 1976),

24–29. For the most complete history of the Philharmonic, see Howard Shanet, *Philharmonic: A History of New York's Orchestra* (Garden City, N.Y., 1975).

54. Erskine, *The Philharmonic-Symphony*, 23–24; Mueller, *The American Symphony Orchestra*, 69–76; George Martin, *The Damrosch Dynasty: America's First Family of Music* (New York, 1983), 47–48, 187–200, 264–269, 305–314.

55. Frances Anne Wister, *Twenty-five Years of the Philadelphia Orchestra, 1900–1925* (Philadelphia, 1925), written for the friends and supporters of the Philadelphia Orchestra Association to celebrate the orchestra's twenty-fifth anniversary, is an invaluable source containing lists of board members, early programs, newspaper reactions, and a wealth of other information. See also Edward Arian, *Bach, Beethoven, and Bureaucracy: The Case of the Philadelphia Orchestra* (University, Alabama, 1971), chap. 3, for an analysis of the composition of the orchestra's leadership.

56. Hart, *Orpheus in the New World*, 46–47, 66–70; Howe, *The Boston Symphony Orchestra*, 137–139. For brief histories of these early orchestras, see Mueller, *The American Symphony Orchestra*, chap. 3.

57. Krehbiel, *The Philharmonic Society of New York*, 82, 84.

58. *The Diary of George Templeton Strong*, II, 44, 204; III, 504; Finck, *My Adventures in the Golden Age of Music*, 33–38.

59. Otis, *The Chicago Symphony Orchestra*, 162; Rose Fay Thomas, *Memoirs of Theodore Thomas*, 16; Russell, *The American Orchestra and Theodore Thomas*, 88–89, 155. *Dwight's Journal* is quoted in Rose Fay Thomas's *Memoirs*, 20–21.

60. John Sullivan Dwight, "Music as a Means of Culture," *Atlantic Monthly*, 26 (September 1870), 324; *Dwight's Journal of Music*, July 6, 1878, 262–263; January 4, 1879, 6; August 2, 1879, 126–127.

61. Edward Baxter Perry, "Mutual Courtesy between Artist and Audience," *Music*, July 1892, 246–249; Finck, *My Adventures in the Golden Age of Music*, 235–236, 252; George William Curtis, "Editor's Easy Chair," *Harper's New Monthly Magazine*, 64 (February 1882), 467–468.

62. Damrosch, *My Musical Life*, 75–76; H. Earle Johnson, *Symphony Hall, Boston: With a List of Works Performed by the Boston Symphony Orchestra, Compiled by Members of the Staff of Symphony Hall* (Boston, 1950), 26; Finck, *My Adventures in the Golden Age of Music*, 235–236, 252; Thomas, *A Musical Autobiography*, I, 3.

63. Sonneck, *Early Concert Life in America*, 195. Max Maretzek, whose career throws much light on nineteenth-century American culture, published two autobiographical books: *Crochets and Quavers* (New York, 1855) and *Sharps and Flats* (New York, 1890). They have been

reprinted in one volume, *Revelations of an Opera Manager in Nineteenth-Century America* (New York, 1968), with their original pagination. Maretzek's anecdote is recounted in *Crotchets and Quavers*, 71–73. Mahler and the reporter are quoted in Johnson, *Symphony Hall, Boston*, 52, 47.

64. Maretzek, *Sharps and Flats*, 9–10; *The Diary of George Templeton Strong*, IV, 166, 354. The Thomas and Toscanini anecdotes are related respectively in Finck, *My Adventures in the Golden Age of Music*, 180, and John Briggs, *Requiem for a Yellow Brick Brewery* (Boston, 1969), 110–111.

65. *The Diary of George Templeton Strong*, IV, 354; Mueller, *The American Symphony Orchestra*, 48–49, 361–363. Mahler is quoted in Harold Schonberg, "Gustav Mahler as Conductor," *Hi-Fi/Stereo Review*, August 1967, 47. The attacks on Mahler are related in Finck, *My Adventures in the Golden Age of Music*, 425.

66. Mussulman, *Music in the Cultured Generation*, chap. 10; *Atlantic Monthly*, 68 (October 1891), 575; "The Decline of the Amateur," *Atlantic Monthly*, 73 (June 1894), 859; Olga Samaroff Stokowski, *An American Musician's Story* (New York, 1939), 260–262.

67. Rose Fay Thomas, *Memoirs of Theodore Thomas*, 328–329; Charles E. Ives, *Memos*, ed. John Kirkpatrick (New York, 1972), 52, 71, 131–132; J. Peter Burkholder, *Charles Ives: The Ideas behind the Music* (New Haven, 1985), 50–52; Stokowski, *An American Musician's Story*, 36.

68. Irving Sablosky, ed., *What They Heard . . . from the Pages of Dwight's Journal of Music*, 37–40; Gottschalk, *Notes of a Pianist*, 44, 48, 118. For an excellent discussion of the discontented state of American composers in mid-nineteenth-century America, see Shanet, *Philharmonic*, chap. 11; Fry is quoted on p. 114.

69. Mark Twain to Joe Twichell, August 22, 1897, quoted in Ives, *Memos*, 88–89; Finck, *My Adventures in the Golden Age of Music*, 401; Dwight, "Our Dark Age in Music," *Atlantic Monthly*, 50 (December 1882), 813–823; Frederick W. Root, "Folk-Music," *International Folk-Lore Congress of the World's Columbian Exposition, Chicago, 1893* (n.d., n.p.), I, 424–425. White, Nast, and Apthorp are quoted in Mussulman, *Music in the Cultured Generation*, 109–110, 114–115.

70. Malcolm Cowley, "The Revolt against Gentility," in Cowley, ed., *After the Genteel Tradition: American Writers, 1910–1930* (1937; repr., Carbondale, Ill., 1964), 6, 12–13; Randolph Bourne, "Trans-national America," in Carl Resek, ed., *War and the Intellectuals* (New York, 1964), 107. Lewis and Garland are quoted in Cowley's book.

71. Russell, *The American Orchestra and Theodore Thomas*, 174–175.

Norton is quoted in Green, *The Problem of Boston*, 139. James is quoted in Marc Pachter, "American Cosmopolitanism, 1870–1910," in Marc Chenetier and Rob Kroes, eds., *Impressions of a Gilded Age: The American Fin de Siècle* (Amsterdam, 1983), 29. Cole is quoted in Barbara Novak, *Nature and Culture: American Landscape and Painting, 1825–1875* (New York, 1980), 206. Adams is quoted in Horowitz, *Culture and the City*, 67.

72. *Harper's New Monthly Magazine*, 34 (January 1867), 261.

73. Neil Harris, *Humbug: The Art of P. T. Barnum* (Chicago, 1973), 78. See the excellent accounts of Peale's museum in Edward P. Alexander, *Museum Masters: Their Museums and Their Influence* (Nashville, 1983), chap. 3, and Charles Coleman Sellers, *Mr. Peale's Museum: Charles Willson Peale and the First Popular Museum of Natural Science and Art* (New York, 1980). Johnson's definition is in Alexander, *Museum Masters*, 3.

74. H. Earle Johnson, *Musical Interludes in Boston, 1795–1830* (New York, 1943), 20–27; Alexander, *Museum Masters*, chap. 3; Sellers, *Mr. Peale's Museum*, 236–237.

75. *Scribner's Monthly*, 14 (September 1877), 716. The other quotations in this paragraph come from Neil Harris, *The Artist in American Society*, chap. 12, and Roger B. Stein, *John Ruskin and Aesthetic Thought in America, 1840–1900* (Cambridge, Mass., 1967), 76, 77, 79, 105, 109, 132–133, 146, 214.

76. This paragraph is based upon material in Walter Muir Whitehill, *Museum of Fine Arts, Boston: A Centennial History*, 2 vols. (Cambridge, Mass., 1970), I, chaps. 1–2; Theodore Lewis Low, *The Educational Philosophy and Practice of Art Museums in the United States* (New York, 1948), chap. 1; and Neil Harris, "The Gilded Age Revisited: Boston and the Museum Movement," *American Quarterly*, 14 (Winter 1962), 545–566. The speech of Mayor Cobb, as well as other dedicatory speeches, can be found in *Dwight's Journal of Music*, July 22, 1876, 267–268. For Paul DiMaggio's argument, see his articles "Cultural Entrepreneurship in Nineteenth-Century Boston: The Creation of an Organizational Base for High Culture in America," and "Cultural Entrepreneurship in Nineteenth-Century Boston, Part II: The Classification and Framing of American Art," *Media, Culture and Society*, 4 (1982), 33–50, 303–322. For a different point of view, see Neil Harris's article cited above.

77. This account of the struggle in the Boston Museum is based upon the detailed history in Whitehill, *Museum of Fine Arts, Boston*, I, esp. chap. 6.

78. The Boston trustees' statement is in Whitehill, *Museum of Fine*

Arts, Boston, I, 60; Prichard's statement is on p. 212; for figures showing how much greater attendance was on free days, see p. 40, and for a description of the new building, see chap. 7. Gilman's statement comes from his essay "Dr. Goode's Thesis and Antithesis," in Gilman, *Museum Ideals of Purpose and Method*, 2d ed. (Boston, 1923), 77–81. The Philadelphia trustee is quoted in Daniel M. Fox, *Engines of Culture: Philanthropy and Art Museums* (Madison, 1963), 12.

79. This paragraph is based upon Peter C. Marzio, *The Art Crusade: An Analysis of American Drawing Manuals, 1820–1860* (Washington, D.C., 1976).

80. This account is based upon Wilcomb E. Washburn's excellent articles "Joseph Henry's Conception of the Purpose of the Smithsonian Institution," in *A Cabinet of Curiosities: Five Episodes in the Evolution of American Museums*, with an introduction by Walter Muir Whitehill (Charlottesville, Va., 1967), 106–166, and "The Influence of the Smithsonian Institution on Intellectual Life in Mid-Nineteenth Century Washington," in Francis Coleman Rosenberger, ed., *Records of the Columbia Historical Society of Washington, D.C., 1963–1965* (Washington, D.C., 1966), 96–121.

81. For the policies of Henry's successors, see Edward P. Alexander, "George Brown Goode and the Smithsonian Museums: A National Museum of Cultural History," in Alexander, *Museum Masters*, 292–294, 302. The statement of the Metropolitan Museum founders is in Winifred E. Howe, *A History of the Metropolitan Museum of Art*, 2 vols. (New York, 1913), I, 102.

82. The anecdote about Eliot and Winsor is in Edward P. Alexander, "John Cotton Dana and the Newark Museum: The Museum of Community Service," in Alexander, *Museum Masters*, 382; *Life*, January 17, 1884, reprinted in Harry Miller Lydenberg, *History of the New York Public Library* (New York, 1923), 113–115.

83. Horowitz, *Culture and the City*, 121–125; Dana's career is related in "John Cotton Dana and his Newark Museum," in Alexander, *Museum Masters*, 317–411; Dunne, "The Carnegie Libraries," in *Dissertations by Mr. Dooley* (New York, 1906), 177–182.

84. This account of chromolithography is based upon Peter C. Marzio, *The Democratic Art: Pictures for a Nineteenth-Century America* (Boston, 1979). For Godkin's views, see "Chromo-Civilization," *Nation*, September 24, 1874. For a sense of the animated debate over whether wood engraving was an art, see *Scribner's Monthly*, 16 (June 1878), 237–242, 291–292.

85. Alfred Stieglitz, "Pictorial Photography," *Scribner's Monthly*, 26 (November 1899), 528–537. Baudelaire is quoted in Allan Sekula, "On

the Invention of Photographic Meaning," in Sekula, *Photography against the Grain: Essays and Photo Works, 1973–1983* (Halifax, Nova Scotia, 1984), 11–12.

86. *Appleton's Journal*, November 3, 1875, 630; W. J. Stillman, "The Revival of Art," *Atlantic Monthly*, 70 (August 1892), 251; Joseph Pennell, "Is Photography among the Fine Arts?" *Living Age*, 216 (January 1, 1898), 99–108; Peter Henry Emerson, *Naturalistic Photography*, 3d ed. (1899; repr., New York, 1973), 56, 63; Charles H. Caffin, *Photography as a Fine Art: The Achievements and Possibilities of Photographic Art in America* (New York, 1901); *Nation*, 73 (December 19, 1901), 475–476. For the parallel debate in Europe, see Naomi Rosenblum, *A World History of Photography* (New York, 1981), chaps. 5, 7.

87. Stieglitz, "Pictorial Photography," *Scribner's Monthly*, 26 (November 1899), 528–537; Alfred Stieglitz, "Modern Pictorial Photography," *Century Magazine*, 64 (October 1902), 822–825; Allan Sekula, "On the Invention of Photographic Meaning," in Sekula, *Photography against the Grain*, 12; Arthur Rothstein, *Documentary Photography* (Boston, 1986), xvii.

88. John Philip Sousa, "The Menace of Mechanical Music," *Appleton's Journal*, September 1906, 278–284. Sousa's recordings are mentioned in Schwartz, *Bands of America*, 241. Sousa's views on radio are in his autobiography, *Marching Along*, 356–357. His radio broadcasts are mentioned in Paul E. Bierley, *John Philip Sousa: American Phenomenon* (New York, 1973), 20. Hapgood's statement is in *Collier's*, 32 (December 26, 1903), 23.

89. Susan Sontag, "Against Interpretation," in Sontag, *Against Interpretation and Other Essays* (1966; repr., New York, 1982), 297; Benjamin, "The Work of Art in the Age of Mechanical Reproduction," in Benjamin, *Illuminations*, 217–251. Arnold is quoted in Raymond Williams, *Culture and Society: 1780–1950* (New York, 1983), 118–119.

90. *Dwight's Journal of Music*, August 2, 1856, 141; Finck, *My Adventures in the Golden Age of Music*, 34. The three *New York Times* editorials were entitled "Coney Island," July 18, 1880, "The Brass Instrument Habit," July 28, 1880, and "The American Brass Band," August 25, 1880. The attacks on Gilmore are related in Harris, "John Philip Sousa and the Culture of Reassurance," in Newsom, ed., *Perspectives on John Philip Sousa*, 61.

91. The best account of reactions to Sousa, and the source of the newspaper quotations, is Harris, "John Philip Sousa and the Culture of Reassurance," in Newsom, ed., *Perspectives on John Philip Sousa*. Sousa's missionary statement is quoted in Pauline Norton, "Nineteenth-Century American March Music and John Philip Sousa," in Newsom,

ed., *Perspectives on John Philip Sousa*, 48. Victor Herbert is quoted in Jon Newsom, "The American Brass Band Movement," *Quarterly Journal of the Library of Congress*, 36 (Spring 1979), 119–120. The fullest account of Sousa's life and ideas is Paul E. Bierley, *John Philip Sousa: American Phenomenon* (New York, 1973). The most valuable source for Sousa's attitudes toward music and the American people is his autobiography, *Marching Along*.

92. Joseph Horowitz, *Understanding Toscanini* (New York, 1987), 102, 368–372. Lamb's views are discussed above, in "William Shakespeare in America."

93. Frank Capra, *The Name above the Title: An Autobiography* (New York, 1971), 486, and *passim*.

94. G. W. F. Hegel, *The Philosophy of Fine Art*, trans. F. P. B. Osmaston, 2 vols. (1920; repr., New York, 1975) I, 12.

Three · Order, Hierarchy, and Culture

1. *The Education of Henry Adams*, 457, 238; Henry James, *The American Scene* (1907; repr., New York, 1946), 71, 131, 265–266.

2. James, *The American Scene*, 80, 85, 125, 126, 132, 230–232.

3. Ibid., 54, 64, 67, 76, 79–80, 83–84, 86–87, 158, 232–233.

4. *The Diary of Philip Hone*, I, 261, 435–436, 451, 508; II, 600–601, 825.

5. *The Diary of George Templeton Strong*, I, 293; II, 316–379; III, 335–336, 567; IV, 232, 236, 245, 317.

6. Charles Eliot Norton, "James Russell Lowell," *Harper's New Monthly Magazine*, 86 (May 1893), 848–849. Henry May's characterization of Norton is in his study *The End of American Innocence: A Study of the First Years of Our Own Time, 1912–1917* (New York, 1959), 35. The other quotations in this paragraph come from Frederick Cople Jaher, *The Urban Establishment: Upper Strata in Boston, New York, Charleston, Chicago, and Los Angeles* (Urbana, 1982), 276, and "The Boston Brahmins in the Age of Industrial Capitalism," in Jaher, ed., *The Age of Industrialism in America* (New York, 1968), 206–207.

7. James, *The American Scene*, 87; Green, *The Problem of Boston*, 141. For an excellent study of the tensions that pervaded public life on the streets of a nineteenth-century city, see Susan G. Davis, *Parades and Power: Street Theatre in Nineteenth-Century Philadelphia* (Philadelphia, 1986). There are also many fine examples in Christine Stansell, *City of Women: Sex and Class in New York, 1789–1860* (New York, 1986), see esp. chap. 10.

8. This account is based upon material in Harris, "John Philip Sousa

and the Culture of Reassurance," in Newsom ed., *Perspectives on John Philip Sousa*. See also Sousa, *Marching Along*, 339–340.

9. *America* is quoted in May, *The End of American Innocence*, 45; Higginson is quoted in Johnson, *Symphony Hall, Boston*, 66–67.

10. Sonneck, *Early Concert Life in America*, 168, 53–54, 164, 67, 109–110.

11. *New York Mirror*, April 23, 1836; The *Boston Weekly Magazine* and the New Orleans judge are quoted in Grimsted, *Melodrama Unveiled*, 67–68.

12. Maretzek, *Crochets and Quavers*, 30–47.

13. Henry Irving, "The American Audience," *Fortnightly Review*, 43 (February 1, 1885), 199. The El Paso incident was reported in the *New York Times*, March 4, 1907, and the *San Francisco Chronicle*, March 4, 1907. For another view of the Astor Place operatic row, see *The Diary of George Templeton Strong* I, 336.

14. Gottschalk, *Notes of a Pianist*, 129, 161; Finck, *My Adventures in the Golden Age of Music*, 33–34; *The Diary of George Templeton Strong*, II, 389, 467; IV, 257.

15. *Dwight's Journal of Music*, November 3, 1855, 37; Mueller, *The American Symphony Orchestra*, 354. The Stadt Theatre incident is related in *Scribner's Monthly*, May 1871, 22–23, and quoted in Burton Peretti, "Richard Wagner and the Transformation of American Culture, 1860–1910," unpublished seminar paper, University of California, Berkeley, December 1983, p. 2. Mrs. Cutting's transgressions were reported in the *New York Times*, January 28, 1899. For the Metropolitan Opera's plea for order, see Kolodin, *The Metropolitan Opera*, 53, 100.

16. Calvin Tomkins, *Merchants and Masterpieces: The Story of the Metropolitan Museum of Art* (New York, 1970), 78; Winifred E. Howe, *A History of the Metropolitan Museum of Art*, 2 vols. (New York, 1913), I, 244; *New York Times*, June 1, 1891; see also the issues for May 19, 29, 1891, June 8, 15, 1891.

17. Frederick Law Olmsted, *Forty Years of Landscape Architecture: Central Park*, ed. Frederick Law Olmsted, Jr., and Theodora Kimball (1928; repr., Cambridge, Mass., 1973), 58–59, 438–439; Henry Hope Reed and Sophia Duckworth, *Central Park: A History and a Guide* (New York, 1972), 35; Washburn, "The Influence of the Smithsonian Institution on Intellectual Life in Mid-Nineteenth Century Washington," in Rosenberger, ed., *Records of the Columbia Historical Society of Washington, D.C.*, 112–113.

18. Conrad is quoted in Jonas Barish, *The Anti-theatrical Prejudice* (Berkeley and Los Angeles, 1981), 343–344.

19. Howe, *The Metropolitan Museum of Art*, I, 244–245; Tomkins, *Merchants and Masterpieces*, 84–85.

20. Frederick Law Olmsted, *Public Parks and the Enlargement of Towns* (Brookline, Mass., 1902), 69; Buckley, "To the Opera House," (Ph.D. diss., State University of New York at Stony Brook, 1984), chap. 7; Reed and Duckworth, *Central Park*, 35, 53; Olmsted, *Forty Years of Landscape Architecture*, 406–410, 458, 464–465; John Brinckerhoff Jackson, *American Space: The Centennial Years, 1865–1876* (New York, 1972), 213; Robert Weyeneth, "Moral Spaces: Reforming the Landscape of Leisure in Urban America, 1850–1920," (Ph.D. diss., University of California, Berkeley, 1984), chap. 2.

21. *The Diary of George Templeton Strong*, IV, 327, 330, 340, 353–354.

22. Thomas, *A Musical Autobiography*, I, 133–134, 222; Russell, *The American Orchestra and Theodore Thomas*, 83; *Harper's New Monthly Magazine*, 72 (April 1886), 803; Lili Lehmann, *My Path through Life* trans. Alice Benedict Seligman (New York, 1914), 345–346. For Thomas's views on encores, punctuality, and other aspects of audience behavior, see his Introduction in *A Musical Autobiography*, II.

23. *Harper's New Monthly Magazine*, 72 (April 1886), 802–803; Briggs, *Requiem for a Yellow Brick Brewery*, 112; Mueller, *The American Symphony Orchestra*, 355, 356, 359. See also Joseph Horowitz, *Understanding Toscanini* (New York, 1987), 46, 48, 54. The Victor Herbert incident is recounted in the *New York Times*, May 21, 1911.

24. Thomas, *A Musical Autobiography*, I, 234–235, 171; "The Chicago Orchestra," *Dial*, 22 (May 1, 1897), 269–271.

25. Mueller, *The American Symphony Orchestra*, 29; DiMaggio, "Cultural Entrepreneurship in Nineteenth-Century Boston, Part II," *Media, Culture and Society*, 4 (1982), 312.

26. Edward Baxter Perry, "Mutual Courtesy between Artist and Audience," *Music*, 2 (July 1892), 252–255; Johnson, *Symphony Hall, Boston*, 29, 55; Mueller, *The American Symphony Orchestra*, 356; DiMaggio, "Cultural Entrepreneurship in Nineteenth-Century Boston, Part II," 32n6; Howe, *The Boston Symphony Orchestra*, 80; *New York Times*, January 15, 1908.

27. *New York Times*, November 20, 1881, April 4, 1896, January 3, 1909; Johnson, *Symphony Hall, Boston*, 27, 54–55; *Boston Evening Transcript*, October 31, 1908, November 2, 20, 1908.

28. George Gladden, "Is Applause Necessary?" *Music*, 8 (September 1895), 431–436; Mueller, *The American Symphony Orchestra*, 132–133, 356–357; *Dwight's Journal of Music*, 36 (April 29, 1876), 217; Thomas, *A Musical Autobiography*, I, 133, 222; II, 18–23; *New York Times*, October 15, 1899, November 19, 1899.

29. Theodore Thomas, "Music in Chicago," *Chicago Tribune*, Janu-

ary 23, 1894, reprinted in Thomas, *A Musical Autobiography*, I, 278–279; E. Irenaeus Stevenson, "Music and Manners," *Harper's Weekly*, 41 (June 5, 1897), 570; Karleton Hackett, "A Word to the American Audience," *Music*, 5 (February 1894), 280–282.

30. *New York Mirror*, January 2, 1836; Joseph Hatton, "American Audiences and Actors," *Theatre*, 3 (May 1881), 257; *New York Times*, January 10, 1909, January 24, 1911, December 1, 1911; Gatti-Casazza was quoted in the *New York Times*, Sunday, November 29, 1908, pt. 5.

31. Richard Sennett, *The Fall of Public Man* (New York, 1978), 230, 261. See also Mueller, *The American Symphony Orchestra*, 286.

32. B. F. Keith, "The Vogue of Vaudeville," *National Magazine*, 9 (November 1898), 146–153, reprinted in Charles W. Stein, ed., *American Vaudeville as Seen by Its Contemporaries* (New York, 1984), 17; *Boston Evening Transcript*, March 27, 1894; Albert F. McLean, *American Vaudeville as Ritual* (Lexington, Ky., 1965), 206–208; Edwin Milton Royle, "The Vaudeville Theatre," *Scribner's Magazine*, 26 (October 1899), reprinted in Stein, ed., *American Vaudeville as Seen by Its Contemporaries*, 25; The Drama Committee of the Twentieth Century Club, *The Amusement Situation in the City of Boston*, 15.

33. Jane Addams, *The Spirit of Youth and the City Streets* (1909; repr., New York, 1930), chap. 4; Mary Kingsbury Simkhovitch, *The City Worker's World in America* (New York, 1917), 123–124.

34. Walter Prichard Eaton, "The Menace of the Movies," *American Magazine*, September 1913, 60; Olivia Howard Dunbar, "The Lure of the Films," *Harper's Weekly*, 57 (January 18, 1913), 20; Lewis E. Palmer, "The World in Motion," *Survey*, June 5, 1909, 356. Zukor is quoted in Lary May, *Screening out the Past: The Birth of Mass Culture and the Motion Picture Industry* (New York, 1980), 148.

35. Norbert Elias, *The Civilizing Process: The History of Manners*, trans. Edmund Jephcott (German ed., 1939; translated ed., New York, 1978); John Kasson, "Civility and Rudeness: Urban Etiquette and the Bourgeois Social Order in Nineteenth-Century America," *Prospects*, 9 (1984), 143–167. See also Arthur M. Schlesinger, *Learning How to Behave: A Historical Study of American Etiquette Books* (New York, 1946).

36. Johnson, *Symphony Hall, Boston*, 68–69.

37. *Old and New*, 11 (December 1874), 686.

38. John Sullivan Dwight, "Music as a Means of Culture," *Atlantic Monthly*, 26 (September 1870), 321–331; *The Diary of George Templeton Strong*, IV, 249–250; *Century Magazine*, 10 (June 1875), 254; Charles Edward Russell, *The American Orchestra and Theodore Thomas*, vii. Cragin and Upton are quoted in Mussulman, *Music in the Cultured Gen-*

eration, 89–91. See also Henry T. Finck, "Music and Morals," in Finck, *Chopin and Other Works* (New York, 1910), 143–182.

39. *New York Times*, May 19, 1891, November 6, 1894. For Bryant's speech, see Howe, *A History of the Metropolitan Museum of Art*, I, 106–112. Choate's address is in the *New York Herald*, March 31, 1880.

40. Olmsted, *Public Parks and the Enlargement of Towns*, 46–48, 71; Buckley, "To the Opera House," (Ph.D. diss., State University of New York at Stony Brook, 1984), chap. 7; Laura Wood Roper, *FLO: A Biography of Frederick Law Olmsted* (Baltimore, 1973), 328–329; Galen Cranz, *The Politics of Park Design: A History of Urban Parks in America* (Cambridge, Mass., 1982), 8; Olmsted, *Forty Years of Landscape Architecture*, 247–248. Pintard is quoted in Jaher, *The Urban Establishment*, 236.

41. Charles Loring Brace, *The Dangerous Classes of New York, and Twenty Years' Work among Them* (New York, 1872), 68–69. The material on Boston and San Francisco parks comes from Weyeneth, "Moral Spaces," (Ph.D. diss., University of California, Berkeley, 1984), chap. 2. Olmsted's complaints about federal architecture are quoted in Geoffrey Blodgett, "Frederick Law Olmsted: Landscape Architecture as Conservative Reform," *Journal of American History*, 62 (March 1976), 875–876. For Burnham's role, see Thomas S. Hines, *Burnham of Chicago: Architect and Planner* (Chicago, 1979).

42. "Certain Dangerous Tendencies in American Life," *Atlantic Monthly*, 42 (October 1878), 385–402; Perry, *Life and Letters of Henry Lee Higginson*, 328–329.

43. Gareth Stedman Jones, "Class Expression versus Social Control? A Critique of Recent Trends in the Social History of 'Leisure,'" *History Workshop*, no. 4 (Autumn 1977), 162–170.

44. James, *The American Scene*, 117–118; Annie Nathan Meyer, "The Vanishing Actor: And After," *Atlantic Monthly*, 113 (January 1914), 96.

45. *The Education of Henry Adams*, 340. In addition to the contemporary press, my sense of the Columbian Exposition was derived from Reid Badger, *The Great American Fair: The World's Columbian Exposition and American Culture* (Chicago, 1979), David F. Burg, *Chicago's White City of 1893* (Lexington, Ky., 1976), Robert W. Rydell, *All the World's a Fair: Visions of Empire at American International Expositions, 1876–1916* (Chicago, 1985), Norman T. Newton, *Design on the Land: The Development of Landscape Architecture* (Cambridge, Mass., 1971), chap. 24, and John C. Cawelti, "America on Display: The World's Fairs of 1876, 1893, 1933," in Jaher, ed., *The Age of Industrialism in America*, 317–363.

46. "The Midway Plaisance," *Frank Leslie's Weekly*, July 13, 1893, 25; M. G. Van Rensselaer, "At the Fair," *Century Magazine*, 46 (May 1893), 3–13. The president of the exposition's board is quoted in Horowitz, *Culture and the City*, 99. Catherwood's comments and Gilder's poem are contained in the interesting collection of "Literary Tributes to the World's Fair," *Dial*, 15 (October 1, 1893), 176–178.

47. Christopher Lasch, *The Culture of Narcissism: American Life in an Age of Diminishing Expectations* (New York, 1978), 228–229; Mary Tucker Magill, "A Georgian at the Opera," *Harper's New Monthly Magazine*, 71 (June 1885), 135–139; H. E. Krehbiel, "How to Listen to Wagner's Music," *Harper's New Monthly Magazine*, 80 (March 1890), 530; W. J. Henderson, "To Persons Desiring to Cultivate a Taste in Music," *Century Magazine*, 45 (December 1892), 312–314; *Collier's Weekly*, 32 (December 26, 1903), 22–23; Helen Noe, "Art's Devotees," *Munsey's Magazine*, 25 (June 1901), 391.

48. Van Wyck Brooks, *The Ordeal of Mark Twain* (London, 1922), 218 and *passim*. Matthews and Arnold are quoted in Henry Nash Smith, "The Publication of *Huckleberry Finn*: A Centennial Retrospect," *Bulletin of the American Academy of Arts and Sciences*, 37 (February 1984), 19.

49. Hamlin Garland, *A Son of the Middle Border* (New York, 1928), 458–461.

50. Thomas Wentworth Higginson, "A Plea for Culture," *Atlantic Monthly*, 19 (January 1867), 29–37. At the end of the year Higginson had more to say on related topics in "Literature as an Art," *Atlantic Monthly*, 20 (December 1867), 745–754.

51. *Frank Leslie's Illustrated Newspaper*, November 10, 1883, 178; "About Poetry in America," *Appleton's Journal*, September 18, 1869, 150–151; *New York Times*, February 22, 1880, quoted in Harris, "The Gilded Age Revisited: Boston and the Museum Movement," *American Quarterly*, 14 (Winter 1962), 558; *The Diary of George Templeton Strong*, I, 225; III, 30.

52. James's litany is in Henry James, *Hawthorne* (1879; repr., Ithaca, 1967), 34–35; his comment about culture is quoted in Marc Pachter, "American Cosmopolitanism," in Chenetier and Kroes, eds., *Impressions of a Gilded Age*, 29; Sydney Smith's attack was published in the *Edinburgh Review*, January 1820, 79–80; Charles Eliot Norton, "A Definition of Fine Arts," *Forum*, 7 (1889), 36; Cooper is quoted in Marzio, *The Art Crusade*, 19; O. B. Frothingham, "Art and Wealth," *Atlantic Monthly*, 50 (December 1882), 741–750; William F. Apthorp, "Music," *Atlantic Monthly*, 35 (January 1875), 122–124.

53. Apthorp, "Music," *Atlantic Monthly*, 35 (January 1875), 122–

124; *The Outlook,* December 2, 1893, 989–990; "'High-Brow,'" *Dial,* 56 (April 1, 1914), 287–288; T. R. Sullivan, "A Standard Theatre," *Atlantic Monthly,* 75 (May 1895), 686–689; Aline Gorren, "The Superfluous Critic," *Century Magazine,* 55 (April 1898), 874–877; Gerald Stanley Lee, "Making the Crowd Beautiful," *Atlantic Monthly,* 87 (February 1901), 240–253. For the views of Putnam and Bancroft, see Marzio, *The Art Crusade,* chap. 2.

54. W. J. Henderson, "Music," *New York Times—Illustrated Magazine,* October 25, 1898, 4; Harry Thurston Peck, "The Drama of Disintegration," *Cosmopolitan,* 28 (March 1900), 513–515. Guild is quoted in H. Earle Johnson, *Hallelujah, Amen! The Story of the Handel and Haydn Society of Boston* (Boston, 1965), 197. Horowitz is quoted in Frank Browning, "The Strange Journey of David Horowitz," *Mother Jones,* May 1987, 28.

55. *Atlantic Monthly,* 40 (November 1877), 624–625; John Sullivan Dwight, "Mere Music and the Art of Music," *Dwight's Journal of Music,* July 26, 1873, 62–63; W. J. Stillman, "Journalism and Literature," *Atlantic Monthly,* 68 (November 1891), 687–695; James L. Ford, "The Fad of Imitation Culture," *Munsey's Magazine,* 24 (October 1900), 153–157; *Independent,* 47 (June 27, 1895), 11, as quoted in Frank Luther Mott, *A History of American Magazines* 5 vols. (Cambridge, Mass., 1930–1968), IV, 7; *Collier's,* 36 (November 4, 1905), 7; Katharine Fullerton Gerould, "The Extirpation of Culture," *Atlantic Monthly,* 116 (October 1915), 445–455.

56. Gail Hamilton, "Camilla's Concert," *Atlantic Monthly,* 11 (June 1863), 756–766. The *New York Herald* is quoted in Harris, *Humbug,* 318n25, and Gladys Denny Shultz, *Jenny Lind: The Swedish Nightingale* (Philadelphia and New York, 1962), 200. Dwight is quoted in Willis, *Memoranda of the Life of Jenny Lind,* 123–124. See also *Dwight's Journal of Music,* April 10, 1852, 12; May 15, 1852, 42–43; December 4, 1852, 67–68.

57. *Atlantic Monthly,* November 1857, 125–128; March 1858, 636; and Mabel Dodge are quoted in Burton Peretti, "Richard Wagner and the Transformation of American Culture, 1860–1910," (unpublished seminar paper, University of California, Berkeley, 1983), 34–35, 37; *New York Daily Tribune,* December 29, 1884; William Francis Allen, "Italophobia," *Dwight's Journal of Music,* February 1, 1879, 21; Simeon Strunsky, "The Highbrow—An Appeal to Zoölogists," *Century Magazine,* 89 (February 1915), 639. For the dominance of German opera at the Metropolitan, see Kolodin, *The Metropolitan Opera,* 87–105, and Briggs, *Requiem for a Yellow Brick Brewery,* chap. 4. *Metropolitan Opera Annals,* compiled by William H. Seltsam (New York, 1949), is a valu-

able year by year listing of all operas performed at the Metropolitan, along with the casts and excerpts from reviews. In his history of the Metropolitan, Kolodin includes a useful appendix, "The Metropolitan Repertory, 1883–1966," which compiles the number of times each opera was performed in each season. For Wagner, see Anne Dzamba Sessa, "At Wagner's Shrine: British and American Wagnerians," in David C. Large and William Weber, eds., *Wagnerism in European Culture and Politics* (Ithaca, 1984).

58. *New Orleans Times-Picayune*, June 20, 1918.

59. Nast is quoted in Mussulman, *Music in the Cultured Generation*, 106; Sidney Lanier, "The Proper Basis of English Culture," *Atlantic Monthly*, 82 (August 1898), 165–174; *The Education of Henry Adams*, 237.

60. For the derivation of these terms see the Oxford English Dictionary *Supplement*; for the illustration see John D. Davies, *Phrenology: Fad and Science—A Nineteenth-Century American Crusade* (New Haven, 1955), frontispiece.

61. Matthew Arnold, *Culture and Anarchy* (New York, 1875), 44, 47; *Harper's New Monthly Magazine*, 34 (January 1867), 261. My account of Arnold's impact upon the United States is derived from John Henry Raleigh, *Matthew Arnold and American Culture* (Berkeley and Los Angeles, 1957), 37, 58–61, 137, 153–154, 246, and *passim*.

62. Noah Webster, *An American Dictionary of the English Language*, 2 vols. (New York, 1828); see also the 1839 edition published in New York. Noah Webster, *An American Dictionary of the English Language*, revised and enlarged by Chauncey A. Goodrich (New York, 1852); Noah Webster, *An American Dictionary of the English Language*, thoroughly revised and greatly enlarged and improved by Chauncey A. Goodrich and Noah Porter (Springfield, Mass., 1869); Noah Webster, *A Dictionary of the English Language*, as revised by Chauncey A. Goodrich, Noah Porter, and William A. Wheeler (Springfield, Mass., 1887); *Webster's Collegiate Dictionary: A Dictionary of the English Language* (Springfield, Mass., 1898); *Webster's International Dictionary of the English Language: Being the Authentic Edition of Webster's Unabridged Dictionary Comprising the Issues of 1864, 1879, and 1884*, thoroughly revised and enlarged under the supervision of Noah Porter (Springfield, Mass., 1899); *The People's Webster Pronouncing Dictionary and Spelling Guide* (Chicago, 1898); *Webster's Army and Navy Dictionary* (Springfield, Mass., 1919); *Webster's New Standard Dictionary, Elementary School Edition* (Chicago, 1919); *Webster's Collegiate Dictionary*, 3d ed., Merriam Series (Springfield, Mass., 1919).

63. Hiram M. Stanley, "A Suggestion as to Popular Amusements,"

Century Magazine, 47 (January 1894), 476–477; Van Wyck Brooks, *America's Coming-of-Age* (New York, 1915), 6–7; James is quoted in Montrose J. Moses, *The Fabulous Forrest: The Record of an American Actor* (Boston, 1929), 246. For the changes in meaning that were occurring, see the discussion of such terms as AESTHETIC, ART, CIVILIZATION, CLASS, COMMON, CREATIVE, CULTURE, MASSES, POPULAR, and TASTE in Raymond Williams, *Keywords: A Vocabulary of Culture and Society*, rev. ed. (New York, 1985).

64. Whitman, *Democratic Vistas*, in Kaplan, ed., *Whitman: Poetry and Prose*, 950–951, 961–962; Veblen, *The Theory of the Leisure Class* (1899; repr., New York, 1979), 45, 397–398.

65. Brougham is quoted in David Vincent, "The Decline of the Oral Tradition in Popular Culture," in Robert Storch, ed., *Popular Culture and Custom in Nineteenth-Century England* (London, 1982), 28.

66. Lawrence W. Levine, "African Culture and U.S. Slavery," in Joseph E. Harris, ed., *Global Dimensions of the African Diaspora* (Washington, D.C., 1982), 128–129.

67. For a discussion of the distinctions between social and cultural authority, see Paul Starr, *The Social Transformation of American Medicine* (New York, 1982), 13–14.

68. For several interesting and suggestive attempts to understand the phenomenon of invented tradition, see the essays in Eric Hobsbawm and Terence Ranger, eds., *The Invention of Tradition* (Cambridge, England, 1983); Hobsbawm's statement comes from his essay "Mass-Producing Traditions: Europe, 1870–1914," 297.

69. Mozart is quoted in Mueller, *The American Symphony Orchestra*, 287.

70. Max Weber, *Economy and Society*, II, 937.

71. *Harper's Monthly Magazine*, 12 (September 1912), 634; "A Democratic Art," *Nation*, 97 (August 28, 1913), 193.

72. *The Diary of George Templeton Strong*, IV, 290–291; Virgil Thomson, "George Gershwin," originally published in *Modern Music*, November 1935, and reprinted in Virgil Thomson, *A Virgil Thomson Reader* (Boston, 1981), 25.

73. Martin Jay, "Hierarchy and the Humanities: The Radical Implications of a Conservative Idea," *Telos*, no. 62 (Winter 1984–85), 144. For interesting examples of shifting cultural categories, see Russell Lynes, *The Tastemakers: The Shaping of American Popular Taste* (1955; repr., New York, 1980), chap. 17 and Afterword.

74. Charles W. Eliot, "A New Definition of the Cultivated Man," *World's Work*, 6 (August 1903), 3806–11; Green, *The Problem of Boston*, 65–66.

75. Whitman, *Democratic Vistas*, in Kaplan, ed., *Whitman: Poetry and Prose*, 950–951, 961–963; Charles Dudley Warner, "What Is Your Culture to Me?" *Scribner's Monthly*, 4 (August 1872), 470–478; Theodore Roosevelt, "What 'Americanism' Means," *Forum*, 17 (April 1894), 196–206. See also Charles Edward Russell, "The Growth of Caste in America," *Cosmopolitan*, 42 (March 1907), 524–534.

76. Plunkitt, *Plunkitt of Tammany Hall*, 52, 71; Sousa, *Marching Along*, 132, 274–275, 294–296, 341; see also 109–110. Sousa's statements to the reporters and the *Topeka Daily Herald*'s views are quoted in Harris, "John Philip Sousa and the Culture of Reassurance," in Newsom, ed., *Perspectives on John Philip Sousa*, 62, 64, 70, 78.

77. Milton "Mezz" Mezzrow and Bernard Wolfe, *Really the Blues* (New York, 1946), 124–125.

78. *Appleton's Journal*, September 11, 1875, 340–341. For newspaper opinion, see Jackson, *American Space*, 214. The *Evening Transcript* is quoted in Olmsted, *Forty Years of Landscape Architecture*, 109; this collection of Olmsted's writings on Central Park contains many details of his political travails; see esp. pt. I, chaps. 7, 9, 10. The debates over the use of parks throughout the country during these years can be traced in Galen Cranz, *The Politics of Park Design*, chap. 1 and *passim*.

79. John William Ward, *Andrew Jackson—Symbol for an Age* (New York, 1955), 213.

80. DiMaggio, "Cultural Entrepreneurship in Nineteenth-Century Boston, Part II," *Media, Culture and Society*, 4 (1982), 320.

81. Paul Whiteman and Mary Margaret McBride, *Jazz* (New York, 1928), 128.

Epilogue

1. *New York Times*, Sunday, December 22, 1985, section 2; Sunday, November 23, 1986, section 2.

2. "When Michael Tilson Thomas Looks at Music in America," *U.S. News & World Report*, 81 (December 27, 1976), 65; Ellington's statements come from *Time*, 97 (June 7, 1971), 67, and from his autobiography, *Music Is My Mistress* (Garden City, N.Y., 1973), 452; Ross Russell, *Bird Lives!: The High Life and Hard Times of Charlie (Yardbird) Parker* (New York, 1973), 293; Dizzy Gillespie with Al Fraser, *To BE, or Not . . . to BOP: Memoirs* (Garden City, N.Y., 1979), 492–493; Clarke is quoted in Gillespie's *Memoirs*, p. 142.

3. *New York Times*, December 31, 1987, July 26, 1987; Sontag, *Against Interpretation*, 302–304.

4. Scott E. Brown, *James P. Johnson: A Case of Mistaken Identity*

(Metuchen, N.J., 1986), 86–87; Gene Lees, "Jazz: Pop or Classical?" *High Fidelity*, 27 (May 1977), 22.

5. Playbill, Goodman Theatre, Chicago, January 14–February 27, 1983; *New York Times*, Sunday, May 24, 1987, section 2.

6. "The Subtle Work of Making Supertitles," *New York Times*, Sunday, July 27, 1986, section 2; "Many U.S. Orchestras Are in Financial Straits," ibid., January 19, 1987; "Arts Groups Seek Ethnically Broader Audience," ibid., January 1, 1987.

7. "Arts Groups Seek Ethnically Broader Audience," *New York Times*, January 1, 1987; "Plaster Casts of Statues: From Storage into Vogue," ibid.; "Andy Warhol Is Dead at 58," ibid., February 23, 1987; John Russell, "The Man Who Turned Art Upside Down, Inside Out," ibid; "The Modern Prepares for the Twenty-first Century," ibid., Sunday, March 6, 1988, section 2.

8. See E. D. Hirsch, Jr., Joseph Kett, and James Trefl, "What Literate Americans Know: A Preliminary List," in E. D. Hirsch, Jr., *Cultural Literacy: What Every American Needs to Know* (Boston, 1987), 146–215.

9. *San Francisco Chronicle*, May 13, 1987; *New York Times*, November 26, 30, 1986, May 13, 1987, June 30, 1987.

10. For the book's sales, see "Best Sellers From 1987's Book Crop," *New York Times*, January 6, 1988. For positive responses to Bloom's book, see *Wall Street Journal*, April 22, 1987; *New York Times*, March 23, 1987; *New York Times Book Review*, April 5, 1987; *The Economist*, May 16, 1987; *Time*, August 17, 1987; and the extensive coverage in *Insight*, May 11, 1987. Martha Nussbaum's critique was published in *New York Review of Books*, November 5, 1987. For other negative responses, see *The Nation*, May 30, 1987; *The New Republic*, May 25, 1987; and *Harper's Magazine*, January 1988.

11. Allan Bloom, *The Closing of the American Mind* (New York, 1987), 185–188.

12. Ibid., 346, 51.

13. Ibid., 322, 68–81.

14. Ibid., 346–347, 381, 341, 344.

15. Ibid., 346–347, 337–339, 59–60.

16. Ibid., 381.

17. Jonathan Yardley, "Paradise Tossed: The Fall of Literary Standards," *Washington Post*, January 11, 1988; Bennett's speech was reported in the *San Francisco Chronicle*, February 5, 1988.

18. "Classical Music: What Next?" *New York Times*, Sunday, January 31, 1988, section 2; Nureyev is quoted in the *Washington Post*, July 24, 1986; Yehudi Menuhin, "A Virtuoso Reflects upon Aspects of His

Art," *New York Times,* Sunday, June 1, 1986, section 2; Will Crutchfield, "James Levine: New Era at the Met," *New York Times Magazine,* September 22, 1985, 38; Donal Henahan, "Could Veblen Explain Today's Opera?" *New York Times,* Sunday, April 19, 1987, section 2; Vickers is quoted in Thomas Brown, "Eminently Otello," *Dial,* January 1987, 32.

19. Ralph Ellison, *Shadow and Act* (New York, 1964), 123; Bloom, *The Closing of the American Mind,* 68–81; Bellow is quoted in James Atlas, "Chicago's Grumpy Guru: Best-Selling Professor Allan Bloom and the Chicago Intellectuals," *New York Times Magazine,* January 3, 1988, 31.

Index

p. 202

S → crítica de bottom (1, 2) ? o →
embodied "z" ?

No tiene voluntad de reformar.
cultura no mecha proselytic.
Cultura pasiv, pero +
sympathetic emigranten f
otros ?